James Frederick Schön

Grammar of the Hausa Language

James Frederick Schön

Grammar of the Hausa Language

ISBN/EAN: 9783744670715

Printed in Europe, USA, Canada, Australia, Japan

Cover: Foto ©Thomas Meinert / pixelio.de

More available books at **www.hansebooks.com**

GRAMMAR

OF THE

HAUSA LANGUAGE.

BY

REV. J. F. SCHÖN,

CHAPLAIN OF MELVILLE HOSPITAL, CHATHAM;
MEMBER OF THE GERMAN ORIENTAL SOCIETY; AND
LATE MISSIONARY OF THE CHURCH MISSIONARY SOCIETY.

LONDON:
CHURCH MISSIONARY HOUSE,
SALISBURY SQUARE.
1862.

וְנִבְרְכוּ בְךָ כֹּל מִשְׁפְּחֹת הָאֲדָמָה׃

GENESIS xii. 3.

כּוּשׁ תָּרִיץ יָדָיו לֵאלֹהִים׃

PSALM lxviii. 31.

Καὶ ἐξῆλθε νικῶν καὶ ἵνα νικήσῃ.

REVELATION vi. 2.

W. M. WATTS, CROWN COURT, TEMPLE BAR

PREFATORY REMARKS.

THE language, a Grammar of which is now presented to the public, is called the Hausa. The origin of the name itself I have not been able to ascertain, nor has Dr. Barth[1] been more successful than myself in the endeavour to settle the question. It may be mentioned, however, that the word Hausa is explained by some as denoting the language rather than the people, and that my interpreters at Sierra Leone insisted on rendering the passages referring to the miraculous gift of tongues by " speaking another Hausa ;" but as we must say " yi magana-n-Hausa," or " yi magana-n-Hausawa," that is, to speak the language of the Hausa country, or of the Hausa people, this individual assertion carries little weight. And the fact that a Hausa man is called " bahauše,"[2] which forms its plural regularly into " hausawa," seems to deprive it of all appearance of probability.

The extent of the territory in which the Hausa is the vernacular language, and the notoriety it has attained among other nations being of much greater importance than the origin of its name, I shall endeavour to exhibit these two subjects at some length, as it will be seen thereby that so much time, labour, and expense, bestowed upon the reduction of this language, have not been misapplied by the Committee of the Church Missionary Society, to whose perseverance and forethought the accomplishment of this present work is attributable. I am convinced that the future—and that probably no distant one—will recognise the hand of Providence in directing attention to the reduction of this language, which is calculated to render it accessible to Missionaries, travellers, and commer-

---

[1] Barth's Travels, vol. ii. page 72. [2] See Grammar, § 19.

cial men as the medium of communication with the inhabitants of Central Africa. The territory in which the Hausa is the vernacular language may with some limitation be said to be the Soudan.[1] The Hausas themselves divide their country into seven provinces, generally called "Hausa bokoi:" the names of all the seven I have never been able to ascertain correctly from natives: one or two were sometimes missing, or different names given by different informants. A rivalry for the honour of belonging to them induced some to number their own native countries amongst them; and it was often amusing to witness with what warmth they would argue and stigmatize each other's countries, as "Bansa Hausa," that is, with Dr. Barth,[2] "Bastard Hausa." I therefore take the liberty to avail myself of the labours of Barth in quoting the names of seven provinces as recorded by him. They are the following—"Biram, Doura, Gober, Kano, Rano, Katsena, and Zegzeg; and the seven other provinces or countries, in which the Hausa language has spread to a great extent, although it is not the original language of the inhabitants, are, Zanfara, Kebbi, Nupe, Gwari, Youri, Yariba, and Kororofa." Among the northern provinces, I find in my collections Zinder, and among the western, Rabba, and Sokoto, mentioned. A glance at the map in Dr. Barth's most instructive Travels will show that the territory in which the Hausa is the vernacular language is of considerable extent, probably greater than that occupied by any other language in Central Africa. It is, moreover, not only in those parts that this language is known and understood, and serving as the medium of communication: it has, from various causes, such as the dispersion of Hausas among other nations, through the slave-trade, the commercial pursuits of the natives of the Soudan, and the beauty of the language itself, become, as it were, to Africa, what the French is to Europe; and that this is no vague assertion of my own will

---

[1] Compare Dialogues, and a small portion of the New Testament in the English, Arabic, Hausa (or Sudanese), and Bornu languages. London, 1853.

[2] Vol. ii. page 72.

be proved by many undeniable facts, and by the testimonies of travellers. Sierra Leone contains many of every province of Hausa. Near Cape Coast a little village was pointed out to me inhabited by Hausas, and I have met some at the island of Fernando-Po. At Cape Coast, Lander engaged his faithful Paskoe, the Hausa interpreter, with whom he commenced his travels at Badagry; and there is every reason to conclude that the Hausa language has been the only medium of communication and intercourse with people, chiefs, and kings, from Badagry to Borgou, Rabba, Boosa, Yaouri, Egga, and down the Niger to the Ibo country. No native words are found in Lander's three interesting volumes except such as are Hausa, and the author himself very frequently refers to the extent of the Hausa language. "It is understood," he says,[1] "by the generality of the natives of Borgou, both young and old, almost as well as their mother tongue, and it is spoken by the majority of them with considerable fluency." At Gunga only it was that *even* the Hausa language was not understood.[6] I can corroborate the above statement from my own experience and observation in the River Niger as far as Eggan.

Leaving the west for the present, and passing over the above-mentioned seven provinces to the north, it is most gratifying to find that it has there also spread far and wide, and obtained the same notoriety as in the west, every traveller bearing testimony to this fact. Clapperton's incidental allusions to the importance of the Hausa language are numerous. Oberweg congratulates the Expedition in having met with an interpreter who was master of Afnu, that is, the Hausa language. Barth,[2] writing to Professor Lepsius from Ai-Salah, speaks of the absolute necessity of mastering the Hausa language, and of his inability on that account to pay much attention to the Tuareg, observing that it was the less to be regretted, since all Asbenawas spoke the Hausa, and used it

---

[1] Lander's Travels, vol. ii. page 2.
[2] Vol. iii. page 19; compare, however, pages 49, 78, 82, &c. &c.

even more generally than the Targia.[1] Numerous allusions to the paramount importance of this language from Barth's Correspondence and Travels might be quoted; but as the philological labours of that accomplished scholar may shortly be expected, I would rather refer the reader to his own statements, being convinced that my observations will be confirmed by him.

Dorugu, whom I shall introduce shortly, speaks (in the interesting narrative of his life and travels) of meeting Hausas everywhere from Kukawa to Tripoli; and in the last-mentioned place he met liberated Hausas in great numbers, inhabiting a separate village, and desirous of returning to their own country if they could obtain the means of doing so. On the steamer from Tripoli to Malta he met Hausas, from whom he learnt that there were many of their nation to be found in Egypt, and even in Stambul, or Constantinople; and the very same thing I was told at Sierra Leone by a traveller, who had visited those parts, by the name of Ari Babaribari.

With a view to ascertain whether Hausa was known in the countries along the Tshadda, from the confluence of that river and the Niger, I consulted Crowther[2]; and found that from the Confluence to Hamaruwa, a distance of *three hundred miles*, the Hausa was understood, and of immense service to the Expedition. But Crowther's own summary, in the Appendix, speaks so entirely the conviction of my own mind, that I cannot do better than to quote his own words. "The Hausa," (after enumerating *twelve* languages in which the Bible ought to be translated,) he says,[3] " is the most important of all: it is the commercial language of Central Africa.

" At Oru, in the Delta, we already commenced meeting with

[1] Gumprecht's, Barth's, and Oberweg's Untersuchungs Reise nach dem Tshad See, und in das Innere von Afrika, Berlin 1852: compare pages 40, 41, 59, 62, 93, 116, 145, 146, 147, 148, 150, 151, 160, 168, 169, and many more incidental expressions throughout the whole work.
[2] Journal of an Expedition to the Niger and Tshadda Rivers, 1854.
[3] Pages 202, 203.

solitary opportunities of communicating with the people through Hausa slaves. From Abo we engaged a Hausa interpreter, who was very serviceable to us throughout the Expedition. At Idda we found that the Hausa language was becoming more generally spoken by the inhabitants: salutations in that language generally sounded in our ears. At Igbegbe, near the Confluence, the Hausa is one of the prevailing languages spoken by the mixed population of that market town, and it is the chief medium of communication in commercial transactions, though Igbira is the language of the place.

"At Yimaha in the Igbira country, at Oruku in the Bassa country, at Doma, also among the hitherto unknown Mitshis, among the inhabitants of the extensive Kororofo, and with the Fulanis of Hamaruwa, the Hausa language was the chief medium of communication, both with the chiefs and with the people whom we visited during the late Expedition; and I was told that the knowledge of Hausa will bring any one to Mecca. From Igara and upwards, though each language must ultimately be learnt, and translations be made into it, there can be no doubt that a good translation into the Hausa language, for the general use of travelling Missionaries among the nations above mentioned, will be of inestimable advantage. *This language seems to be destined by God to be the general medium of imparting the knowledge of Christianity, to a very great extent, among the nations by whom it is spoken,* when we take into consideration the Hausas themselves, of Kano, Katsina, Zanfara, and other tribes speaking the language as their own.

"All the Mohammedans understand and speak the Hausa language, and through it the Koran is explained and interpreted in their own mosques throughout Yoruba; so that from Lagos, Badagry, and Porto Novo, and upwards to the Niger, where Mohammedans are found, the Hausa language is spoken by them. Now, if we glance at the map, it will at once be seen to what extent the language is spoken, and how generally useful a knowledge of it is likely to be. I may suggest, therefore, that the reduction of the Hausa language is of very great importance, especially if there is any probability of annual visits to the Niger and Binue by steam-vessels, for the purpose of commerce, and even if no attempt can yet be made to commence Missionary operations about the confluence of the Kwora and Tshadda. Such translations will be of general use among whatever tribes the travellers go.

Schön's Vocabulary[1] needs to be revised and improved:[2] I shall be ready to contribute what I have now in possession towards such improvements when required."

Enough has been said and quoted to prove the importance of the reduction and study of the Hausa language; the necessity of translating the sacred Scriptures into it; and no further apology seems necessary for bestowing so much time upon it. But there are other questions arising, and other suggestions presenting themselves to my mind, which I do not feel at liberty to suppress. If all who have any knowledge of this subject are agreed that an acquaintance with Hausa is of

[1] "A Vocabulary of the Hausa Language, with Grammatical Elements prefixed," London 1843.

[2] A revised and improved edition is nearly ready for the press. I take the liberty to quote the opinion expressed on my first attempts by Barth. He writes from Gummel, March 15, 1851, to Professor Lepsius, in Berlin (Gumprecht, page 144—45)—"All the people here understand Hausa, though their language among themselves is the Bornu, or, as they call it, Kánori. I have made so much progress in the Hausa language that I can express myself fluently on every subject. You inquire as to the meaning of Afnu and Hausa. They are indentical: Afnu is only the Bornu name for Hausa. The Hausa is a beautifully rich and sonorous language, often exceeding the European languages in delicacy. The variation of dialects is considerable, the importance of intonation extraordinary, the variety of forms great, but the verb meagre.(?) Schön's Vocabulary, preceded by a short Grammar, is, on the whole, excellent, although not the purest Katshena. He is perfect master of the language." I have since had the pleasure of reading Dr. Barth's Travels in Africa: he introduces Hausa words, very rarely sentences. I compared all his quotations carefully with my own collections, and must confess that I have not met with any thing that could convince me of the correctness of his remark. His philological work I have not yet seen, still I regret that all his references should be to my elementary work only.

such infinite importance, should not all Missionaries, commercial agents, and travellers in those parts of Africa, make themselves familiar with it, now that it is made accessible to every one that can read English? Are translations into it of so much importance as the means of imparting a knowledge of Christianity among numerous tribes who understand it? Should not those already made be introduced at every Missionary station in the Yoruba country and on the banks of the Niger? Should not every means calculated to advance and facilitate the thorough reduction of it be employed? Is it right to let a Hausa literature, collected with so much labour, be laid aside, merely because it has no direct bearing on Missionary or commercial pursuits, or for want of funds to defray the expense of publication? Is it not a matter in which *all* Missionary Societies are equally interested? Ought not African-Aid, Ethnographical, Geographical, Oriental, and Philological Societies render some assistance?

A few words must be added respecting the occasion, progress, and completion of this work, and my own connection with the Hausa language in general. My attention was first called to it in the year 1840, when I was requested by the Church Missionary Society to accompany the Niger Expedition. I addressed myself to the study of the Ibo and Hausa languages. I soon discovered that the latter was of more importance than the former, and published the results of my inquiries, in the Vocabulary above mentioned, after my return to England in the year 1843. On my returning to Sierra Leone in the spring of the same year, I was requested to pursue the study of the Hausa, and to prepare translations of portions of Scripture into it. Three Gospels and the Acts of the Apostles were translated, and materials collected for a Grammar and Dictionary, amidst many interruptions from fever and other circumstances. In the spring of 1847 I was obliged to return to Europe through ill health : in fact, during the last three years of my residence in Sierra Leone, I do not think I ever enjoyed more than tolerable health to prosecute my labours for a month together.

On presenting the results of my labours to the Committee of the Church Missionary Society, I confess I was not a little disappointed at its decision, " that as the translations were not required for Sierra Leone, and as there was no prospect of commencing a Mission in the interior, the Committee could not recommend them for publication." Consequently, all was put aside, or at all events very little attention paid to it, until the year 1856, when I was informed by the Rev. H. Venn, who has always taken the warmest interest in these undertakings, and encouraged me in every possible manner, that Dr. Barth, who had just returned from Africa, had spoken favourably of my labours, and that my translations and other collections should now be published. Satisfactory as this news was to me on the one hand, it was no less embarrassing on the other. Ten years my papers had been lying in the dust: I had nearly forgotten the language. I began to long and to pray for help in the person of a Hausa man, and the thought of how to get one engaged me day and night; when, to my astonishment and delight, I learnt that Dr. Barth had brought to London with him two Hausa lads, whom I saw, and Dr. Barth very obligingly allowed one of them, Dorugu, to spend a few weeks with me, and, soon after, both of them were placed under my care. It was the Lord's doing, and it is marvellous in our eyes!

The two lads were called Abbega and Dorugu: both were Mohammedans, and could not speak English, which was just as I could wish it. With them the work was begun afresh. I discovered very soon that Abbega spoke Hausa like a foreigner, being a Margi by birth; but being very communicative, I obtained many new words from him, besides collecting a small vocabulary and some stories in his own native tongue, the Margi. Dorugu is a real Hausa, speaks the language fluently and beautifully. Never was there an African coming to this country that was of greater use; full of information for his age, probably not more than 16 or 17 years old, energetic and lively in his habits, always ready to speak. He began relating stories to me, or rather dictating them, giving me a description of his own life and travels in Africa in his own language, very often dictating to me for hours together, and even till late in the night; so that I had soon a Hausa literature of several hundred pages before me, by which my memory was refreshed and stored with new matter, so that I could judge of the correctness of my former collections, by the documents before me, of one who could not understand a word of English, and whose Hausa diction laboured under no disadvantages from that quarter, as is the case with people at Sierra Leone. Having worked myself afresh into Hausa, my translations were read to them and by them.[1] They understood them, and, through much conversation with them, I could discover where a sentence was wanting in perspicuity, or another liable to be misunderstood, and for a third a more idiomatic expression was suggested. In a few instances they could not understand the meaning of a word, but invariably protested against altering it, observing that my interpreters at Sierra Leone were old men, and they themselves but youths. Still I altered and accommodated it to their understanding, and struck out all self-coined words, however legitimately formed after given analogies. And considering all these things, and the many improvements introduced, as well as the more uniform character the translations have assumed under this process,

[1] For I had made it my first business to teach them to read their own language by the use of a little Primer, published 1848. But I must mention the assistance I have derived from Koelle's books in the Bornu language. As both these lads spoke the Bornu language, they were able in a very short time to read the Bornu stories, fables, &c. &c. Nothing could be more suited to their taste, nor so likely to encourage them in their studies as the discovery of the practical use of mastering the formidable A B C, and to see that they could at once understand what they read. They read the book through in a very short time, communicated to me in Hausa what they read in Bornu; and, comparing it with the English translations, I have had an opportunity of testing its correctness which probably no other person ever had. I cannot withhold this testimony to the value of Koelle's labours. So much for those who are for ever dwelling upon some errors in his "Polyglotta Africana," but cannot discover its invaluable treasures.

I devoutly thank the Lord of his Church for sending these young men to this country. It was no chance, but Providence: they have been sent, and Dorugu more especially, for this very work; they have endeavoured to assist according to their power in *watering* others, and have derived the greatest benefit for themselves. The Gospel has proved the power of God unto salvation to their own souls: they have learnt to believe in Him who is the Saviour of all men, and especially of them that believe; they have made public confession of their faith, being admitted by baptism to Christ's flock. Abbega has returned to Africa with the Gospels in his hand, has given evidence of his zeal for the conversion of others, and has hitherto maintained his Christian character. Dorugu is still with me, reading and studying, and, by God's blessing, preparing himself for still greater usefulness. I am quite aware that I have digressed from my subject in dwelling so long upon the translations and the circumstances connected with them, and would ask the reader's indulgence. The rules of the British and Foreign Bible Society allowing no introductions to translations, I availed myself of this opportunity of saying a few words.

In my labours in the Hausa language, I have had no forerunner. What I have given, and what is still in hand, I have collected from the natives of the country. It is true I have met with short vocabularies of travellers, as in Lander's and Clapperton's works, but they have added nothing to my stock.

The orthography in which the Hausa books appear is that which has approved itself to my mind, through years of observation, as most suitable. I may be charged with inconsistency in the spelling of some words, and more especially for introducing double consonants again, after having discountenanced them in the earlier translations, still I am convinced that double consonants are necessary in *taffi, filta, fitto, sigga, godda*, &c. &c. In some words it is difficult to a *German* to decide as to whether they should be written with *s*, or the *English* *z*, the sharp *s* in German, as in the word "same," being in fact the English *z*. In doubtful cases I have generally given both ways. That there are great dialectic differences has been mentioned above, and will surprise no one; but I believe I have pointed out in the first chapter, however briefly, in what they principally consist among *real* Hausas. The differences are still greater among other tribes, who have adopted Hausa as foreigners, but no man of common sense would make his collections from them. It is with them not only in the enunciation that they differ, but also in grammar: it will generally be found that they confuse gender, number, and tenses, besides introducing words from their own languages.

I have given numerous examples under every rule in the grammar, with an *almost* literal translation, throughout the work, and am convinced that in so doing I have best consulted the interest of the student. He will have no difficulty in ascertaining the *exact* meaning of every word. To give merely some equivalent expression in *classical* English causes much trouble to the learner, and must often mislead him as to the real meaning of the respective word. I will mention a few instances in illustration of my meaning, and quote a few sentences to show how inaccuracy in the translation must cause an immense deal of trouble, (not to depreciate the exertion of any one, but merely to show how every one acts on first commencing to write a hitherto unwritten language,) thus: *Ka zakka yansu*, translation, "come in a minute." The student finds that *ka zakka* means "come thou," and supposes that *yansu* must mean "a minute," but *yansu* means "now." *Sadu kiah besah du ba comme*, "put the baggage on the camel." The vocabulary collected from this sentence is: *sadu* "to put," *kiah*, "baggage," *besah*, "on," *du? ba? comme*, is it camel? but when he is able to analyze the sentence, he will find that it ought to be written, *sa dukia bissa ga rakumi*. Another sentence: *Reši ndama ya hanna mu na aiki*, "business hinders my work." What means business? is it *reši?* then what means *dama?* and is *muna aiki*, "my work?" All is confusion in the sentence; but give the literal translation, "want of health hinders us to do the work," and all is plain. *Na sami dama ni yi aiki*, "I have time, I will do the work." What means time? *dama?* Translate it correctly, "I am better (I received health)," &c. &c. and all is plain. *Rua suna wutšewa*, "the river flows rapidly;" but *rua* means "water" and not "river," and there is nothing for "rapidly" in the sentence. *Sariki nan šina da alheri*, "this is a bad king;" the very reverse, because it means "this king is possessed of kindness."

The hyphen, used in the Grammar to mark the genitive case, and between the verbal pronouns and the verb, has been discontinued in the stories, the student being thought sufficiently informed on the subject.

I cannot conclude without expressing my sincere gratitude to Professor Lepsius for the invaluable assistance I have derived from his "Standard Alphabet." It has facilitated the reduction of this language very much. No one can duly appreciate the importance of such a Standard but those who have had to struggle with the innumerable difficulties, and the conflicting systems of orthography introduced by various writers of languages reduced for the first time to writing.

I have ventured (on grounds which may be deemed insufficient by others) to style the Hausa a Semitic language. The comparisons on which the opinion is founded have been made with the Hebrew alone: the identities discovered may, in some cases, and probably with greater propriety, be referred to the Arabic, which would not set aside my opinion. The absence of guttural letters seems a more serious objection to my view. I will not quarrel with those who may form a different opinion, and whose learning may enable them to institute more extensive investigations and comparisons. I have occasionally drawn attention to the affinities and identities in the Grammar between the two languages, and shall now add a few more, skimmed, as it were, merely from the surface, to show that I had some reason for the conclusion I have arrived at of the Semitic origin of the language. The pronouns are the most striking part. Compare §§ 29. 83.

The distinction of gender into masculine and feminine (so unlike other African languages), the *almost* identity in form of the subjunctive and future tense, the derivation of different classes of verbs from the same root, &c. &c.; and to these grounds the identity of some words, as—

Mutum, "man," compare מֵת or מָת. Gesenius *Metusala*, or related to מָוֶת, or מוּת, "to die," hence *mutum*="mortal being;" its pl. *mutane*=מֵתִים, See Isa. xli. 14. *Mantše*, "to forget," and מַנְשֶׁה "who makes forget." *Hawaye*, "tear"= אָוָה= *awagi*, "to cry, to howl," and *ufu*, "to scream." *Itše*, "tree" =עֵץ. *Kamma*=כְּמוֹ, "like, as," "like as." *Kammani*=כָּמוֹנִי, "as I," "like me." *Kammaka* = כָּמוֹךָ, "as thou." *Kammamu* כָּמוֹנוּ, "as we," "like us." *Daši*, "desert," "field"=שָׂדֶה, transposition of letters. *Makaranta*, "school"=מִקְרָא, "assembly," "convocation." *Kirra*, "to call"=קָרָא. *Takirani*=תִקְרָאֵנִי, "she called me;" and *karatu*, "to read." *Daffa, backen, kochen*=אָפָה. *Kadan*, "little"=קָטָן. *Alfadara*, "mule"=פִּרְדָּה. *Gona*, "farm"= גַּן, "garden," "farm." *Kafada*, "shoulder"=כָּתֵף; pl. *kafadu*=כְּתֵפוֹת. *Maraki*, "calf"=מַרְבֵּק. *Mi?* "what?" מִי "who?" *Azumi*, "to fast"=צוּם. *Gaferta*, "to forgive," "pass over," "excuse"=כָּפַר. *Rami*, "hole"=מְעָרָה. *Malake*, "to reign," "to rule," "govern"=מֶלֶךְ. *Sariki*, "king" = שַׂר "prince." *Halal*, "ceremonially clean," "lawful"=חָלָל. *Haram*, "what is unlawful" = חָרַם. *Malaiki*, "angel"=מַלְאָךְ. *Ebilisi*, "devil" = διαβολος. *Oba*, father=אָב. *Anabi* "prophet" נָבִיא.

In devoting myself to these labours, I have had no other end in view than to promote the great cause of Christian Missions in Africa, and to prepare the way for the Message of the Gospel to those who are still sitting in heathen darkness, or in the delusions of the false prophet; and while I am persuaded in my own mind that the present work will contribute, in some measure, towards the accomplishment of this glorious object, I am not the less sensible of its many imperfections.

Still, it is one step towards the realization of the Christian's prayer for Africa, that the promise "Ethiopia shall soon stretch out her hands unto God," may be fulfilled. The signs of the times are encouraging. Much has been done for Africa of late years ; and the present aspect of things is such as to encourage the hope that the slave trade will soon be destroyed ; the sons of Africa be employed in the peaceful pursuits of agriculture and legitimate commerce, and in the enjoyment of the blessings of Christianity. For this glorious end it is our privilege to pray and to labour, in the assurance *" that we may look for Divine countenance and help. I see no reason for despair. What has been done may be done again; and it is matter of history, that from superstitions as bloody, from a state of intellect as rude, and from the slave trade itself, a nation has been reclaimed, and now enjoys, in comparison with Africa, a blaze of light, liberty, religion, and happiness. That nation is great Britain. What we find the Africans, the Romans found us ; and it is not unreasonable to hope that even Africa will enjoy, at length, in the evening of her days, those blessings which have descended so bountifully upon us in a much earlier period of the world."*[1]

JAMES FREDERICK SCHÖN.

Palm Cottage, Gillingham, Kent.
20 *January,* 1862.

---

[1] The African Slave Trade and its Remedy. Sir T. F. Buxton, page 62.

CONTENTS.

PART I.

CHAPTER I.

SECT.		PAGE
1. Orthography		1
1. Letters and Sounds		1
3. Pronunciation of Vowels		2
4. ,, Diphthongs		3
5. ,, simple Consonants		3
6. ,, double ,,		5
7. Combination of Consonants and Division of Syllables,		6
8. Accentuation		7
9. Intonation		7

PART II.

CHAPTER II.

Substantives—

10. Primitives or Derivatives			8
11. Abstract: derived by the suffix *tši*			8
12. ,, ,, *ma*			9
13. ,, ,, *ta*			10
14. Derivatives by *abin*			11
15. ,, *wuri*			11
16. ,, *mai*, pl. *masu*			11
17. ,, *dā*			12
Diminutives by *da*			12
18. Derivatives by *ga*			12
19. Patricial Nouns by *ba*			12

GENDER OF SUBSTANTIVES—
SECT.   PAGE
20. Masculine and Feminine   ...   13
    1. Expressed by different words   13
    2.   ,,   additional ,, ...   14
    3.   ,,   different terminations   14
NUMBER—
21.—26. Singular and Plural, how formed   ...15—20
CASES—
27.—28.   ...   ...20—21

CHAPTER III.
PRONOUNS—
29. Separable or inseparable   21
    1. Personal, simple forms   22
    2.   ,,   compound   ...   23
30. Possessive, simple and compound   24
    1. Inseparable   24
    2. Separable   25
31. Demonstrative—
    1. *Nga, nan, wonnan*   ...   25
    2. *Wonga, wogga,* referring to person   26
    3. Adverbial—*nana, daga nan, tšan*   26
    4. *Abin da*   26
32. Interrogative   ...26—28
33. Indefinite   ...28, 29
34. Relative   ...   29
35. Reciprocal   30

CHAPTER IV.
ADJECTIVES—
36. Nature of   ...   30
37. Formation of Plural   30
38. Characteristic termination of the Feminine ... 30
39.   *a.* by reduplication, corresponding to Past Parti-
         ciples in English   31
      b. by prefixing *a*   32
40. Formed by *da*   33
41.   ,,   *mai*, plural *masu*   33
42. Negative   34

CHAPTER V.

NUMERALS—

SECT.		PAGE
43.	Cardinal	35
44.	Ordinals	39
45.	Adverbial	40
46.	Distributive ...	41
47.	Fractional	41

CHAPTER VI.

VERBS—

48.	Nature of ...	42
49.	Derivation of	42
50.	In form the same with the Noun	42
51.	a. *Yi*	43
	b. *Kawa*	43
	c. *Si* ...	43
	d. Derived by *ta*	44
	e. ,, *wo*	44
	f. ,, *ye* ...	44
52.	Frequentitive and Intensive ...	44
53—55.	Derived by suffixes	...45—48
56.	Nature and quality of	48
57.	Transitive and Intransitive, expressed by different forms,	49
58.	Different forms of, instead of Prepositions	50

MOODS—

59.	Nature of	50
60.	Infinitive	51
61.	Imperative	52
62.	Subjunctive ...	52
63.	Conditional	53
64.	Permissive or Concessive	54
65.	Tenses	55
66—68.	Verbal Pronouns	...55—57
69.	,, ,, tabular exhibition of	...57, 58
70.	Conjugations of	59
	The Aorist ...	59
71.	,, Negative	62
72.	,, Imperative	62

SECT.	PAGE
73. Imperfect	63
74—76. Present	...64—67
77. Perfect	68
78. Participial form, or indefinite past tense	68
78. Future	...69—71
78. ,, Form II. (Participial Mood)	72
80. ,, Second	72
81. Formation of the Passive	...72—75
82. List of Verbs	...76—78

CHAPTER VII.

83. Prepositions	79

CHAPTER VIII.

84—89. Adverbs	...81—85

CHAPTER IX.

90—92. Conjunctions	...85—87

CHAPTER X.

93. Interjections	87

PART III.

CHAPTER XI.

SYNTAX—

94. Nature of	88
95. Subject and Predicate	88
96. (1) ,, grammatical	88
96. (2) ,, logical	89
97. ,, simple	90
98. ,, compound	90
99. Predicate	
,, grammatical	90
,, logical	91
100. (1) ,, simple	91
(2) ,, compound	91

SECT.		PAGE
101. Sentences, different kinds of—		
102. Negative		92
103. Interrogative		93
104. Imperative	...	93
105. Compound		...94, 95

CHAPTER XII.

106. Substantives, nature of	96
107. ,, concordance of	96
108. Genitive Case	97
109. Dative	99
110. Accusative	101
111. Vocative	102
112. Ablative	102
113. Number	102
114. Gender	104

CHAPTER XIII.

Pronouns—

115. Personal	106
116. Possessive	107
117. Objective	108
118. Demonstrative	109
119. Adjective Demonstrative	110
120. Interrogative	113
121. Relative	114
122. Indefinite	115

CHAPTER XIV.

123. Adjectives	118
124. ,, Comparison of	121
,, Comparative	121
125. ,, Superlative	123

CHAPTER XV.

126. Numerals, mode of counting	124

CHAPTER XVI.

SECT.	PAGE
131. Verbs, nature of	129
132. Tenses of—	
133—136. Presence	130—132
137. Imperfect	132
138. Participial form, or indefinite past tense	133
139, 140. Aorist	135
141. Perfect	137
142, 143. Future (Subjunctive Future)	137
144. Pluperfect and Second Future	139
145. Moods	140
146, 147. Government of Verbs : Transitive	140
148. *Verba sentiendi et declarandi*	141
149. Participle in the form of final Verb	142
150. Idiomatic use of some Verbs	144

CHAPTER XVII.

151. Particles—	
152. Simple Adverbs	145
153. Verbs including the force of Adverbs	146
154. Locality	147
155. ,, use of Substantives	147
156. Adverbs of Place	148
157, 158. ,, Time	151
159. ,, Manner	154
160, 161. Negative Particles	155

CHAPTER XVIII.

162. Conjunctions	157—163

APPENDIX.

		PAGE
1. Narrative of a Hunting Match	.. .. ..	165
2. The Story of the Hyena and the Fox	.. ..	168
3. The Story of the Priest and the Fox	.. ..	172
4. The Story of the Two Girls who had the same Father and the same Master	..	176
5. The Story of the Mother and her Boy	..	189
6. The Story of an Englishman and his Stick	.. ..	193
7. The Story of the Girl and the Four Bachelors	..	195
8. The Story of the Woman and her Husband	.. ..	198
9. The Story of the Origin of Monkeys	.. ..	204
10. A Story about Two Men	.. .. ..	206
11. The Story of a Woman, her Daughter, and their Dogs,		207
12. The Story about a Woman	.. .. ..	210
13. A Tale of a Fox, Hyena, and Fish	..	212
The Life and Travels of Dorugu, 1st Chapter	.. ..	216

CORRIGENDA.

Page	Line						
3	11	from above,	read	*akoi*	for	*akọi*
3	19	,,	,,	,,	*Hausa*	,,	*Haussa*
6	16	,,	below,	,,	*Consonant*	,,	*Consanant*
10	6	,,	,,	,,	ה	,,	ה
24	13	,,	,,	,,	*dokita*	,,	*dokia*
29	4	,,	above,	,,	*kiwo*	,,	*kiwọ*
29	6	,,	,,	,,	*woddanan*	,,	*waddanan*
33	2	,,	below,	,,	*tends*	,,	*attends*
46	16	,,	,,	,,	*transitive*	,,	*causative*
48	15	,,	,,	,,	*šida*	,,	*sida*
51	1	,,	above,	,,	*no*	,,	*n*
64	12	,,	,,	,,	*suffix*	,,	*affix*
69	3	,,	,,	,,	*women*	,,	*woman*
85	6	,,	,,	,,	*kurdinsa*	,,	*kurdinša*
87	2	,,	,,	,,	*tambayésu*	,,	*tambayẹ́su*
92	16	,,	above,	,,	*nan*	,,	*nun*
93	9	,,	,,	,,	*serpent*	,,	*serpen*
112	12	,,	below,	,,	*zaki*	,,	*ya-ki*
117	12	,,	above,	,,	*tšiki*	,,	*tsiki*
123	13	,,	,,	,,	*mun*	,,	*mnn*
148	7	,,	,,	,,	*daga*	,,	*daia*
167	4	,,	,,	,,	*šina*	,,	*sina*
170	12	,,	,,	,,	.	,,	?
182	1	,,	,,	,,	*wota*	,,	*wata*
183	8	,,	,,	,,	*nan*	,,	*an*
185	4	,,	,,	,,	*dádi*	,,	*dáda*
185	4	,,	,,	,,	*gaši*	,,	*taši*
185	7	,,	,,	,,	*šido*	,,	*sido*
185	7	,,	,,	,,	*tše*	,,	*tši*
192	7	,,	,,	,,	*kašši*	,,	*kašsi*
198	5	,,	,,	,,	*saši*	,,	*sasi*
200	2	,,	,,	,,	*wota*	,,	*wata*
210	11	,,	,,	,,	*mata*	,,	*mat*
217	15	,,	,,	,,	*da muka*	,,	*damu ka*
218	6	,,	,,	,,	*daga*	,,	*da ya*
221	2	,,	,,	,,	*mutane*	,,	*matane*

PART I.

ORTHOGRAPHY.

CHAPTER I.

§ 1. THE *Orthography* of the Hausa books already printed, as well as of this Grammar, is that proposed by Professor Lepsius, of Berlin, and recommended by the Church Missionary and the principal Missionary Societies in England, France, Germany, and America. It is adopted in this work as far as the peculiar character of the Hausa language seemed to render it necessary and desirable. In this Grammar, chiefly designed for native teachers, and such as may enter practically upon the study of the language by intercourse with natives of the country, much relating to that system is omitted which might otherwise have proved useful and interesting; but there is nothing introduced which is not in harmony with the method proposed for the reduction of unwritten languages in the Standard Alphabet, the careful study of which we would earnestly recommend to all who are engaged in such labours.

LETTERS AND SOUNDS OF THE HAUSA LANGUAGE.

§ 2. The signs required for writing the Hausa language may be represented by the following scheme:—

1. *Vowels.*
   1. Fundamental Vowels: *i, a, u.*
   2. Subordinate Vowels: *ę, e, ĕ, i, ĭa, a, o, ǫ.*
2. *Consonants.*

	GUTTURALS.	LINGUALS.	LABIALS.
1. Liquids,	*ṅ*	*l n r*	*m*
2. Mutes—			
(*a*) *fortis*	*k*	*t*	*p*
(*b*) *lenis*	*g*	*d*	*b*
3. Spirants,	*y h*	*s š z ž*	*w f*
4. Double Consonants,	*ds, dz, dž, ts, tš, gb, kw.*		

PRONUNCIATION.

§ 3. PRONUNCIATION OF VOWELS.

The *ą* and *ę* introduced in the translations of portions of the Sacred Scriptures are pectoral sounds resembling the letter *i* in the English words 'girl,' and 'fir,' as in *bęr, gęrta.* The sound of the *ą* is that of the Hebrew ע somewhat modified, as in *ḱáka*, and occurs but in very few words chiefly of Arabic origin, as in *Albęrka.* This mark under these respective letters having now a different office assigned to it in the Standard Alphabet, will be henceforth discontinued.

The Vowels are either long or short. The long Vowels are marked with a horizontal stroke over them as:— *ā, ē, īō, ō, ū;* the short Vowels are not distinguished, except where pointed out as such below.

The letters *e* and *i* are sometimes exceedingly short; when that is the case they are represented as *ĕ* and *ĭ*; they also approach each other so closely, as to leave it doubtful whether we ought to write *ĕ* or *ĭ*, that is *Kĕao,* or *Kĭao,* or whether we ought to omit them altogether, and write *Kafri* or *Kafĕri, sarki* or *sarĭki.* The same may also be said with regard to the near approximation of the sound between *a* and *e*, as in *sarki* or *serki*, and *dare* or *dere*, *dayawa* or *deyawa*.

The *ǫ* (seldom heard) is pronounced like *a* in 'water' or in 'law,' or the *a* in *ja*=*yǫ* in the southern parts of Germany; as in *dǫka*, 'law'.

PRONUNCIATION OF THE DIPHTHONGS.

§ 4. The Diphthongs are *ai, au, ei,* and *oi*. It is necessary to observe that these are *real* diphthongs but in very few words, as in *kaí,* head, *rai,* 'life,' *dei,* 'must'; *daia,* 'one', *akǫi,* 'there is', *bokoi,* 'seven,' and in a few more besides. *Au* occurs only in a few Proper names, as *Šatau*. The best rule respecting the pronunciation of these so-called diphthongs, or rather combination of vowels is: let each vowel be distinctly enunciated in somewhat rapid succession; thus: *kĕdo* read *kĕ-d-o*; *keauta,* *ke-a-ŭ-ta*; *saraunia,* *sa-ra-ŭ-ni-a*; *Haŭsa* (sometimes written by travellers *Haousa* to prevent its being tortured into *Housa*) read *Ha-ŭ-sa*: the *ŭ* being long, shows that to spell it Houssa would be incorrect.

NOTE.—It is characteristic of the Hausa, as of all Semitic languages, that it is rich in vowels. The contraction of two vowels into one, or the ejection of one so frequent in other African languages, is rarely met with in the Hausa. As instances we may mention *Kaina,* 'my head,' 'myself,' which forms *kánka,* 'thyself' instead of *kainka*; *raina,* 'my life,' forms *ránka,* 'thy life,' instead of *rainka*; also *almaširánna,* instead of *almaširaina*. Otherwise the language admits of two and more vowels meeting, and all being pronounced separately: as an instance we may mention *zāauikĕsi,* read *zā-a-a-i-kĕsi,* 'he is about, or going to be sent.'

PRONUNCIATION OF SIMPLE CONSONANTS.

§ 5. The Consonants exhibited above according to the organism of a language, are subject to the same laws as in other languages, and especially as in the Kanuri (See Koelle). The changes they undergo, and the combinations in which they occur, together with some dialectic differences, and pronunciations will be briefly explained here.

b is like *b* in 'be.' It is combined with *m* instead of *n*, before *b*, as, *ambani*, instead of *anbani*. In different dialects it is sometimes exchanged with *f*, as: *fusari*, where others say, *busari*.

d is pronounced like *d* in 'do,' and combines with *ń*, and *n*, as: *nda* or *enda*, and *gańgań*.

f is like *f* in 'find' (see *b*), combined with *ń*, as *ańfani*. *F* and *p* are sometimes exchanged the one for the other, and that not only in different dialects, but by the same individual, as: *fansa=pansa*, 'ransom,' and *faše=paše*, 'to break.'

g is like *g* in 'go,' 'give' and never like *g* in 'gem:' it combines with *ń*: as in *ńga*, *woddańga*.

h is like *h* in 'hothouse,' as, *haske*, 'light,' *haram*, what is unlawful.

k is like *k* in 'king,' 'key:' it combines with *ń* as in *hańkuri*.

kw is introduced instead of *Qu* in 'queen;' as *kwana*, *kwanaki*, *kwarai*.

l as in 'lamb.' *L* and *r* are often exchanged in different dialects; but to say: *lua* instead of *rua*, *budulua* instead of *budurua*, *balibali* instead of *Baribari*, &c., is ridiculed as the language of slaves by those who speak the purest Hausa.

n is like *n* in 'name,' as, *náma*, and combines with *g* and *k*, as in *nga* and *kanka*.

ń is like *ng* in 'king,' as, *yuńwa*, instead of *yungwa*; *ańfani* instead of *angfani*.

The dialectic differences are very great with regard to the use of this nasal sound. By some of the natives it is distinctly pronounced in many words which those who speak

PRONUNCIATION OF SIMPLE CONSONANTS. 5

the purest Hausa will merely pronounce as the simple *n*, as, *doṅ=don; doṅwonnan=donwonnan; kaṅka, suṅka, suṅ*, instead of *kanka, sunka, sun*, &c.

p is like *p* in 'pay.' The *p* is but of very limited use in the language, and in some dialects it is probably never heard. (See *f*).

r the *r* is not the guttural or Hanoverian of the throat, but rather the dental *r* of the southern parts of Germany and in the English word ring, as in *ruṅfa, rafonia, rakia*.

s is like *s* in 'see,' In some words it is more like *s* in the German word *sonne, i.e.* more like *z*, in English.

š is pronounced like *sh* in 'shame,' or the German *sch* in '*Schaar*.'

t is like *t* in 'top,' as *toffi*.

w is not exactly the English double *u*, as in 'wild,' more like in 'wind,' It is sometimes heard indistinctly, and may easily be confounded with *u*; hence some will write *baua*, instead of *bawa, kau* instead of *kawo*. It is plain that it partakes somewhat of the character of a semi-vowel.

y is like *y* in 'yes,' 'year,' always a consonant; as, *yáro*, 'boy,' *yarínia*, 'girl.'

z is like *z* in 'zeal,' not like the German *z* in '*zeit*.'

ž is the strongly aspirated *z* in 'azure,' chiefly combined with *d*, as *dža*, 'red.' Heard also more like *ža*, and by others it is pronounced almost like *dy* or *ty*.

PRONUNCIATION OF DOUBLE CONSONANTS.

§ 6. There are *Five* double Consonants in the Hausa language, as, *gb*, which requires *g* sounded very gently before the *b* (not as in the *Yoruba*), as in *gbata*. An ear not familiar with the language will hardly perceive it.

ds comes nearest in sound to the German *z* in '*zeit*,' as in *dsóro*, 'to fear.'

dz is but sparingly introduced, and the difference between *ds* and *dz* is hardly definable.

dž (see *ž*)

ts is not introduced in our books.

tš supplies the place of the German *tsch* or the English *ch* in 'church,' 'chide,' or *j* in 'jest,' and of *g* in 'ginger.' It is necessary to notice that the dialectic differences with regard to this double letter (as in fact with regard to the sibilants in general) are very great among the numerous tribes speaking Hausa. Some use *š* or even the simple *s* for *tš*: the same word may therefore be heard either as *tši, ši* or *si;* *tšia, šia; ša, šia,* &c. Still *si* seems to be used in this case only by persons speaking Hausa as foreigners.

COMBINATION OF CONSONANTS AND DIVISION OF SYLLABLES.

§ 7. The Hausa, like most of the languages of Western and Central Africa, requires every word to terminate in a Vowel, though it may begin with any one of the Consanants. But in this case also, as in other languages, the liquids *l m n ṅ* and *r*, and the spirants maintain their character as semi-vowels, and the labials *b f* and *p* can terminate syllables without the mediation of a Vowel; hence it happens that terminations like the following are of frequent occurrence, as, *mutum*, 'man,' but *mutumeˌ* is also used, *kadán,* 'little ;' and *kádan*, 'if ;' *hal,* 'till,' *halše,* 'tongue ;' *wohalda,* trouble, *alberka,* 'blessing,' *bamda,* 'besides,' *kamši,* 'sweet smell,' *tambaya,* 'question,' *aḫin,* 'thing,' *bansa,* 'in vain,' *hanśi,* 'bowels,' *haṅkali,* 'sense,' *háṅkūri,* 'patience,' *woṅya,* 'this,' *ber* and *beri,* 'to leave,' *berdo,* 'dove ;' *haske,* 'light,' *fuska,* 'face,' *hiska,* 'wind ;' *habši*= *hafši (leben*='life') 'to bark' ; *tapši*=*tafši,* 'soft,' *šiebda*= *šiepta*=*šiefta,* *makafta,* 'blindness;' *makoftši*=*makoptši ma-* *kobtši*=*makoptši,* 'neighbour ;' *tapki* or *tepki* 'pool.'

There are but two words in our collection which end in a mute *t*, namely, *daket*, 'with difficulty,' *fet*, as in *farifet*, 'very bright.'

§ 8. The accented syllable is indicated by the acute accent, *i.e. māgána* 'the word ;' *hánikári*, ' patience ;' *sáfia*, 'morning.'

INTONATION.

§ 9. The Intonation of the language must be distinguished from accentuation, neither of which is sufficiently ascertained to enable us to lay down rules. The few lines we can give with regard to the former are designed to direct the attention of the learner to the subject, rather than to develope the system. Besides this, we may safely assert that it is altogether impossible to represent intonation by any marks or signs. It consists in the raising or sinking of the voice, (not so prominent in the Hausa language as in the Ibo and others,) and dwelling upon and prolonging one syllable according to the will of the speaker. Adverbs are more especially subject to it : we mention one of frequent occurrence, *i.e. dayáwa* 'much, very much, many :' the speaker intending to convey the idea of 'very very much,' must raise his voice, dwell upon the accented syllable *á*, sing it rather than speak it, and the higher the degree of greatness or multiplicity, the longer will he dwell upon the *á*. So likewise with Adverbs expressing rapidity, he must not only double the Adverb *massa* into *massamassa*, but pronounce them together as rapidly as possible.

PART II.

ETYMOLOGY.

CHAPTER II.

SUBSTANTIVES.

§ 10. Substantives are either Primitives or Derivatives. Primitive Nouns are those whose origin cannot be traced any further; as, *rua*, 'water;' *gona*, 'farm;' *samna*, 'sit down.' Derivatives are such nouns as can be traced to their original source, or primary parts; as:

Maígona, 'farmer;' *masamni*, 'seat.'

NOTE.—All Infinitives may be used substantively, and are treated as such; e. g. *kēdáyansa da wúya*, 'to count it is difficult='the counting of it is difficult;' and *tšinsa da dádi*, 'it is sweet to eat'='the eating of it is sweet.'

Derivation of Substantives takes place by means of Prefixes and Suffixes, and sometimes by both in the very same word.

§ 11. Abstract Substantives are derived from Concrete Nouns by means of the suffix *tši*, which is sometimes preceded by the connecting or binding liquid letter *n* and the terminational Vowel is frequently changed, or altogether ejected. Examples:—

Anabántši, 'prophecy' from *anábi*, 'prophet.'
Bawántši, 'slavery,' derived from *bawa*, 'slave.'
Bākóntši, the place in which one is a stranger, from *báko*, 'stranger.'

Mallamantši, and } 'priesthood, the office and work of a
mallamtši } priest,' from *mallami* 'priest.'
Turántši, pl. *turawa*, 'what belongs to the Arabs,' as *magána-n-turántši* (*ko turantši*) 'the Arabic language.'
Hausantši, pl. *hausawa*, 'what belongs to the Hausas,' *i.e.* *magana-n hausawa* (*ko hausantši*) 'the Hausa language.'
Fadántši, 'the work or office of the *mafáda*, King's minister or counsellor.'
Fulantši, 'belonging to the Phula nation ;' *magana-n-fulani* (*ko fulantši*,) 'the Phula language.'
Ragontši, 'idleness,' from *rágó*, 'idle.'
Wawantši, 'folly, foolishness,' from *wawa*, 'fool.'

a) words ending in *a*, and *wa* form also derivatives with other changes ; as,

Diautši or } 'liberty, freedom,' from *dia*, 'free born, free.'
Diyautši, }
Bautši, 'slavery,' from *bawa*, 'slave.'

§ 12. Substantives are derived from verbs:

a) by means of the Prefix *ma* (מ,) and the Suffix *tši*, added to the infinitive of the verb, *e.g. makelatši*, 'a cruel fellow.'

Magátši, 'overseer,' from *ga* or *ganni*, 'to see.'
Mafaútši, 'slaughtering,' from *fawa*, 'to slaughter.'
Maaikátši, 'labour and labourer,' 'the place where work is performed,' from *aiki*, 'to work.'
Marokátši, 'begging, and beggar,' from *roko*, 'to beg.'
Madsorátši, 'cowardice,' from *dsóro*, 'to fear,' or *dsorata*, 'to frighten.'
Mafútši, *wúri nda ake-kétare-n-ruá*, (§ 28, 3.) 'the place at which one crosses a river=ferry.'
Marowátši, 'greediness,' from *rowa*, 'to be greedy.'

b) the Suffix *tši* is dropped, and the vowel changed into *i*; *e.g.*

Madúbi, 'glass, looking-glass,' from *duba*, 'to behold.'
Makári, 'end,' from *káre*, 'to finish.'
Masamni, 'seat,' from *samna*, 'to sit down.'

Mašídi, 'inn,' from *šída*, 'to encamp, sojourn, alight at a place.'

Makíyi, 'enemy,' (literally, one that hates), from *kī*, 'to hate,' and *yi*, 'to do.'

Mākámi, as *mākámi-n-kífi*, 'one that catches fish=fisher.'

Mākéri, 'blacksmith,' from *kíra*, 'to forge.'

Masáki, 'a weaver,' from *saka*, 'to weave.'

Masesekí, 'carpenter.'

Magballí, 'fastening, knot,' from *gballa*, 'to fasten, button, tie.'

Makublí, 'key,' from *kuble*, 'to lock.'

Makoyí, 'one that teaches,' from *koyo*, 'to teach.'

Maaikatší, *wuri nda ake yi-n-aiki*, 'the place where work is done.' Words beginning with *ma* denote, besides the action and the actor, sometimes also the place where the action is performed. Another example is *masasaka*, the place where carpentering or weaving, &c. is performed.

Maso, 'one that loves,' from *so*, 'to love.'

Makiáyi, 'shepherd,' from *kíwo*, 'to feed, or tend cattle,' and *yi*, 'to do.'

Makiaší or *makiaží*, lit. 'one who refuses to hear,' from *kī*, 'to refuse,' and *ší* or *ží*, 'to hear=disobedient.'

Mādáffi, *wuri nda ake daffa*, 'the place where cooking is done=kitchen.'

Madsayi, 'standing-place,' from *dsaya*, 'to stand.'

Mahayi, 'something to mount on=steps, ladder,' from *hawa*, 'to mount.'

Mahanni, 'hindrance,' from *hanna*, 'to hinder, to prevent.'

§ 13. Abstract Substantives are also formed by the Suffix *ta* (—ㅠ—*ta kirrata*, she called her) from Nouns and Adjectives : *e.g.*

Bauta, 'slavery,' from *bawa*, 'slave.'

Gašiérta, 'shortness,' from *gašiére*, 'short.'

Kariáta, 'falsehood,' from *karia*, 'false.'

Kčaúta, 'gift, present,' from *kědo*, 'good.'

Kuturta, 'leprosy,' from *kuturu,* ' to be leprous, leprous.'
Kasamta, ' uncleanness, pollution,' from *kasámi,* 'unclean.'
Makafta, ' blindness,' from *mákáfo,* 'blind person.'
Mūgúnta, ' badness, wickedness,' from *mugu,* bad, ' wicked.'
Tšiwuta, ' sickness,' from *tšiwo,* ' to be sick, sick.'
Wauta, ' foolishness,' from *wawa,* ' fool.'
Saraúta, ' kingdom, dominion, authority,' from *saríki,* ' king.'

§ 14. Derivatives are formed by combining the substantive *abin* (§ 28, 3), 'thing,' with the infinitive of verbs; as,
Abin-dsoro, ' something inspiring with fear.'
Abin-mámáki, ' something wonderful=wonder, miracle.'
Abin ša, ' something to drink, drink.'
Abin-tši, ' something to eat, food.'
Abin-worigi, ' something to play with, plaything, toy.'
Abin-sára, 'some cause or matter of accusation, accusation.'
Abin-hawa, 'something to mount on=steps, staircase,' from *hawa,* ' to mount.'

§ 15. Derivatives are formed by means of the substantive *wári,* 'place,' combined with the infinitive of verbs ; as,
Wíri-n-kwána, (§ 23. 3) 'place to sleep=bedroom, chamber.'
Wúri-n-kíwo, 'place where cattle are feeding=pasture, field.'
Wuri-n-rubutu, ' a place to write, table, room, office.'
Wuri-n-máta, ' a place assigned to women.'
Wuri n yini, 'a place to rest, resting-place;' so also,
Wuri-n-sabka, and *wuri-n-šída.*

§ 16. Derivatives are formed from Nouns, Adjectives, and Verbs, by the help of the Prefix *mai,* pl. *masu,* (בַּעַל) most intimately connected with an action, so that a word thus formed might be always resolved, at least as to its origin, into a particular relative Proposition ; as,

Maigona, ' one who possesses or cultivates a farm= farmer,' from *gona,* 'farm.'
Maihalbi, ' a marksman,' from *halbi,* ' to shoot.'
Maidóki, ' one that owns, or attends to a horse.'

Maiaski, ' one that shaves=barber,' from *aska*, ' to shave.'
Maigaskia, ' a man of truth,' from *gaskia*, ' truth.'
Maikoyo, ' one that learns,' from *koyo*, ' to learn.'
Maikīwuya, from *kī*, to 'hate,' and *wuya*, ' trouble, molestation, *ein Arbeitsscheuer Mensch*=idler.'
Maiwayo, ' one that is cunning or prudent,' from *wáyo*, ' cunning, or cunningness.'

§ 17. Derivation is effected by prefixing *dă*, signifying ' child, offspring, breed, native, or inhabitant of a place;' as,

Da-m-birni, ' a native of the town.'
Da-n-Dawura, ' a native of Dawura.'
Da-n-Katšina, ' a native of Katshina.'
Dóki da-n-Asbon, ' a horse of Tuarik breed.'

The word *da* is also employed to form diminutives; as,

Da-n-tšiako, 'the child of the hen=chick.'
Da-n-akwia,   „   ' goat=kid.'
Da-n-dumkia, „   ' sheep=lamb'
Da-n-záki,   ,, ' lion=lion's whelp.'
Da-n-zunzua, „   ' bird=young bird.'
Da-n-uwana,   „   ' my mother, an expression of endearment and affection=my brother.'

18. Derivatives are formed by the Prefix *ga* with the infinitive of verbs; as,

Garikua, ' that which holds the arrows=quiver ;' and
Garike-n-šánu, ' a place where cows are kept=cow-house,' from *rike*, ' to hold.'
Garika, ' enclosed place, enclosure, garden.'

§ 19. Patricial Nouns are formed by the Prefix *ba*; as,

Bahauše, ' a man of the Hausa nation.'
Bafilatše, ' a Phula.'
Babaribari, ' a Kanuri or Bornuman.'
Bayafude, ' a Jew.'
Ba laraba, pl. *larabawa*, ' Arab.'
Bature, pl. *turawa*, ' an Arab or European, white-man.'

One more may be mentioned, of which one word only has been found, because it is not unlikely that more may be found, namely, *barantaka*, 'service;' *yi barantaka*, 'to do service,' from *bara*, ' servant.'

GENDER OF SUBSTANTIVES.

§ 20. The Hausa language differs from most of the African languages, as regards the distinction of Gender. Almost all of them know of no distinction except a physical one, *i.e.* where it exists in nature, and then it is invariably expressed by different words: but the Hausa has developed a Feminine to a much greater extent, as will be seen in the course of this Grammar; and a careful consideration of this, and of many other peculiarities, seem to indicate the Semitic origin of the Hausa. The method by which the Gender is distinguished by the termination in *a*, and the use of *ta*, to denote the feminine Gender, seem to point even more distinctly to the Semitic origin (*ta kirrata*, she called her).

There are but two Genders in the Hausa language, viz. the Masculine and the Feminine. They are distinguished and expressed in three different ways:

1 By using *different* words, especially where Gender exists in nature, and which may be called the *physical* distinction; as,

Ōbá, ' father.'	*Uwá*, ' mother.'
Wā, ' elder brother.'	*Ya* or *Iya*, ' elder sister.'
Kāné, ' younger brother.'	*Kanua*, ' younger sister.'
Mutum (מיח mortal) ' man.'	*Matše*, ' woman.'
Rākumí, ' camel.'	*Tagua*, ' female camel.'
Bunsuru, ' he-goat.'	*Akwia*, ' she-goat.'
Dóki, ' horse.'	*Godia*, ' mare.'
Zakkara, ' cock.'	*Kasa*, or *kaza*, ' hen.'
Bašimi, and *Takarikari* } ' bull.'	*Sania*, ' cow.'
Rago, ' ram.'	*Dumkia*, or *tumkia*, ' sheep.'

Sărmáyi, 'youth.'   Budurua, 'maid.'
Aṅgo, 'bridegroom.'   Amaria, 'bride.'
Tóro, 'the male, and   Gíwa, the 'female elephant.'
Obangiši, 'master.'   Uworigidda, and Uworigišia, 'mistress of the house.'

2. The Gender is distinguished by *additional* words, such, namely, as correspond to our male and female; as, *Miši*, or *Nămíši*, 'male,' and *Matše*,' female ;' *e. g.*

Dă nămíši, ' male child = boy.'

Dia matše, 'female child = girl;' though *da* and *dia* are also used independently for son and daughter.

Da-n-záki, a 'lion's whelp, a young lion' (masc.): and *Da-n-zakainya*, (fem.)

Namiši-n-gádo, ' boar ;' *Matše-n-gádo*, ' sow.'

Da-n-úwa, ' mother's child = brother.'

Dia uwáta, ' mother's daughter = sister.'

3. The Gender is distinguished by different *terminations:* the masculine may end in any vowel, but the characteristic termination of the feminine is *a*, which, influenced by euphonical laws, may be *ia*, *ania*, *nia*, or *unia* ; *e. g.*

Babe, m. *bábánia*, f. ' locust.'
Mutum, or *mulumé*, ' man,' *mutumnia*, ' woman.'
Saríki, ' king,' *saraúnia*, ' queen.'
Yáro, ' boy,' *yurínia*, ' girl.'
Da, ' son,' *dia*, ' daughter.'
Kane, ' younger brother,' *kanua*, ' younger sister.'
Sa, ' bull,' *sania*, ' cow.'
Maraki, m. *maraka*, f. ' calf.'
Bardo, m. *baraúnia*, f. ' thief.'
Karre, ' dog,' *kăria*, or *kariya*, ' bitch.'
Bara, ' male,' *baránia*, ' female servant.'
Mayi, ' wizard,' *mayia*, ' witch.'
Šariri, m. *šariria*, f. ' infant.'
Zofo, ' old man,' *zofua*, ' old woman.'
Gado, ' pig,' *gadonia*, ' sow.'
Alfadori, ' mule,' *alfadara*, f. (פֶּרֶד m. פִּרְדָה f.)

Goburo, 'widower,' *goburánia*, 'widow.'
Anabi, 'prophet,' *anabia*, 'prophetess' (נָבִיא and נְבִיאָה.)

NUMBER OF SUBSTANTIVES.

§ 21. The Hausa has developed two numbers, viz., the Singular and the Plural, in the former only Gender is distinguished. The formation of the plural presents a great diversity, and on that account also no small difficulty. It may, however, be said to be formed *a*) either by a change of the terminating vowel of the singular; or *b*) by adding certain particles to the singular; or *c*) by dropping the last vowel, and adding some particle to the root (*i.e.* the last consonant of the noun); or *d*) a reduplication of the last syllable takes place. In the following enumeration of plural forms it will be observed that some words occur under several heads, and that their plurals are formed in two, or even in three different ways. All we can do is to give an extensive list of the various forms collected, instead of laying down rules for the *formation* of such as are still wanting. And it may also be noticed here, that almost all nouns are used as collectives, and construed as plurals.

1. *a*) The *a*, terminating the singular, is changed into *ai, oi*, or *u;* or the particles *ne, ki, naki,* or *ye*, are added to the word; as,

Alúra, pl. *alurai*, 'needle.'
Albassa, pl. *albassai*, 'onion.'
Bára, pl. *báruá,* 'servant.'
Búdurúa, pl. *budurai*, 'maid, virgin.'
Dórína, pl. *dorinai*, 'hippopotamus.'
Fakára, pl. *fakarai*, (' owl') ' partridge.'
Tasúnía, pl. *tasunai*, ' tale, story.'
Hankáka, pl. *hankáki*, ' quail.'
Tágua, or *táguwá*, pl. *taguai* or *taguwai*, ' female camel.'

b) The *a* is changed into *u;* as,
Alšifa, pl. *alšifu*, ' pocket, bag.'

Šiékāra, pl. šiékāru, ' year.'
Tantábera, pl. tantaberu, ' dove.'
c) Ne is added to the singular.
Oba, pl. obane, ' father.'
Túkūnia, pl. túkuāne, ' pot, earthen vessel.'
d) Ki or naki added to the singular; as,
Akwia, forms its pl. into āwáki, ' she-goat.'
Kwana, pl. kwanaki, ' day.'
Gona, pl. gonaki, ' farm.'
Suna, pl. sunanaki, ' name.'
e) ye is annexed to the singular; as,
Kura, pl. kuraye, ' hyena.'
Rua, pl. ruaye, ' water.'
Gauta, pl gautaye, ' egg-plant,'
Gíwa, pl. giwayé, ' elephant.'
Gainya, pl. gainyaye, ' green herbs.'
Uwa, pl. uwaye, ' mother.'
Kaya, forms its pl. kayayeki, ' things.' Geräthe.

2. The a is dropped in the singular, and some kind of irregular reduplication of the last syllable takes place; as,
Albassa, pl. albasoši, ' onion.'
Yása, pl. yasosi, ' finger.'
Danga, pl. dangógi, ' garden.'
Gúga, pl. gugógi, ' bucket.'
Hainya, pl. hainyóyi, ' road.'
Tasunia pl. tasunióyi, ' tale.'
Igia, pl. igoi or igóyi, ' rope, string.'
Kugi, pl. kugógi, ' hook, fish-hook.'
Maraya, pl. marayóyi, ' orphan.'
Muria pl. murioyi, ' voice.'
Fuska, pl. fuskóki, ' face, countenance.'
Hiska, pl. hiskóki, ' wind.'
Iáka. pl. iakóki, ' boundary.'
Karikia, pl. karikóki, ' girl.'
Kaka, pl. kakoki, ' grandfather.'

Sarika, pl. *Sarikoki*, 'chain.'
Zuma, pl. *zumoki*, ' rags.'
Kafa, pl. *kafafu*, 'foot.'
Kofa, pl. *kofófi*, ' door, the hole for the door.'
Tufa, pl. *tufófi*, ' clothes, garments.'
Murda, pl. *murdodi*, ' snuff-box.'

Exceptions:

Gidda, pl. *giddaše*, ' house, premises.'
Bissa, pl. *bissaše*, ' beasts, creatures.'
Kuda, pl, *kudaše*, ' fly, insect.'
Kaza, or *kasa*, forms its plural *káši*, ' hen.'

3. The *a* of the singular is dropped and *una* appended to the root; as,

Ganga, pl. *gāngúna*, ' drum.'
Gāriká, pl. *gārikúna*, ' enclosed place, garden.'
Gúga, pl. *guguna*, ' bucket.'
Kataruka, pl. *katarukuna*, ' bridge.'
Riga, pl. *riguna*, ' garment, coat.'
Sinda, pl. *sāndúna*, ' stick.'
Šikka, pl. *šikkuna*, ' sack.'
Tōka, pl. *tōkúna*, ' ashes.'

Magana inverts the *una* into *anu*, and forms its pl. *māgánganú*, ' word, history,' &c.

§ 22. Words terminating in *e* in the Singular form the pl. *a*) either by a reduplication of the last syllable, or *b*) adding the syllable *aye*, and dropping the last vowel:

Wake, pl. *wakeke*, and *wakuna*, ' bean.'
Furé, pl. *furaye*, ' blossom.'
Lañye, pl. *langaye*, 'feathers.'

Exceptions:

Itše and *itatše*, pl. *itatua*, ' tree, wood.'
Matše, pl. *máta*, ' woman.'
Karre, pl. *karnuka*, ' dog.'

D

§ 23. Words ending in *i* in the Singular, change the *i* into *a, ai,* and *are;* as,

a) *Aboki*, pl. *abokai*, 'friend.'
Takalmi, pl. *takalma*, 'shoe, sandal.'
Rakumi, pl. *rakuma*, 'camel.'
Šariri, pl. *šarirai*, 'infant.'
Takarikari, pl. *takarikarai*, 'bullock.'
Iri, pl. *irare*, 'nation, seed, kind.'
Wuri, pl. *wurare*, 'place.'
Márari forms the pl. into *máraré*, 'orphan.'

b) The *i* is dropped and *una* added to the root; as,
Baki, pl. *bakuna*, 'mouth.'
Daki, pl. *dakuna*, 'house, room.'
Taiki, pl. *taikuna*, 'sack, measure.'
Kai, pl. *kaúna*, 'head.'
Rami, pl. *ramuna*, 'hole.'
Rawani, pl. *rawuna*, 'turban, head-dress, bandage.'
Sariki, pl. *saráki, sarakai,* and *sarakuna*, 'king.'
Surdi, pl. *surduna*, 'saddle.'
Zani, pl. *zanua*, 'cloth.'
Zobi, pl. *zobuna*, 'ring.'

Exceptions:

Sarmáyi, pl. *samári*, 'young man, bachelor.'
Gari, pl. *garurua*, 'country, town.'
Hakki, pl. *hakkukua*, 'grass.'

c) The *i* is dropped and *aye* added to the root; as,
Kifi, pl. *kifaye*, 'fish.'
Biri, pl. *biraye*, 'monkey.'
Kwami, pl. *kwamaye*, 'flame.'

Exceptions:

Akoši, pl. *akusa*, 'dish, bowl.'
Miši, or *namiši*, pl. *másu*, 'man, male.'

NUMBER OF SUBSTANTIVES.

Gáši, pl. *gasusuka*, ' hair, feathers.'
Doki, pl. *dawaki*, ' horse.'

§ 24. Words ending in *o* change it into *a* or *i*; as,

a) *Yáro*, pl. *yára* (also *yayaye* occurs), ' boy.'
Zófo, pl. *zofi*, ' aged person.'
Bākó, pl. *baki*, and *bakuna*, ' stranger.'
Rufogo, pl. *rufogi*, ' barn, store-house.'
Exceptions:
Tšigo, pl. *tšigogi*, ' gallows.'
Kwado, pl. *kwadia*, and *kwaduna*, ' frog, or toad.'
Gadó, pl. *gadaše*, ' bed.'

b) The *o* falls out and *aye* is added to the root; as,
Gádo, pl. *gadaye*, ' hog.'
Rágo, pl. *raguaye*, ' idler.'
Berdo, pl. *berdaye*, ' pigeon.'

c) The *o* is omitted and *anu* or *unu* joined to the root; as,
Ido, pl. *īdánu*, ' eye.'
Sanfo, pl. *sanfuna*, ' basket.'
Rago, pl. *raguna*, ' ram.'

d) *ni* or *ri* are joined to the root; as,
Kafo, pl. *kafóni*, ' horn.'
Taro, pl. *tarori*, ' heap, multitude.'
Kasko, forms *kasku*, ' cup, mug.'

§ 25. Words ending in *u* in the singular take *a* or *na* in the plural; as,

Hanu, pl. *hanua*, ' hand.'
Lambu, pl. *lambuna*, ' dry season garden.'
Yimbu, pl. *yimbuna*, ' potter's clay.'
Rumbu, pl. *rumbuna*, ' store-house.'
Mutum forms the pl. *mutane*, ' person, people.'

§ 26. Nouns compounded with the prefix *mai* form the plural in *masu*; as,

Maimagani, pl. *masumagani*, 'doctor.'

Maitalautši, pl. *masutalautši*, 'poor person.'
Maigona, pl. *masugona*, 'farmer.'
Maitši, pl. *masutši*, 'one that eats much.'
Maihaŋkali, pl. *masuhaŋkali*, 'wise person.'

CASES OF SUBSTANTIVES.

§. 27. There being no Cases in the sense in which the word is used in Greek and Latin, the explanation of the method by which this language compensates for this apparent deficiency may be referred to the Syntax: still it will be necessary to explain in this place, however briefly, at least the Genitive Case.

§ 28. The Genitive or Construct Case. This relation is expressed in various ways.

1. It is indicated by the *position* which the modified substantive occupies in the sentence. Thus the noun which reaches its idea and end in the word next following, is placed before and pronounced rapidly with the following, as though they formed but one word, and this is more especially the case, when the second word begins with one of the liquid letters. At the same time we cannot help thinking that in many instances it may be attributed to carelessness in the speaker, or want of perception in the hearer. A few examples will be sufficient to arrest the reader's attention; as,

Diamatše=dia-n-matše, 'the woman's daughter.'
Rua Madina=rua-n-Madina, 'the water of Medina.'
Magana namiši, 'the man's word.'
Dia rana, 'the daughter of the sun.'
Magana bako da matšiši-n-rua, 'the story of the stranger and of the water-serpent.'

2. The particles *na* (masc.), and *ta* (fem.), are employed to indicate the relation of the Genitive, and that more especially when the emphasis lies on the *na*, so that it may frequently be translated by 'that of,' or 'those of;' examples:

Riga ta Abbega, 'Abbega's coat;' *i.e.* not of any one else.
Kwára na šinkaffa, 'grain of rice;' *i.e.* no other grain.
Magana ta bākinsa, 'the word of his mouth.'
Da-n-záki šina-gōlgodáwa kāfánsa da na ūwása, 'the child of the lion was comparing (measuring) his foot with that of his mother.'

3. In the rapidity of pronunciation the *a* in *na* is frequently dropped, and the *n* forms the sign of the Genitive between two substantives. This *n* is therefore joined to the first word in our publications, and without the hyphen introduced in this Grammar only, to show the necessity of reading the words ending with *n* rapidly together with the next following; as,

Oba-n-giši, literally, 'father of the house,' *i.e.* 'master, owner, proprietor.'
Dā-n-ūwána, 'child of my mother=brother.'
Nama-n-zunzua, 'the flesh of the bird.'
Suna-n-yáro, 'the name of the boy.'
Mutane-n-gari nan, 'the people of this country.'
Daiansu, 'one of them.'
Sília ta alharini, 'a chain of silk.'

The other Cases see Syntax.

CHAPTER III.

PRONOUNS.

§ 29. The Hausa language has developed six classes of Pronouns, viz.: Personal, Reflective, Relative, Interrogative, Demonstrative, and Indefinite Pronouns. They are (like the pronouns in Hebrew to which they bear some affinity, as, נִי *ni,* ךְ and כָּה *ka,* ךְ and כִי *ki;* and מוּ *mu* בִי, תְ *ta,*) either *Separable* or *Inseparable.* To the latter class belong the simple form of the *Possessive* and of the *Objective* Pronouns.

1. **Personal or Substantive Pronouns:**

They are chiefly formed from the personal characteristics as used in the conjugation of the verb, and are necessary for the inflection of the verb in the imperative mood, and otherwise, as will be explained when we come to speak of the verb.

To avoid frequent repetition, we notice that the first person sing. and all the persons in the pl. are of common gender, while in the second and third persons gender is distinguished by different forms.

Personal or Substantive and Objective Pronouns.

Singular.

Person.	Absolute. Separable.	Inseparable.	Separable.
1	na, I.	ni, me, to me.	máni, garéni, to me
2 m.	kai; ka, thou.	ka, thee, to thee	máka, gareka, to thee
2 f.	ke; ki, thou.	ki, thee, to thee.	máki, gareki, to thee
3 m.	ši (ya), he.	ši, sa, him, to him.	mása, garása and garésa, gareši.
3 f.	ita, ta, she.	ta, her, to her.	máta, garata, and garéta.

Plural.

1	mu, we.	mu (muna) us.	mamu, garemu.
2	ku, ye.	ku (muku) you.	maku, gareku.
3	su, they.	su (musu) them.	masu, garésu.

NOTE.—To enable the student of Hausa to pursue his studies with greater facility, the following conjugation of the verb bā and bāda, 'to give,' is given in anticipation:—

Singular.

Person.

1	na-báka, I give thee.	na-báda maka, or garéka, I give to thee.
2 m.	ka-báni, thou givest me.	ka-bada maní, or gureni, thou givest to me.
2 f.	ki-baši, thou givest him.	ki-bada masa, or garasa, or garesa, thou givest him.
3 m.	ya-bata, he gives her.	ya-bada mata, or garata, or gareta, he gives her.
3 f.	ta-baši, she gives him.	ta-bada mata, or garasa, or garesa, she gives him.

Plural.

1	mu-baku, we give you.	mu-bada muku, or garéku.
2	ku-bamu, ye give us.	ku-bada muna, or garemu.
3	su-basu, they give them.	su-bada masu, or garemu.

2. Personal Pronouns, Compound Form.

There is another class of Compound Pronouns, which is formed by prefixing *kai*, 'head,' to the simple form of the Possessive Pronouns; as, *kaina*, lit. my head=myself. In the rapidity of pronunciation the *i* is sometimes ejected in all other except in the first person sing. (See § 4 Note); and a third class, increasing the emphasis, and excluding every person but the speaker, is formed by prefixing the Personal Pronouns and the syllable *da* before *kaina*; as,

Singular.

Person.	Second Class.	Third Class.
1	káina, myself.	ni da kaina, I myself.
2 m.	kanka, thyself.	kai da kanka, thou thyself.
2 f.	kanki, thyself.	ki da kanki, thou thyself.
3 m.	kansa, himself.	ši da kansa, he himself.
3 f.	kanta, herself.	ita, or ta da kanta, herself.

Person. Plural.

1 *kaimu*, and *ka'mu* } ourselves.	*mu da kaimu*, or *ka'mu*.
2 *kanku*, yourselves.	*ku da kanku*.
3 *kansu*, themselves.	*su da kansu*.

3. In the same way also is declined a peculiar form, *ni kadai*, I only, or, I alone; as, *ni kadai, ka kadai, ke* or *ki kadai, si kadai, ita* or *ta kadai, mu kadai, ku kadai, su kadai*.

Possessive Pronouns.

§ 30. There are two kinds of Possessive Pronouns, which may be called *Simple*, and *Compound Emphatic*; the former are *Inseparable*, i.e. they are always appended to the Substantives as Suffixes; the latter are *Separable*, and used absolutely. The Gender is distinguished in each person of the Sing.

NOTE.—In a few instances, perhaps through inadvertency, the masculine pronouns of the first person are used with feminine nouns; as, *da-n-uwana*, instead of *uwata*, and *rigana* instead of *rigata*, &c.

1. The Inseparable Possessive Pronouns are:

Person. *Singular.*

1 *na*, my	*dokina*, my horse	*uwána* (?) my mother
1 f. *ta*, my	*dokia*, (?) my ,,	*uwata*, my ,,
2 m. *ka* or *nka*, thy	*dokinka*, thy ,,	*uwanka*, thy ,,
2 f. *ki* or *nki*, thy	*dokinki*, thy ,,	*uwanki*, thy ,,
3 m. *sa* or *nsa*, his	*dokinsa*, his ,,	*uwansa*, his ,,
3 f. *ta* or *nta*, her	*dokinta*, her ,,	*uwanta*, her ,,

Plural.

1 *mu* or *nmu*, our	*dokimu*, our horse	*uwamu*, our mother
2 *ku* or *nku*, your	*dokinku*, your ,,	*uwanku*, your ,,
3 *su* or *nsu*, their	*dokinsu*, their ,,	*uwansu*, their ,,

Dawaki, horses, *uwaye*, mothers.

Dawakina; dawakita (?); *dawakinka; dawakinki; dawakinsa; dawakinta; dawakimu; dawakinku; dawakinsu;* so likewise: *uwayena* (?), *uwayeta*, &c.

Note.—The suffixes combined with *n*, as *nka, nki, nsa*, are equivalent to our Genitive case in the expression 'a friend of mine,' as in *gidda na* (§ 28, 2) *uwánsa*, the 'house *of his* mother;' *dóki na abokinsa*, 'the horse of his friend,' whereas without the *n*, the suffix is merely the adjective pronoun, as *uwásа ta-tše*, 'his mother said;' and *ōbása yabáda mása bindiga da baki biu*, 'his father gave him a gun with two mouths,' (barrels) and *bindiga na obansa šina-da báki biu*, 'his father's gun has two mouths,' and *kára ta muriansa ta-báda mani dsóro*, 'the sound of his voice frightened me;' and *muriasa ba kammanta matše ba ta-ke*, 'his voice is not like that of a woman.' This distinction, however, is not observed in common conversation, and there occur, therefore, suffixes with *n* combined merely as adjective pronouns.

2. Separable Possessive Pronouns:

When the Possessive Pronouns refer to a preceding subject which is omitted, and are thus used *absolutely*, corresponding with the German '*der meinige, die meinige, das meinige*,' and the English 'mine, thine,' or, with a stronger emphasis, are like 'my own, thy own,' &c., they assume another form, and are as follows:

m. *Nawa*, 'my own,' 'mine;' f. *nata; näka; naki: nasa; nata; namu; naku; nasu.*

DEMONSTRATIVE PRONOUNS.

§ 31. 1. The Demonstrative Pronouns, indicating *things* near at hand, as well as remote, no distinction like 'this,' and 'that,' being noticed, are: *nga, nan*, and *wonnan*, signifying 'this and these, that and those.' They have no distinct forms for the plural, neither any distinction of Gender. Examples:

Dóki nga, 'this horse.' *Muria nga*, 'this voice.'
Mutume nan, 'this man.' *Matše nan*, 'this woman.'
Letafi wonnan ba wonnan ba, 'this book, not that one.'

2. The Demonstrative Pronouns referring to *persons* or

living beings form a plural, and distinguish the Gender in the Singular, as,

woṅga, m. and
wogga, f. } pl. *woddaṅga*, 'this, these ;' 'that, those.'

Examples:

Yáro wóṅga, 'this boy ;' *yārínía wogga*, 'this girl ;' pl. *yárawoddoṅga yārana ne*, ' these boys are my boys.'

3. Demonstrative *Adverbial* Pronouns. These are:

Nana, ' here, hither,' and *nan ; nan*, ' here, there ;'

Daganan, ' here, at this place ;' and

Tšan, and *dagatšan*, ' there, yonder.'

4. *Abin da*, lit. the thing which='*das was*,' or, '.that which=what,' may be mentioned also; as: *kána-ganni abin da suna-yi?* ' dost thou see the thing which=that which= what they are doing ?' *abin da na-fadda maka gaskia ne*, ' the thing which=that which=what I told thee is true.' *Ba ka-sanni ba abin da ya-sāméka ga dúnia nan*, ' thou dost not know what may happen to thee in the world.'

INTERROGATIVE PRONOUNS.

§ 32. The Interrogative Pronouns are:

1. *Nia*, ' I, or, is it me ?=you mean me ?'

    Nia na-fadda hakka ? ' did I say so ? was it I that said it ?'

2. *Wa*, pl. *sua ?* ' who, whose,' referring to *persons* of both genders :

    Wa ya-daúki kurdina? ' who took my money ?'

    Wa ya-fadda maka ? ' who told thee ?'

    Mata wa (nwa) ta-kūwá giširi ? ' whose wife was turned into salt ?'

    Tumaki nwa ke nan ? ' whose sheep are these ?'

3. *Wonne ?* ' what ? which ?' *wonne iri-n-letafi ke nan ?* ' what kind of book is this ?'

4. *Wáne*, m. and *wátše*, f. and *wānéne*, referring to *persons* both in the sing. and pl. These are evidently Compound forms of *wa*, ' who ?' and *ne*, m., and *tše*, f., of

the verb 'to be,' 'to exist;' for in many cases it is
necessary to construe them in English, as such compounds, and to say, ' who is it that?' or, ' what is it that?'
as, *wane šina-ía sāyénsa?* ' who can buy it ?' *wānéne
kana-so ya-fi wonnan* ? 'what dost thou want better
than this?' *wanene nakuduka ya-tšainye níma dúka ?*
'who is that' *nakuduka,* (for all of you) ' who did eat
all the meat ?'

5. *Mi ?* 'what' (מִי)? *mi kuna-yi daši ?* ' what are you doing
with it ?' *mi ya-sāméka ?* 'what is the matter with
thee ? what aileth thee ?'

6. *Míne* and *mīnéne?*' ' who ?' or, ' what ?' or, ' who is it,' or,
what is it that ? (See 4, above.) *Minéne šina-tši tūmáki-
na ?* ' who is it, or what is it, that destroys my sheep ?'

Míne da Engliž ? 'what is it in English ?'
Minene sūnsuá nan túna-fadda máni ? ' what is it that this
bird is telling to me ?'
Fadda mani minene su ? ' tell me what they are ?'

7. *Káka ?* ' how ? or what ?'
Káka múna-yi da dūkia nan ? ' what shall we do ?=how
shall we deal with his property ?'
Kaka īyálinka dúka ? ' how is all thy family ?'

8. *Dómi ?* ' why ?'
Domi kina-wórigi da muršan ? ' why dost thou play with
the coral ?'
Domi ba ka-so ži abin nan ? ' why dost thou not like to
hear that ?'

9. Adverbial Interrogative Pronouns. These are:
Enna ? ' where, whence ?' *dagaenna ?* ' whence ?'
Enna abokinka ? ' where is thy friend ?'
Daga enna ka-fitto ? ' whence dost thou come from ?'
Yaúše ? ' when ?' *yaúše kána-táffia ?* ' when art thou going ?'
Nawá ? ' how much, how many ?'

Kurdinsa nawá? 'how much money for it? = what is the price of it?'

Mutane nawá? 'how many persons?'

INDEFINITE PRONOUNS.

§ 33. The Indefinite Pronouns are formed from the Interrogative forms, by prefixing the *intensive* particle *kō*; as, *wa?* 'who?' *kówa,* ' any one, every one;' so also *kowaddane,* 'some, any.'

1. *Kówa,* 'every one, any one, any, all.'
2. *Kōwáne,* m., and *kowatše,* f., referring to *persons* only, 'every, every one, any, any one, all.'
3. *Kówonne,* m., and *kowotše,* f., referring to persons and things, ' every, every one, any, any one, all.'
4. *Kómi,* ' something, any thing, every thing, whatever, whatsoever.'

Kómi, ya-fádda maki ki-yi, ' whatsoever he tells thee, do.'

Negatively expressed by *ba, babu,* 'no, not, not any thing.' (*Babu,* contraction of *abu,* or *abin,* 'thing,' and the negative particle *ba,*' not,' *babu*=*ba abu*=*babu,* though *babu abu* is also used.)

Ba ši-yi maki kómi, ' it will do thee no harm.'

Babu komi, 'no matter, of no consequence.'

Babu wonda ya-sannši, ' there was no one that knew him.'

5. *Kōminé,* 'whatever, whatsoever=whatsoever it be or was.'

Kōminé ta-roko Alla, Alla ya-báta, ' whatsoever it was that she asked of God, God gave her.'

6. *Wonni,* m., *wota,* f.,' some, some one, a certain, another;' pl. *wosu; wonni, wonni,* ' the one, the other, some some.'

It has frequently to be rendered by the Indefinite Article, or, ' the one, the other.' Examples:

Dia ta wonni matše tána-da keáo, ta wonni matše dianta babu keáo, the daughter of one woman=the one was beautiful, the daughter of the other was not beautiful.

7. *Wóddansu*, 'some (lit. some of them), correlative, some : 'some, some—others.'

Ní koya ga woddansu, 'I shall teach others.'

Wóddansu mutane súna-kíwo rakuma, woddansu súna-nóma, 'some mind camels, others attend to their farms.'

So also *waddanan*, these; as,

Mu woddanan úku an-haifému ga gari daía, 'we (these) three were born at the same place.'

8. *Hakka*, 'so=the same,' and *síne*, 'it is he=the same.'
9. *Adverbial Indefinite Pronouns.* These are:

a) Of place:

Kōenna, 'anywhere, any whither, somewhere, wheresoever, whithersoever.'

Ki-taffi kōenna ki-ke so, 'go whithersoever it may please thee.'

b) Of time:

Kōyaúše, 'at any time, always.'

Ina-túnawa koyauše, 'I am always remembering it.'

Uwaye koyauše suna-so su-koya ga diánsu, 'mothers always like to teach their children.'

RELATIVE PRONOUNS.

§ 34. There are but *two* Relative Pronoun forms, viz. *Wonné*, and *wonda*, m., *wodda*, f., pl. *woddanda* (*woddanan*) of which *da* and *nda* are abbreviated forms for both numbers and both genders—'who, which.' Examples :

Wonné gari ne da ūwáka zata-káika? 'which is the place to which thy mother is going to take thee?'

Abintši wonda ši-ke so, 'the food which he is fond of.'

Wonda ya-sāyému daga Bornu, 'he who bought us in Bornu.'

Ba ši sanní ba wonda ya-dauki kurdinsa, 'he did not know who it was that took his money.'

RECIPROCAL PRONOUNS.

§ 35. There is but one; as, *siúna, einander*, ' each other ;' *sabbaba girimansu ba su-ia wutše siúna*, ' they cannot pass one the other on account of their size ;' *suna-raba kurdi ga siúnansu*, ' they divide the money among each other ;' *tumaki suna tunkuda-n šiúnansu*, ' the sheep are pushing each other.'

CHAPTER IV.

ADJECTIVES.

§ 36. Adjectives are either *Simple* or *Compound, Original* or *Derived*. They are employed both as attributes, *i.e.* qualifying nouns, and as predicatives, *i.e.* standing in the place of a verb, and expressing the predicate of a sentence. Example: *babá sariki*, the 'great king;' and *sariki babá ne*, ' the king is great.' Simple adjectives qualifying the noun are generally placed before the noun, while the compound forms, expressing the qualification or attribute by means of prefixed particles, as *da* and *mai*, follow the noun, being regarded as abstract substantives (*yawa-n-rai*, ' length of life=long life.') in apposition, and must frequently be construed by a relative sentence.

§ 37. The formation of the plural differs from that of the substantive, and ends almost invariably in *ye* or *u*.

§ 38. The characteristic termination of the feminine gender is *a*, but, influenced by euphonical laws, it may be *ia, una,* or *unia*.

Nāgari, tagari, and *nākwarai, takwarai*, ' well, good,' indicating the gender at the beginning by *na* and *ta*, seem to be the only exceptions to this rule. We shall now give a comprehensive list of most of the Adjectives occurring in our collection.

Baba, pl. irregular, *mainya*, 'great, large.' The reduplication expresses what we express by the adverb *very*, as, *mutane mainya mainya*, 'very great, high, or respectable people.'

Bakki (baki), f. *bakka*, pl. *babaku*, 'black;' *mutane babaku*, 'black people,' more frequently, *babaku mutane*.

Dōgo, f. *dogua*, pl. *dōgayé*, 'high, tall, dense, large;' *dogo itatše*, pl. *itatua dogaye*, 'high tree;' *dógo-n-dáši*, 'dense forest.'

Fari, f. *fara*, pl. *farufarú*, also, *farare* and *faráye*, 'white.'

Gašiére, f. *gašiéra*, pl. *gašiéru*, 'short, small;' likewise *gašéria wáka*, 'a short song.'

Girima, 'great;' *giririma*, 'very great.'

Kadan, f. *kadana*, (קטן) 'little, small.'

Kananú, pl. *kanané*, 'little, small;' and: *kankana karnuka*, 'little dogs.'

Karami, f. *karama*, and *karamia*, pl. *karamai*, 'little, small, young;' *Yáro karami*, 'little boy;' *Yarínia karámia mugúniá*, 'little naughty girl;' *tagia karama*, 'little cap.'

Mugu, f. *mugunia*, pl. irregular, *mīágu*, 'bad, wicked;' *Mugu mutum*; *mīágu mutane*; *mugunia matše*, *mīagu máta*.

Rama and *ramame*, f. *ramamia*, 'thin, lean, emaciated;' *yarínia ta-tše ga kánuàta: ni ramamia? na-fíki da kibba*. *Yaro ya-amsa: ni rāmamé, na-fiki da kibba*, 'The girl said to her sister: am I lean? I surpass thee in fatness. The boy answered,' &c.

Wáwa, pl. *wawaye*, 'foolish, senseless.'

Zofo, f. *zofua*, pl. *zofi*, 'old;' used substantively also.

Kekaše, f. *kekasa* and *kekasašia*, pl. *kekasu*, 'dry, dried.'

§ 39. Adjectives corresponding in sense to the Past Participle in English are formed from verbs.

a) by a kind of irregular reduplication of the last syllable; as,

Dafafe, pl. *dafafu*, 'cooked,' from *daffa*, ' to cook.
Bie or *biye*, pl. *biyu*, 'followed,' from *bi*, ' to follow.'
Dsarare, pl. *dsararu*, ' drawn, as a sword.'
Haifafe ,, *u*, 'born,' from *haifi*, ' to beget, to give birth.'
Karikatše ,, *u*, ' bent, crooked,' from *karikata*, ' to bend.'
Kōnáne ,, *u*, 'burned,' from *kóne*, 'to burn.'
Matatše ,, *u*, ' dead,' from *mutu* (מות), 'to die.'
Nína, *nináne*, pl. *ninanu*, ' ripe, ripened, cooked.'
Šaidade pl. *šaidadu*, ' approved,' from *šaida*, ' to prove; bear testimony.'
Kirraye pl. *kirrayu*, ' called,' from *kirra* (קרא), ' to call.'
Širiaye, and *širaye*, pl. *širiyeyu*, and *aširiye*, ' prepared, ready,' from *širia*, ' to prepare.'
Tšietátše, pl. *tšiétatu*, ' saved,' from *tšieto, tšietšie*, ' to save.'
Yirdade, pl. *yirdadu*, ' accredited;' likewise, ' active, one who believes = believer.'

b) *a* is prefixed to the infinitive, giving it the sense of a passive, or of a neuter participle; as,

Aságe, ' drawn;' *tamma asage*, ' a drawn sword.'
Akwantše, ' laid down.'
Aratáye, '.hanged, hanging.'
Adarime, ' bound.'
Adsaye, ' standing erect.'
Akaffe, ' sticking to, fastened.'
Awanka, ' washed.'
Akuntše, ' untied.'
Amatše, ' dead.'
Aširige, ' laden;' as, *širigi aširige da mutane*.
Ašike, ' melted, wet.'
Amantše, ' forgotten.'
Asanntše, ' understood, known.'
Akassa, ' on foot,'
Ahadie, ' swallowed.'
Atauše, ' pressed.'

Atšikke, 'filled.'
Asamne, 'sitting down.'

§ 40. The verb *da*, signifying 'to have,' or 'to possess,' 'to be,' or 'to exist,' and as preposition 'with,' forms Adjectives expressing the possession or the existence of the thing, to whose names it is prefixed; as,

Da anfani, lit. 'having use = being useful, profitable, beneficial; with profit, or with benefit, or advantage.'

Da yunwa, 'having hunger, hungry;' *suna-mutua da yunwa*, 'they are dying of hunger.'

Da rua, 'having water, watery;' *da wuta*, 'having fire = fiery.'

Da rai, 'having life, being alive;' *da wuya*, 'being difficult.'

Da rairai, 'having sand, sandy;' *da kaifi*, 'having edge = sharp.'

Da nauyi, 'having weight, heavy;' *da kedo*, 'having beauty, beautiful.'

Namiši da matše, 'a man that has a wife = married man.'

Matše da namiši, 'a woman that has a husband = married woman.'

Mutum da hankali, 'a man that has good sense = sensible man.'

Mutum da kondo dagá hanunsa, 'a man with, or having a basket in his hand.'

§ 41. The Prefix *mai*, pl. *masu* (§ 16) forms Adjectives denoting the occupation with the thing expressed by the substantive, or verb; as,

Maimagani, 'one who is practising the medical art = doctor.'

Maikiwo, 'one that attends cattle = shepherd, herdsman.'

Maikúnu, 'one that boils gruel.'

Máimugu-n-halli, 'one that has a bad temper, insolent or irritable person.'

Wata maizakkua, the 'month which is coming=next month.'

Mai and *masu* are also connected with Adverbs and other Adjectives, increasing the strength or intensity of the original idea; as,

Maidzíni, 'being very sharp, or pointed.'

Farítši maidzíni, ko farítši da dzini, kammada báki-n-alúra, 'having finger-nails as sharp as the point of a needle.'

Gidda maikedo, 'the house, the fine one=very fine.'

Gari mainésa, 'a far distant country.'

(See also § 26 and § 28, 2, *na* and *ta*.)

§ 42. The negative (see § 33, 4) is expressed by: *ba, babu,* and *maras,* pl. *marasa;* as,

Babu ūwá, 'without mother=mother-less.'

Babu maitaffia ga ríšia da dere, 'no one goes to the well by night.'

Maras hankali, pl. *marasahankali*, 'senseless person, insensible.'

Maraskatšia, 'uncircumcised.'

Maraskarifi, 'powerless, helpless, without strength.'

Respecting such Adjectives as indicate the country to which one belongs, *i.e.* Patricial Adjectives, compare § 19.

CHAPTER V.

THE NUMERALS.

§ 43. The Cardinal Numbers are as follow:—

1 daía.
2 biú.
3 úku.
4 fúdu, or húdu.
5 biál, or biár, or biat.
6 šidda
7 bokoi
8 tokos.
9 tára.
10 góma.
11 goma ša daía, or ša daía.
12 goma šabiu, or ša biú.
13 goma ša úku, or ša úku.
14 goma ša fudu, or ša fudu.
15 goma ša bial, or ša biál, biar, biat.
16 goma ša šidda, or ša šidda
17 goma ša bokoi, or ša bokoi.
18 goma ša tókos, or ša tókos.
19 goma ša tara, or ša tara.
20 íširin, or áširin; עֶשְׂרִים, عشرين.
21 íširin da daía.
22 iširin da biú.
23 íširin da úku.
24 íširin da fudu.
25 íširin da bial, biar, biat.
26 íširin da šidda.
27 iširin da bokoi.
28 iširin da tókos.
29 iširin da tára.
30 tallátin ثلاثين.
31 tallátin da daía.
32 tallatin da biú.
33 tallátin da úku.
34 tallatin da fúdu.
35 tallatin da bial, biar, biat.
36 tallatin da šidda.
37 tallatin da bokoi.
38 tallatin da tókos.
39 tallatin da tára.
40 arbaín אַרְבָּעִים; اربعين.
41 arbain da daía.
42 arbain da biú.
43 arbain da úku.
44 arbain da fúdu.
45 arbain da biál, biar, biát.
46 arbain da šidda.

47 arbain da bokoi.
48 arbain da tókos.
49 arbain da tára.
50 hamsin חֲמִשִׁים, خَمْسِين
51 hamsin da daía.
52 hamsin da biú.
53 hamsin da úku.
54 hamsin da fúdu.
55 hamsin da bial, biar, biat.
56 hamsin da šídda.
57 hamsin da bokoi.
58 hamsin da tókos.
59 hamsin da tára.
60 settin שִׁשִּׁים, سِتِّين
61 settin da daía.
62 settin da biú.
63 settin da úku.
64 settin da fúdu.
65 settin da bial, biar, biat
66 settin da šídda.
67 settin da bokoi.
68 settin da tókos.
69 settin da tára.
70 sebbain, or sabbain שִׁבְעִים, سَبْعِين.
71 sebbain da daía.
72 sebbain da biú.
73 sebbain da úku.
74 sebbain da fúdu.
75 sebbain da bial, biar, biat.
76 sebbain da šídda.
77 sebbain da bokoi.
78 sebbain da tókos.
79 sebbain da tára.

80 tamánin ثَمَانِين
81 tamánin da daía.
82 tamánin da biu.
83 tamánin da úku.
84 tamánin da fúdu.
85 tamánin da bial, biar, biat.
86 tamánin da šídda.
87 tamánin da bokoi.
88 tamánin da tókos.
89 tamánin da tara.
90 tissain תִּשְׁעִים; تِسْعِين
91 tissain da daía.
92 tissain da biú.
93 tissain da úku.
94 tissain da fúdu.
95 tissain da bial, biar, biat.
96 tissain da šídda.
97 tissain da bokoi.
98 tissain da tókos.
99 tissain da tára.
100 darí.
101 darí da daía.
110 darí da góma.
111 darí da gómā ša daía.
120 darí da tširin.
121 darí da tširin da daía.
130 darí da tallátin.
131 darí da tallátin da daía.
140 darí da arbaín.
141 darí da arbain da daía.
150 darí da hámsin.
151 darí da hamsin da daía.

THE NUMERALS.

152 darí da hamsin da biú.
160 dari da settin.
161 darí da settin da daía.
170 darí da sebbain.
171 dari da sebbain da daía.
180 darí da tamánin.
181 darí da tamánin da daía.
190 darí da tíssain.
191 darí da tíssain da daia.
200 métin מָאתַיִם, ميتَين
 (also, dšaugu biú and darí biú.
201 metin da daía (dsaugu biú da daía) dari biú da daía.
210 métin da góma.
220 métin da íširin, or áširin.
230 metin da tallatin.
240 metin da arbain.
250 metin da hamsin.
260 metin da settin.
270 metin da sebbain, or sabbain.
280 metin da tamánin.
290 metin da téssain.
300 darí úku.
301 darí úku da daía.
310 darí úku da góma.
311 darí úku da góma ša daía.
312 darí úku da goma ša biú.
319 darí úkú da góma ša tára.

400 darí fúdu.
401 darí fúdu da daía.
410 darí fuda da goma.
500 darí bial, and hamsinonía; خَمْسُمِائة.
600 darí šídda.
700 darí bokoí.
800 dari tókos.
900 darí tára.
1000 dúbu, or samber.
1001 dubu da daía, or samber da daía
1010 dubu da goma, or samber da goma.
1110 dubu darí da goma.
1111 dubu daía da goma ša daía.
1999 dubu darí da téssain da tára.
2000 dubu biú, or álfin, اَلْفَين الفَرِين.
2001 dubu biú da daía, or alfin da daía.
2010 dubu biú da goma, or alfin da góma.
3000 dubu úku, or samber úku, or talláta.
3001 dubu úku da daía, or samber úku da daía, or talláta da daia.
3010 dubu úku da goma, or samber úku da goma, or talláta da goma.
4000 dubu fúdu, or samber fudu.

4001	dubu fudu da daía.	90,000	dubu tíssain, or samber tíssain.
4010	dubu fudu da goma, or samber fudu da goma	200,000	dubu darí biú, or samber dari biú.
5000	dubu bial (biar, biat) or samber bial.	300,000	dubu darí úku, or samber darí úku.
5001	dubu bial da daía, or samber bial da daía.	400,000	dubu darí fúdu, or samber darí fúdu.
5010	dubu bial da goma, or samber bial da góma.	500,000	dubu darí bial, or samber darí biál.
6000	dubu šídda, or saber šídda.	600,000	dubu darí šídda, or samber darí šídda.
7000	dubu bokoí, or samber bokoí.	700,000	dubu darí bokoí, or samber darí boko
8000	dubu tókos, or samber tókos	800,000	dubu darí tókos, or samber darí tókos.
9000	dubu tára, or samber tára.	900,000	dubu darí tára, or samber dari tára.
10,000	dubu goma, or samber goma.	1,000,000	dubu darí goma.
20,000	dubu iširin, or samber iširin.	2,000,000	dubu darí goma biú.
30,000	dubu tallátin, or samber tallatin.	3,000,000	dubu darí goma ukú.
40,000	dubu arbain, or samber arbain.	4,000,000	dubu darí goma fúdu.
50,000	dubu hámsin, or samber hámsin.	5,000,000	dubu darí goma bial (biar, biát).
60,000	dubu settin, or samber settin.	6,000,000	dubu darí goma šídda.
70,000	dubu sebbain, or samber sebbain.	7,000,000	dubu darí goma bokoí.
80,000	dubu tamánin, or samber tamánin.	9,000,000	dubu darí goma tára.

NOTE 1.—In the common way of counting, the numerals from 11 to 19 appear in a contracted form; as, instead of *goma ša daía*, merely *ša daía* 11, *ša biú* 12, *ša úku* 13, &c.

NOTE 2.—18 and 19 ; 28 and 29, and in the same way all decades up to 98 and 99, are also expressed in a different manner ; as, *iširin biu babu*, ' twenty less two,' and *iširin daia babu*, or *babu daia*, 'twenty less one;' *tallatin biu babu*, ' thirty less two,' &c.

For the tenths from 20 to 90, some use a plural form of *góma*, 10; as, *gómia*, with the units to 9, and say : *gómia biú* 20 ; *gomia uku* 30 ; *gomia fúdu* 40 ; *gomia bial* 50 ; *gomia šidda* 60 ; *gomia bókoi* 70 ; *gomia tókos* 80 ; *gomia tara* 90. There can be no doubt but that this method is the *original* Hausa way of counting, as it is still used among slaves and the lower classes ; and that the other method has been adopted by the higher classes, and especially by merchants, from the Arabs.

Ordinal Numbers.

§ 44. The *Ordinals* are formed from the Cardinals by means of the prefixes *na* and *ta*, which combine two offices, viz., the formation of the Ordinals, and the distinction of Gender. ' The *first*' has no connection with the Cardinal ' *daía*,' but is irregular, as, *nafári*, m., *tafári*, f., and is probably derived from the verb *fára*, ' to begin,' hence, as it were, the beginner=the first. In this sense *nafári* is ' the first-born son,' and *tafári* the ' first-born daughter.' When it signifies superiority in rank and position, ' the second,' unless followed by other Ordinals, is not *nabiú*, but *nabáya*, derived from *báya*, ' back,' ' behind,' that is, the one that comes after another, or is below in rank and position, as it were, ' the one behind,' and hence, also, ' the last.'

The 1st m. *nafári*, f. *tafári*.
2nd m. *nabiu*, f. *tabiú*, and *nabáya*, *tabaya*.

3rd m. *naúku*, f. *taúku*.
4th m. *nafudu*, f. *tafúdu*.
5th m. *nabial*, f. *tabial*.
6th m. *našidda*, f. *tašiddā*.
7th m. *nabokoí*, f. *tabókoi*.
8th m. *natókos*, f. *tatókos*.
9th m. *natára*, f. *tatára*.
10th m. *nagóma*, f. *tagóma*.
11th m. *nagóma ša daía*, f. *tagóma ša daía*.
12th m. *nagóma ša biú*, f. *tagóma ša biú*.

NOTE.—In the numbers above ten a preference is manifested in the language for the use of the Cardinals instead of the Ordinals, though the latter do also occur; it is very likely, however, merely from inattention.

Adverbial Numbers.

§ 45. The Adverbial Numerals, in answer to the question, How often? are formed from the Cardinals by means of the word *saa* or *sā*, 'time,' prefixed. The second *a* is changed into *o* or *u*, as *saodaía*, or *saudaía*:

saudaía or *saodaia*, 'once.'
saubiú, 'twice.'
sauúku, 'three times.'
saúfudu, 'four times.'
sau biál, biár, biat, 'five times.'
sao šídda, 'six times.'
sau bokoí, 'seven times.'
sau tokos, 'eight times.'
sautára, 'nine times.'
saugoma, 'ten times.'
saugoma šadaía, 'eleven times.'
saugoma ša biu, 'twelve times.'
sautširin, 'twenty times.'
sautallátin, 'thirty times.'
sauarbain, 'forty times.'
sauhamsin, 'fifty times.'
sausettin, 'sixty times.'
sausebbain, 'seventy times.'
sautamánin, 'eighty times.'
sautissain, 'ninety times.'
saudarí, 'hundred times.'

THE NUMERALS. 41

Distributive Numerals.

§ 46. The *Distributive Numerals* in answer to the question 'how many to each?' are expressed by a repetition of the Cardinals; as, *ya-aikesu biu biu,* ' he sent them two and two.' *Ya-bada daía daía ga kōwanḗnsu,* 'he gave one to each of them.'

Fractional Numbers.

§ 47. No other Fractional Numbers have been discovered by the writer than such as may be formed by the word *šáše,* ' half,' more properly, ' part or portion ;' as, *ya-báni šáše,* ' he gave me half;' and *sun-báni šaše-n-úku,* ' they gave me (the third part) three parts.'

NOTE.—There occur but two or three instances in our collection of stories, fables, and proverbs, in which *ana* is combined with Cardinal numerals to express an Ordinal sense; as, *da sunka-kētaré daía, biú, anauku sunka-issa wúri-n-kássa,* ' when they had crossed one, two, after the third, they arrived on dry ground.' And, *yáro ya-yi súkua rākumí sāuúku, anafudu ya-taffó, ya-dauki yārínia ya-āšiéta bíssa rākuminsa,* ' the boy galloped the camel three times ; the fourth time he came, he took the girl, he put her on his camel.'

CHAPTER VI.

THE VERB.

§ 48. There are in Hausa, as in every language, *Primitive Verbs*; i.e. such the origin of which cannot be ascertained; as, *tši*, ' to eat;' *ša*, ' to drink;' *ši* or *ži*, ' to hear;' and there are *Derived* Verbs, or such as find their primary elements in other parts of speech.

§ 49. Derivation takes place either by a combination with other verbs (form verbs), as a kind of auxiliary (not of moods or tenses), but completing and modifying the verbal idea required: or derivatives are formed by the addition to the root of the primitive form of formative suffixes (prefixes there are none except the verbal personal pronouns), which will be noticed in their proper place.

§ 50. *a*) In the first place it is necessary to observe that the same word may occur as a substantive or as a verb (§ 9 Note), without undergoing any change as regards its form: Thus,

Māgána, ' to speak,' *s*. word, ' speech, story, history.'
Aiki, ' to work,' *s*. ' work, labour.'
Ganni, ' to see,' *s*. ' sight.'
Sayi, ' to sell,' *s*. ' sale.'
Kiddi, ' to drum,' *s*. ' drum.'
Taya, ' to help,' *s*. ' help, assistance.'

b) The same rule applies likewise to *Adjectives* implying an existence or expressing a state; hence we find, *girima* 'great,' and ' to be great,' and ' to grow;' *kussa*, 'near,' and ' to be near;' *karami*, ' little,' and ' to be little.'

c) Or by the Substantive verbs *ke*, *ne*, and *tše*, to express the predicative relation; as, *ni talaka ne*, ' I am poor;'

ni kárami ne, 'I am little;' *ita kárámia tše,* 'she is little;' *kúra tšc,* impersonal, 'it is a hyena.'

§ 51. *a)* The Verb *yi,* 'to do,' 'to make,' is frequently made use of before substantives, adjectives, and adverbs, to express the verbal notion; as, *yi magana,* 'to speak' (*verba facere*); *yi taya,* 'to render help;' *yi kúka,* 'to make or raise a cry;' *yi girima,* 'to make great=to grow;' *yi massa,* 'to be quick, to make haste;' *yi kusa,* 'to be near, to draw near, approach;' *yi širi,* 'to make ready, prepare;' *yi fúši,* 'to be angry, vexed, enraged, to grow mad;' *yi mafalki,* 'to dream;' *yi keáo,* 'to treat well, to do well, to do good;' *da sáfia ya-yi,* 'when it was morning, when morning had come=in the morning;' so also: *da maraëtšie ya-yi,* 'in the evening.'

b) Kawa and *samma,* combined with substantives and adjectives, denote either the being or becoming of that which the noun or adjective implies; as,

Ina-so-n-kawa mallami, 'I wish to become a priest.'

Kana-so ka-kawa maimágani? 'dost thou wish to become a doctor?'

Kádán ka-samma rágo babu maiso ka-taffi giddansa, 'if thou turn out an idle fellow, no one will like thee to come to his house.'

c) The verb *ši (ži dži)* 'to feel,' combined with substantives or adjectives, must likewise, in this connection, be regarded as merely a *formword,* but it expresses the notion of the simple verb. Thus:

Šidšóro, 'to feel fear=to be afraid.'

Šihaúši, 'to feel vexed, to be vexed, annoyed.'

Šitaúsai, 'to feel pity, to pity.'

Ba ka-ši tausaimu, 'you felt no compassion with us, did not pity us.'

Šikúmia, 'to feel shame, to be ashamed.'

Šidádi, 'to feel pleased, to be comfortable, happy, or contented.'

d) Another class of verbs, of which there are but a few in our collection, is derived from nouns and adjectives by means of the suffix *ta;* as,

Dsōráta, 'to frighten one;' from *dsóro,* ' fear.'
Taúrata, 'to harden oneself;' from *taúri,* ' hard.'
Šaworata, ' to hold a consultation;' from *šawora,* ' consultation, deliberation.'

e) Derivation takes place from primitive verbs, varying more or less the primary signification of the simple form, and uniting with it some accessory meaning or modification (that of intensity, violence, rapidity), such, namely, as are expressed in other languages by prepositions or distinct verbs. We mention a few:

Kai, ' to carry, to take to.'
Kao, and *káwo,* ' to bring, or bring back.'
Kírra, ' to call, to name.'
Kírrawo, and *kirraye,* 'to call for one=to summon one.'
Ša, ' to draw, to drink.'
Šainye, ' to drink greedily, or hastily=to swallow with eagerness.'
Tši,' to eat;' *tšainye,*' to eat eagerly, greedily, immoderately.'
Taya, and *tainye,* ' to help.'

FREQUENTITIVE AND INTENSITIVE VERBS.

§ 52. Frequentitive and Intensitive Verbs are formed by a repetition of the verb, or by a reduplication of the first syllable; as,

Šina-taffia šina-taffia, ' he is going on, going on=always walking, and walking on=walking very far.'

Ya-ša ya-ša har ya-samma marashankali, ' he drank, he drank till he became senseless, or lost his senses.'

Bugebuge, ' to strike often, to strike severely,' from *buga,* ' to beat with a stick.'

Fafage, ' to feel much about with the hand in search of some thing.'

THE VERB. 45

Guŝeguŝe, 'to gush out frequently, or continually, or with rapidity.'
Sansantŝe, 'to explain much, to converse much, to understand much,' from *sanni*, 'to know.'
Tŝatŝage, 'to tear to pieces,' from *tŝage*, 'to tear.'
Tatara, 'to pick up, out, to make a selection,' from *tára*, 'to gather.'
Dsasaga, 'to shake much ;' *ka-dsásaga mágani kána ka-ŝa*, 'shake the medicine well before you drink it.'
Tŝĭtŝika, 'to make very full, to fulfil,' from *tŝikka*, 'full.'
Tŝainyetŝainye, 'to eat very much, to eat a long time.'
Sosŏke, 'to prick, to pierce much,' from *sŏke*, 'to spur, to prick.'

Derivation of Verbs by means of Suffixes.

§ 53. From simple or primitive forms of the Verb other verbs are derived, by the addition of certain particles or verbal formative syllables to the root of the first form, which may generally be regarded as the Imperative Mood, second person in the singular. By this means some modifications and shades of different meanings are expressed, according to the analogy of the Hebrew language; and the frequency of their appearance seems to justify the division of the verb into *Radical*, *Relative*, *Reflective*, and *Causative* conjugations, though it must be observed that these meanings are not absolutely fixed or inherent in the form under which they are arranged, and that what in one verb and form is *causative*, in another may be merely *transitive ;* and also that the relative and reflective sense are not always distinctly implied.

§ 54. The Suffixes, or rather formative syllables, made use of in this class of verbs are *four* in number, and are as follow: *da*, *ŝie*, *yes*, or *as ;* and *yesda* or *asda*. Examples of a few verbs combined with these formative suffixes will be given here ; while, for further information, we must refer to the

Dictionary. It is hardly necessary to observe, that of some verbs no derivation of this class can be formed, and of others but one or two; but of few verbs, comparatively speaking, are all the various forms which might be expected actually found. Many more, it is true, may be discovered in the course of time, but ought not to be formed according to a given analogy, unless actually used by the natives.

1. The *first* suffix, *da*, produces various changes and modifications of the radical verb, but may likewise express no more than the simple root, and this observation is applicable to every form in this class. We will endeavour to illustrate it by a few examples: *sayi* (*sai*), 'to buy,' forms the second form, *saida*, signifying 'to sell,' corresponding with the syllable *ver* in '*kaufen*' und '*verkaufen*;' so also *kawo*, 'to bring,' forms *kauda* (*wo* and *wa* being frequently changed into *u*), 'to take away, annul, abrogate, as a law;' *tši*, ' to eat,' forms *tšída*, (reflective) 'to feed himself, or to maintain oneself;' *táši* (in one or two instances the root occurs as *ta*), ' to rise, to get up, start from a place;' and *táda* is 'to raise,' (causative,) and 'to lift up, to awake one;' *ba*, ' to give as a present;' *báda*, 'to give up what is entrusted to one, to deliver up, give up, convey, to administer medicine;' *báda dária*, ' to cause one to laugh;' *bada dsoro*, ' to cause one to fear, inspire with fear= frighten;' *bada girima*, 'to honour, to exalt;' *bada sanni-n-tšieto*, ' to give knowledge of salvation;' *bada laifi*, and *báda gaskia*, ' give wrong—right=condemn and justify;' *bada aradu, donnern lassen*.

2. The *second* suffix is *šie*. It expresses *causation* when connected with *intransitive* verbs, and corresponds in this sense with the Hiphil in the Hebrew language; but when united with *transitive* verbs, it is more frequently merely *transitive*. A few examples of its use will now be given. *Dsaya* (*dsai*), ' to stand,' forms *dsaišie*, ' to cause to stand, to stop one, or cause one to remain=detain;' *samna*, ' to remain,

sit down, reside,' forms *samšie* (*šie* being appended to the liquid of the root, *na* is dropped), 'to cause to sit, or to lie down;' *ku-samšiesu kassa hamsin hamsin*, ' make them sit down by fifty and fifty;' *tši*, 'to eat;' *tšišie*, 'to cause to eat, feed, maintain others;' *wohalla*, ' to have trouble;' *wohalšie*, ' to cause trouble or pain, to annoy, perplex;' *fitta*, 'to go out of a place;' *fišie* or *fušie*, ' to help one out, to pull out, to extricate one;' and *transitive*, ' to drive out, dismiss, discharge.'

3. The *third* suffix is *yes*, or *as*. Verbs formed by it correspond in signification mostly with the second form in *da*; as, *ka-bāyés ga mutume tšána*, ' give it to the man there;' *ka-sāyés abín da ba ka-ía so*, ' sell that which thou dost not want;' *suna-sayesua dūkiánsu*, ' they are selling their goods;' *abūbuá duka ambāyés garéni*, ' all things are delivered unto me;' *suba*, (*transitive*),' to pour out,' forms *subas* (*intransitive*), ' to gush out of itself;' *šiefa* and *šiefas* are both *transitive*.

4. The *fourth* class of this kind of verbs is formed by the Suffix *yesda* or *asda*. It is difficult to define the exact meaning so as to distinguish it from other forms. Their force will be seen best from some examples: *Bayésda* means ' to give up,' probably with the idea *willingly*, or on one's own accord; *sayésda*, ' to sell off, to dispose of by sale, or to exhibit for sale;' *kawásda*, from *kawo*, 'to bring,' signifies ' to remove, to disperse;' *fittasda*, from *fitta*, ' to go out from some place,' signifies ' to take off;' *ausziehen, ya-fittásda rīgása*, ' he took off his coat;' *subásda mia*, ' to expectorate with great force or violence.'

NOTE.—This method of deriving verbs from the absolute form will not surprise the Hebrew scholar, and others will observe that there is something analogous to this proceeding in other languages, although not to the same extent. as for instance in German, *lernen und lehren; liegen und legen; richten und rechten; fallen und fällen; trinken und tränken*; and in English, 'to lie and to lay;' 'black and blacken;' 'slack and slacken;' 'liquid and liquefy;' 'pure and purify;' and many more.

Deviations from the general rule in the Formation of this class of Verbs.

§ 55. *a*) In the formation of this class of verbs, several variations and irregularities from the general rule must be noticed. A change of the radical vowel takes place; as, *yes*, 'to throw away,' forms its second form in *yáda*; *wohalla* drops one *l*, and forms *wohalda*; *tára* forms *tárda*. *Tše*, as in *kuntše, gbatše, kwantše*, becomes *ta*; as, *kunta*; *gbata*; *kwanta*; and *še* and *ši* are changed into *s*; as, *laše, lasda, koši, kosda, gaši, gasda*. *O* and *wo* are changed into *u*; as, *kao, kauda. Šiefa* forms *šiebda, šiefda*, and *šiepta. Ia*, 'to be able, can,' forms *issa*, 'to be sufficient or enough, to reach to, to arrive at a place;' *ya-issa*, 'it is enough.'

b) The *third* class in *šie*; *Yes* forms *yašie* and *yešie*; *fitta* rejects the last syllable, and forms *fišie*; *samna* forms *samšie*; *sída* has *šišie*; *murda* forms *muršie*; *gamma, gamšie; tara, taršie*; but *amsa* forms *amsašie*, and *lúa, luašie*; and *ía, išie*.

c) The *fourth* class is formed by adding *s* to the radical conjugation, *i.e.* in those verbs which do not take *yes*. Examples: *suba, subas*; *šiefa, šiefas*: *tšieta, tšietas*; *tara, taras*; *gbatše, gbatas*; *kwantše, kwantas*; *o* or *wo* takes likewise *as*; as, *kawo, kawas*; *ía* forms *íyes*.

d) The *fifth* class is invariably formed from the fourth, by adding *da*, whether it terminates in *as* or *yes*, and bears in some respects the same relation to the fourth, which the fourth bears to the second, formed by *da*. Compare Luke xiv. 14.

Nature and quality of Verbs.

§ 56. Verbs are either *Active* or *Passive*; but active verbs may be *transitive* or *intransitive*. The Hausa language has not, at least to any great extent, developed distinct forms for transitive or intransitive verbs; hence it comes that the same form occurs for both, and the signification can only be ascertained from the connection in which it is found. Thus, for instance, is *kíwo*, 'to tend a herd,' and of the herd, 'to feed, to graze;' *gboya*, ' to hide,' and reflective, ' to hide oneself, and to be hid;' *tšikka*, ' to fill, and to be full;' *šieka*, to wet, and to be wet.'

§ 57. In other words, though, comparatively speaking, in very few, a different form is found for the transitive and intransitive signification, and the latter may sometimes be translated impersonally, or by the passive. Verbs of this class, *i.e.* intransitive by nature, terminate in *u*. A list of most of those found in our collection will here be given, with a view to draw the attention of the student to similar appearances in the language, in words which may not have come under our notice. They are the following:

Búdu, 'to be open,' from *buda*, ' to open;' *dadu*, ' to be increased,' from *dade*, ' to lengthen, to prolong, to increase;' *faru*, 'to happen;' *furu*, 'to be burning;' *goddu*, 'to appear,' from *godda*, ' to show ; ' *gammu*, ' to meet,' from *gamma*, ' to join;' *karu*, ' to be added,' from *kara*, 'to add;' *kaffu*, ' to be fastened, stranded;' *kuntu*, ' to be unloosed;' *nadu*, ' to be rolled up, or coiled, entangled;' *mutu*, ' to die;' *madzu*, ' to be squeezed, hemmed in;' *rabu*, 'to depart;' *raba*, ' to divide;' *retu*, ' to be swinging;' *ragu*, ' to be decreasing;' *sannu*, ' to be known;' *subu*, ' gushed out;' *šimfudu*, ' spread;' *taru*, 'assembled;' *wazu*, ' dispersed.'

b) The ending *tše*, of the Radical conjugation, is *generally* intransitive; as,

Gbatše, ' it is spoiled or destroyed;' *kwantše*, ' it lies;' *mantše*, ' to forget;' *wutše*, ' to pass on.'

kubtše, 'to slip;' *ya-kubtše daga hanuna*, ' it slipped out of my hand.'

§ 58. Different forms of the verb compensating in some measure for the absence or disuse of prepositions (a peculiarity of the Hausa language), must be mentioned while we are speaking generally of the nature and quality of verbs. The ending *a* and *e* in some verbs seems to imply *motion towards*, and the ending *o, motion from* a place, besides some other modifications. Examples:

Aike, ' to send to,' and *aiko,* ' to send from.'
Daúka, ' to take,' and *dauko,* ' to take up.'
Dawoya, ' to return to,' and *dawoyo,* ' to return from, come back.'
Koma, ' to go back,' and *komo,* ' to come back.'
Fitta, ' to go out,' and *fitto,* ' to come out, spring up as of seeds.'
Šigga, ' to go in,' and *šiggo,* ' to come in.'
Šída, ' to ascend,' and *šído,* ' to descend.'
Šiefa, 'to throw,' *šiefo,* ' to throw down.'
Taffi, ' to go, go away, leave,' and *taffo,* ' to come.'
Fádi, ' to fall,' *fádo,* ' to fall down.'
Koya, ' to teach,' *koyo,* ' to derive information from'='to learn.'
Koya-n-mágána Kanuri da wúya, ' it is difficult to teach the Kanuri language.'
Koyo-n-magana Enliz da wuya, ' it is difficult to learn the English language.'
Tšíra, ' to pluck, as fruit,' *tširo,* 'to pluck off, take down,' or ' pull down.'

ON THE MOODS.

§ 59. It is plain that in a language which has no *internal inflections* of the Verb, we cannot speak of Moods in the same sense in which the word is used in other languages; and, to speak of prepositions, conjunctions, adverbs, participles or pronouns, as being used to express Moods, is but an accommodation to a system with which we are familiar, but n correct exhibition of the language. Still, as this method has some advantages, a few observations may be made here in explanation of this subject.

THE INFINITIVE.

§ 60. There is no form of the verb by which the *Infinitive* is distinguished from other forms as such; it is known only by the position it occupies in the sentence, and is used much like the German in the word *gehen*; as, *na-taffi kwana, Ich gehe schlafen*. I go (to) sleep; *su-taffi gidda*, they go home; *muka-taffi faraúta*, we went hunting; *sun-taffi tši tuónsu*, '*sie gingen ihr Brot zu essen*, they went to eat their food.' But observe:

a) *Ga* is sometimes used, signifying 'to,' 'in order to,' *zu, um zu*; as, *kai baka girima ba ga aiki*, or *ga yi-n-aiki*, thou art not great enough to work, or to do work; but in the first place, it might be the conjunction *for;* and, *mu-taffi ga ša-n-hiska*, let us go to drink wind, *i.e.* take exercise and airing.

b) *En* is likewise used; as, *to*, in order to; as, *ta-taffi gari en daúka kášia*, she went into the country to get hay; and, *ína-so en kawa mallami, don ina-so en koya ga mutane-n-kassamu*, I wish to become (I may become) a priest, because I wish to teach (that I may teach) the people of our country. But *ga* is evidently a preposition before a noun, and may be rendered 'for work, for doing work,' 'for drinking wind,' &c.; and shows that what in other languages is expressed by the Infinitive, or supine, is expressed in the Hausa by a substantive. The *en* will be explained when we come to speak of the subjunctive.

c) The Hausa language makes use of *co-ordinate* sentences, where in English we use an infinitive; as, *amma mu ba mu-iawa mu-yi aiki*, literally, 'but we, we are not able, we do (to do) work; *šina-so ya-yi faddá da su*, he wishing he (to) fight with them; *muna-zua mu-daúka yārínia nan,* we are going we (to) take this girl; *dadaí ba ka-ganni ba tamraro sina-zua ya-yi magana da abokinsı?* hast thou never seen a star going he (to) speak with his friend?

THE IMPERATIVE.

§ 61. The *Imperative* is indicated by the personal pronouns before the verbal form; as, *ka-taffi,* m., *ki-taffi,* f., *si-taffi,* m., *ta-taffi,* f., *mu-taffi, ku-taffi,* go thou, &c.; and only when person and gender can be understood from the context can the pronouns be omitted. The negative is expressed by *ba* repeated; as, *ba ka-taffi ba,* or, *ba ki-taffi.*

THE SUBJUNCTIVE MOOD.

§ 62. We speak of a *Subjunctive* Mood as we speak of moods in general, and need therefore only observe, that in almost every case where this mood is met with in other languages, as for instance, in indirect interrogative sentences, in depending relative sentences, in incidental sentences in which the verb is governed by conjunctions requiring the subjunctive, the Hausa verb must be *translated* by the same mood, though its form be the same with the indicative.

The first person singular only forms an exception to this rule, it being *en* instead of *ina* or *na*, expressing either an intention or purpose, 'that,' or 'that I may,' (see Infinitive, § 60, *b*). But this *en* in itself must be regarded as a contracted form of *ina* or *na*, and then all the other persons are regular.

NOTE.—*En to,* 'in order to,' that, with the third person, as in the phrase, *matse ta-taffi gari en daúka kásia,* 'a woman went into the field that she might (to) fetch hay,' are very rare.

Examples.—*Na-tse, en taffi, en kāwósi,* I say, may I go,

may I bring him? *uwata ta-tše, en taffi, en wanke ta,* ' my mother said that I should go, that I should (to) wash it.' Indirect: *ta-tše, ta-taffi, ta-wanke,* ' she said, let her go, let her wash it; *ka-bani haiwa en yi nóma,* ' give me a hoe, that I may dig;' *kána en taffi en tši námana,* ' then I would go, I would (to) eat my meat;' *ya-tše : záni en ganni mākári-n-dūniá,* ' he said, I shall go, that I may (to) see the end of the world; *záni en kawo maku wonni abu,* 'I am going to bring you something;' *ya-tše masa ši-ginna masa kušiéya,* ' he told him, that he should (to) dig a grave for him ;' *ba na-so en passa kanka ba,* ' I do not want to break thy head;' *da na taffi en kamaši, ya-kubtše daga hanuna,* ' when I went to lay hold on him, he slipped from my hand.'

So also with the conjunction *kada,* ' that not,' ' lest ;' as, *kada su-mutu,* ' that they should not die ;' *kada ka-tše ga mutane* ' thou shouldest not say to the people;' *kada nama ya-taši,* lest the game should start; *kadan ya-ši mosimu,* ' if it should hear us move.'

THE CONDITIONAL.

§ 63. The Conditional Mood is expressed by the conjunctions *kadan* and *en,* ' if,' and the verb in its simplest form; that is, the verb cannot be preceded by any of the compound verbal prefixes, § 69, but merely by the personal pronouns.

Examples: *kadan ya-baka kada ka-mayes, kadan ka-yi ba zaši-so ba,* ' if he gives thee something, thou must not give it back to him, if thou shouldest do so he would not like it;' *kadan wonga mutum ya-yi guddu šī-fádi,* ' if this man should (attempt to) run, he would fall ;' *kadan ana-rua ba zamutaffia ba,* ' in case it should rain, we should not go ;' *kadan nataffi garesa ši-fadda mani labari,* ' if I should go to him, he would tell me some news.'

PERMISSIVE OR CONCESSIVE MOOD.

§ 64. It is so designated because it may be said to express permission or concession, though it embraces other meanings, as that of usage and habit, and must be rendered by 'use to,' or the German word '*pflegen.*'

Our previous observation respecting the absence of auxiliary or form verbs, to express Moods or Tenses, is here met by some *apparent* limitation, this Mood being formed by the verb *kan*, combined with the simplest form of the pronouns; but if the meaning 'to use to,' 'to be in the habit of,' be assigned to it, it is no longer a form, but a notional word.

(This section might probably bear another heading; but there being no simple term which would embrace its various meanings, we would rather illustrate its use by examples, than dispute about its name.)

Kána ni-kan taffi ni-kan tši tuona, 'then I used to go, I used to eat my food.'

Ki-kan taffi ki-kan kuntšiesu, 'thou canst go, thou canst let them lose.'

Abin da ta-tše mani ni-kan yi mata, 'what she told me I used to do for her.'

Ttatšé ši-kan amsa ši-kan tše: ki-wutše gabá danki babu daya gareni, 'the tree used to answer, it used to say, pass on, thy child is not with me.'

Ta-kan wutše, ta-kan taffi ga wonni itatše, ta-kan tše ga itatše: ka-bani dána, 'she used to pass on, she used to go to another tree, she used to say to the tree, Give me my child.'

VERBAL PRONOUNS. 55

THE TENSES.

§ 65. Hausa verbs may be said to have *five* Tenses:
1 The Aorist.
2 The Imperfect.
3 The Presence. *a.* Finite form. *b.* Participial form.
4 The Perfect. *a.* Finite form. *b.* Participial form.
5 The Future. *a.* Finite form. *b.* Participial form.

VERBAL PRONOUNS.

§ 66. The conjugation of the *persons*, as well as of the *Tenses*, is effected by a special class of *Verbal Pronouns.*[*] These verbal pronouns are composed of the subjective pronouns and particles (suffixes); as, *ina-taffia*, 'I am going;' *kana-taffia*, 'thou art going,' in the Present Tense; and *nina taffi, kaka taffi,* I have gone, thou hast gone, in the Perfect Tense: and for this reason they are called Verbal Pronouns. That they are integral parts of the verb is evident from the fact, that they cannot be rendered unnecessary even by a noun before the finite form of the verb. We cannot say, for instance, *oba taffi,* ' the father goes;' but must say, *oba ya-taffi,* ' the father *he* goes;' *uwa ta-kirrani,* ' the mother *she* calls me;' the verb having always its own subject. And as neither persons, gender, nor tenses are indicated by any inflection in the verb itself, these pronouns are absolutely necessary for this purpose, and make the Conjugation in Tense, Person, and Gender perfect.

NOTE 1.—A few examples occur in which the personal distinction is not expressed after the subject's nominative; as,

Abbega na(=*šina*) *tamaha,* 'Abbega thinking' . . .

---

[*] Compare Becker's Organismus der Sprache Seite, 226. Und; Grundzüge einer Grammatik des Herero von L. Hugo Kahn, Berlin, 1857, where (in §180, compare also § 177) it is said; der Anordnung der Tempora liegen die modificationen des verbal Pronomens zu Grunde.

Kowane na (=*šina*) *ša-n-taba*, 'whoever is smoking tobacco.'

Wata na(=*tana*) *bada haske*, 'the moon giving light.'

Da hiska na(=*šina*) *busawa rairai na*(=*šina*) *šigga ga idanunka*, 'when the wind does blow the sand gets in thy eyes.' And a few more.

NOTE 2.—The author is aware that this arrangement may be objected to on the ground that the verbal notion was being assigned to the pronouns instead of to the verb, and that it may be argued that the particles *na, ka*, as well as *n* and *nka*, ought rather to be regarded as verbal prefixes than pronominal suffixes, and that consequently we ought to write *i nataffia ; ka kataffi, su ntše, su nkatše*, instead of *ina, kaka, sun, sunka*, &c. But a careful consideration of the subject in all its bearings has convinced him, that it is preferable, to say the least, to keep to the arrangement adopted in the books already printed, and more especially for the following reasons:

1. In hearing the natives speak, and taking it down from their own lips, you follow, in so doing, the natural division of words made by them.

2. If *na* were joined to the verb, and separated from the *i*, the latter must have the meaning '*I*' assigned to it, which it has nowhere in the language.

3. The *n* and *nka* prefixed to the verb would create no small confusion in the reading of *sun-taffi*, and *sunka-taffi*, if they were written *su ntaffi*, and *su nkataffi*, &c.

§ 67. The Verbal Pronouns, except when compounds, differ little from the Possessives. The chief difference consists in the Aorist, and in the Imperfect, which take *ya* in the Indicative, and in the Negative and Subjunctive Moods, *ši* for the third person singular masc.; and the Imperfect takes *n* in the pl. and in the second person fem. singular; as, *kin, mun, kun, sun.*

§ 68. There are two forms of the Verbal Pronoun, *i.e.* the Emphatic and the Simple. And as regards their nature, they are either Subjective or Objective. The Simple Objective Pronouns are appended to any part of the Verb except the Infinitive, which, being regarded as a verbal noun, takes the nominal suffixes; as *taffiana*, instead of *taffiani* ; *sĭdánsa*, instead of *sĭdasa*.

Tabular Exhibition of the Verbal Pronouns.

§ 69. To avoid repetition, we notice that the first person singular and all the persons in the plural are of common Gender. The Emphatic Pronouns may be repeated before every tense, though, for the sake of brevity, they are given in one only.

	AORIST.		IMPER-FECT.	PRESENCE.		PERFECT TENSE.		FUTURE.		SUBJUNCTIVE AND CONDITIONAL.	
Emphatic.	Simple			Finite Form.	Participial Form.	Finite Form	Participial Form.	Finite Form.	Participial Form.	Negative.	Concessive.
1 Pers. Singl.											
m. nina	na		na	ni ke	ína	nina	nika	nī or ni-i	zíni	kada en	ni kan
m. kaika	ka		ka	ka ke	kana	kaka	kanka	kā ,, ka-a	záka	,, ka	ka kan
f. ke ki	ki		kin	ki ke	kina	kika	kinka	kī ,, ki-i	záki	,, ki	ki kan
m. ši ya	ya		ya	ši ke	šina	šika	šinka	šī ,, ši-i	záši	,, ši	ši kan
f. íta ta	ta		ta	ta ke	tana	taka	tanka	tá ,, ta-a	záta	,, ta	ta kan
Plural.											
m. mu mu	mu		mun	mu ke	muna	muka	munka	mā ,, mu-u	zámu	,, mu	mu kan
, ku ku	ku		kun	ku ke	kuna	kuka	kunka	kū ,, ku-u	záku	,, ku	ku kan
, su su	su		sun	su ke	suna	suka	sunka	sū ,, su-u	zásu	,, su	su kan
Passive Prefixes.	a		ai	ake	ana	aka	anka	ā			

CONJUGATIONS OF THE VERB.

§ 70. The *Aorist* is the historical tense of the Germans, and is always employed in narration, though not confined to this meaning. With regard to its form, it is the simplest form of the Verb, and has, in fact, no other inflection than that of persons. It takes the simplest form of the Personal Pronouns before the Verb. It is designated Aorist, because it expresses an action or event, without any limitation of time, embracing presence, past, and future. We shall give the conjugation of this tense in full form, through all persons, with the Objective Pronouns, as a specimen; in other tenses we shall only mark the deviations.

Example:

Ba, 'to give,' in its *radical* form; the *second, bada;* the *third, bašie;* the *fourth, bayes;* and the *fifth, bayesda*. In the paradigm *dsaišie*, 'to cause one to stay,' *i e.* 'to detain one,' is substituted for *bašie*, in order to exhibit a *causative* form.

CONJUGATIONS OF THE VERB

Ba, 'to give, gave.'

Singular.

Person.		Form I.	Form II.
		na-bāka, I give thee (m.)	*bādā maka,* I give over to thee (m.)
2	m.	*ka-bani,* thou givest me.	*bada máni,* thou givest up to me.
2	f.	*ki-bata,* thou givest her.	*bada nata,* thou givest up to her.
3	m.	*ya-baki,* he gives thee (f.)	*bada maki,* he gives up to thee (f.)
3	f.	*ta-baši,* she gives him.	*bāda masa,* she gives up to him.

Plural.

1	*mu-baku,* we give you.	*bada maku,* we give up to you.
2	*ku-bamu,* ye give us.	*bada mana,* ye give up to us.
3	*su-basu,* they give them.	*bada masu,* they give up to them.

CONJUGATIONS OF THE VERB. 61

Form III.

Singular.

Person.		
1		na-dsaïsieka, I cause thee to stay
2	m.	ka-dsaïsieni, thou causest me to stay
2	f.	ki-dsaïsieta, thou causest her to stay
3	m.	ya-dsaïsieki, he causes thee to stay
3	f.	ta-dsaïsiesi, she causes him to stay

Plural.

1	nu-dsaïsieku, we cause you to stay
2	ku-dsaïsiemu, ye cause us to stay
3	su-dsaïsiesu, they cause them to stay

Form IV.

Singular.

bāyes garéka, I gave to thee.
bayes garéni, thou gavest me
bayes gareta, thou gavest her.
bayes garéki, he gave thee.
bayes garési, or garasa, she gave him.

Plural.

bayes gareku, we gave you.
bayes garemu, ye gave us.
bayes garesu, they gave them.

Form V.

Singular.

1		na-bayesda, I gave.
2	m.	ka-bayesda, thou gavest.
2	f.	ki-bayesda, thou gavest
3	m.	ya-bayesda, he gave.
3	f.	ta-bayesda, she gave.

Plural.

1 nu-bayesda.
2 ku-bayesda.
3 su-bayesda.

§ 71. The Negative is formed by *ba—ba*. It will be sufficient to exhibit it in one form.

Person.

1 *Ba na-baka ba*, ' I did not give thee.'
2 m. *ba ka-bani ba*, ' thou didst not give me.'
2 f. *ba ki-baši ba*   ,,   ,,   him.'
3 m. *ba ši-bata ba*, he   ,,   ,,   her.'
3 f. *ba ta-baki ba*, she   ,,   ,,   thee.'

NOTE 1.—The first *ba* of the Negative Adverb receives sometimes an *i;* as, *bai ta ba*, ' he was not able ;' *bai kammuta ba*, ' it is not becoming.' This *i* must be regarded as a contraction of *ya*, and stands, therefore, instead of *ba ya-ta ba*, &c.

NOTE 2.—When the negative is used in combination with the Emphatic Pronouns, the pronoun precedes the *ba*; as, *nī ba ni-ne ba sarīki*, ' I am not a king.' In answer to a question, and when a strong negative is to be expressed, *āā*, ' no,' ' by no means,' is used instead of *ba—ba;* as, *obana sarīki ne, obanka kuá sariki ne?* ' My father is a king, is thy father also a king?' *āā, obana talaka ne,* 'No, no, my father is a poor man.'

NOTE 3.—In the first person of the singular the end vowel is dropped, and the *n* annexed to the *ba, e.g. ban sanni ba*, ' I do not know;' and only when the stress is laid on the person, the uncontracted form : *ba na-sanni ba*, ' *I* do not know,' is used.

The Imperative.

§ 72. *Ka-baši*, ' give him.'
Ki-bani, ' give me.'
Ši-baši, ' let him give him '

THE IMPERFECT TENSE.

Ta-baši, 'let her give him.'
Beri mu-baši, 'let us give him.'
Ku-beri ku-baši, 'let ye give him.'
Su-beri su-baši, 'let them give him.'

The Imperfect Tense.

§ 73. The *Imperfect Tense* is used to express an action or event in reference to another, which was either simultaneous with, or antecedent to it; as,

Da muka-fitto daga tšiki-n-gidda mun-gammu da abokimu, 'when we had come out of the house, we met our friend.'

Da šina-tšikawa bindiga na-ganni nama ya-fitta daga tšiki n-sansámi, 'as he was loading the gun, I saw the creature coming from under the leaves.'

Na-tše, gaši šina-fitta, 'I said, see it, it is coming out.'

Conjugation of the Imperfect Tense.

Singular.

Per.
1 *na-taffi,* I went.
2 m. *ka-taffo,* thou camest.
2 f. *kin-tše,* thou didst say.
3 m. *ya-samna,* he sat down.
3 f. *ta-dauki,* she took up.

or *ba, bada, bašie, bayes, na bayesda,* &c.

Plural.

1 *mun-taši,* we arose.
2 *kun-ganni,* ye saw.
3 *sun-rubutu,* they wrote.

The Present Tense.

§ 74. This Tense denotes an action as begun, but not yet completed, or still continuing, and likewise one that has lately passed.

§ 75. The Participial form and the finite verb connected with this tense are not kept very distinct, and the former is conjugated through all the persons like the latter; the sense of the sentence alone must show where the forms ending in *na*, and the verbs ending in *wa*, are to be construed by a relative pronoun, or the particles: '*as, when, indem*,' &c.

The formation of the Present Tense takes place—

a). By joining the verbal affix *na* to the subjective or separate form of the Personal Pronouns; as,

Ina, kana, kina, šina, tana, muna, kuna, suna, 'I am, or was going, seeing, loving, thinking,' &c.

NOTE.—The Particle *na*, as well as *ka*, in the Perfect Tense, may have originated from the substantive verbs *ne* and *ke*, 'to be.'

b). The substantive verb *ke* is placed after the simplest form of the Personal Pronouns, and before the Verb; as,

Ni-ke yi-n-worigi, ' I am playing, do play.'
Mu-ke yi-n-taffia, ' we are travelling, or, do travel.'
Da ši-ke yi-n-taffiasa ya-ši gašiasa, ' as he was travelling he felt his fatigue.'

c). The verb itself undergoes some changes; as for instance: *a* is added to the final vowel; *e.g. taffi* forms *taffia; širi, širia; mutu, mutua*.

d). The end vowel undergoes a change; thus, *a* becomes *ia* or *ua, e.g. dara, daria; fáda, fadua; zakka, zakkua*; or, *e*). The *a* is changed into *e*, as, *samna, samne; dsaya, dsaye*.

f). Verbs of the *fourth* form terminating in the semi-vowel 's,' take likewise *ua*, *e.g. bayes, bayesua; sayes, sayesua; tayes, tayesua; fitas, fitasua; subas, subasua*.

g.) The letter *n* is added to the verb; as,

Ke-yi-n-wáka, ' to be singing.'

Kana-ši-n-tausai, ' thou feelest pity, thou pitiest.'

Suna-tšira-n-tšiáwa, ' they are pulling up the grass.'

Bi, ' to follow,' forms *bie* or *biye*: *šina-biyensa*, ' he is following him.'

NOTE.—The occurrence of the *n* in the above mentioned instances, together with the *nominal* suffixes appended to this form, plainly prove, that the Infinitive form is used, or treated as a substantive.

Conjugation of the Present Tense.

§ 76. From the preceding remarks, it is evident that the inflection of the Present Tense must be exhibited in four different modes, according to the different forms employed. To exhibit it in the first instance with the same verb, *ba*, ' to give,' it is as follows:

Conjugation of the Present Tense.

Singular.

Pers. Radical.	1st Mode. Form I.	II.	III.	IV.	V.	(Participial Form.)
1	niina or ina-ba	bada	baše	bayesua	bayesda	badawa bašiewa
2 m.	kaikana „ kana-ba	bada	baše	bayesua	bayesda	„ „
2 f.	kekina „ kina-ba	bada	baše	bayesua	bayesda	„ „
3 m.	šišina „ šina-ba	bada	baše	bayesua	bayesda	„ „
3 f.	ita, or tana ta, or tana-ba	bada	baše	bayesua	bayesdi	„ „

Plural.

1	mumuna or muna-saye (sell)	saida	saišie	sayesua	sayesda	saidawa saišiewa
2	kukuna „ kuna-taši (rise)	tada	taše	tayesua	tayesda	tadawa tašiewa
3	susuna „ suna-kawo (bring)	kauda	kaše	kawas	kawasda	kaudawa kašiewa

THE PRESENT TENSE.

Conjugation of the Present Tense.

Singular.

Pers.	2nd Mode.	3rd Mode.	4th Mode.
1	ina-taffia, I go, am going	yi-n-wāka, sing, am singing	ni-ke samne, I sit, am sitting down
2 m.	kana-taffo, thou comest	yi-n-daria, thou dost laugh	ka-ke dsaye, thou dost stay
2 f.	kina-tše, thou sayest	yi-n-magana, thou dost speak	ki-ke kwanlše, thou art lying
3 m.	sina-kašše, he kills	yi-n-taffia, he makes a journey	ši-ke karami, he is little
3 f.	tana-samne, she sits down	yi-n-santše, she is conversing	ta-ke karamia, she is little

Plural.

1	muna-dawayowa, we are returning.	yi-n-yaki, we make war	mu-ke samne, we are sitting down.
2	kuna-kama, ye are catching.	yi-n-karatu, ye are reading.	ku-ke ganni, ye are seeing.
3	suna-karewa, they are finishing.	yi-n-rubutu, they are writing.	su-ke ia, they are able.

The Perfect Tense.

§ 77. This Tense expresses an action as performed in the past time, but continuing in its effects and consequences to the present. It is formed by combining the verbal particle *ka* (see § 69), with the simplest form of the Subjective Pronouns, except in the first person singular, which forms *nina* (Emphatic *ninina*) instead of *nika;* as, *nina kašsie Dodo*, ' I have killed Dodo;' as,

Singular.

Pers.	Radical.	Form II.	III.	IV.	V.
1	nina-ba	bada	bašie	bayes	bayesda
2 m.	kaka-saye	saida	saišie	sayes	sayesda
2 f.	kika-saye	dsaida	dsaišie	dsayes	dsayesda
3 m.	šika-tára	tarda	taršie	taras	tarasda
3 f.	taka-taši	tada	tašie	tayes	tayesda
	rise.	raise.	cause to rise.	awake (*intr.*)	wake (*trans.*)

Plural.

1	muka-girigitše	girigida	girigišie	girigitas	girigitasda
2	kuka-gamma	gammada	gamšie	gamayes	gamayesda
3	suka-ia	issa	išie	iyes	iyesda

Participial Form (or Indefinite Past Tense).

§ 78. We have defined this Tense by a more general designation, to indicate the ambiguity of its use. It certainly denotes a past action or event, and is in many instances used as a finite verb; while in other instances it must, with or without the adverb *da*, 'when,' be construed as a Participial Mood, being followed by a finite verb. A few instances will be sufficient to enable the reader to understand it wherever it may occur. Thus: *Sunka-báši bayi iširin ya-wulše*, 'when they had given him twenty slaves, he went his way.' *Máta sunka-taffo ríšia dauka n-rua ya-tše masu,* 'when the woman had come to the well to fetch water, he said to them.' *Kinka-tše : dána ši-ne daga bayana,* 'thou didst say (or likewise a participle) my child is at my back.' *Sunka-taffi, sunka-rabba dukia, sunka-dauka, sunka-taffi garinsu, kówa yasamu ríba kadan kadan,* 'having departed, divided the goods, taken them up, gone to their own towns, each received a little profit.'

NOTE.—It is remarkable that this form never occurs in some of the stories, while in others it seems to be used for the Perfect Tense, so that we might almost arrive at the conclusion, that the insertion or sounding of the *n* before *ka* was but a dialectical difference.

Conjugation.

Singular.

Pers.		
1	*nika*	
2 m.	*kanka*	
2 f.	*kinku*	
3 m.	*šinka*	
3 f.	*tanka*	*ba, bada, bašie, bayes, bayesda.*

Plural.

1	*munka*
2	*kunka*
3	*sunka*

The Future Tense.

§ 79. The Future Tense expresses an action which will be performed at some future time, as well as one that is about, or on the point of being performed. It is formed in various ways:

1. It takes the irregular future of the Substantive verbs: *ne, ke,* and *tše,* which is *samma;* as, *ní samma baba,* 'I shall be, or become great.' *Mū samma talaka,* 'we shall be, or become poor.'

2. The letter *i* is prefixed to the verb; as, *ni-itaśi, ni-itaffi,* 'I will arise, I will go:' or,

3. Which amounts to the same, the end vowel of the pronoun is repeated before the verbal form, but only in the first and third person masculine in the singular, *śi-itaśi, śi-itaffi;* the other persons undergo no change with the exception of the lengthening of the vowels, *more or less distinct or audible,* which does equally apply to the *i* above mentioned. Hence also, and for the sake of uniformity, the same mode of writing is introduced in the first and third persons; that is, *ní, śí,* instead of *ni i, śi i.* e.g. *Ina-tamaha ní-samésa da rai,* ' I hope I shall find him alive.'

4. It is formed by means of the verb, *zua,* ' to go, to be about to go,' in its inflected form (See § 69.) *za, záni.* Example: *Záni-taffia en ganni abokina,* ' I am going, or about to go, to see my friend.' *Da zata mutua ta-tše,* 'when she was going to die, or was about to die, she said.' As regards the form of the verb itself, it will be observed that it takes that of the *presence;* as, *taffia, zakkua, dawoyowa, samne,* &c.

THE FUTURE TENSE.

Conjugation of the Future Tense.

Singular.

Pers.	Form I. Radical.	II.	III.	IV.	V.
1	ni-iba or níba	bada	bašie	bayes	bayesda, 'to give.'*
2 m.	kā-taši	tada	tašie	tayes	tayesda, 'to rise.'
2 f.	ki-fitta		fišie	fitas	fitasda, 'to go out.'
3 m.	ši-dsaye	dsaida	dsaišie or dsaisa	dsayes	dsayesda, 'to stand.'
3 f.	ta-tara	tarda	taršie or tarsa	taras	tarasda, 'to gather.'

Plural.

1	mu-kuntše	kunta	kuntšie	kuntas	kuntasda, 'to loosen.'
2	ku-saye	saida	saišie	sayes	sayesda, 'to sell.'
3	su-kawo	kauda	kaušie	kawas	kawasda, 'to bring.'

* The meaning of the Radical Form only is given; for the signification of the derived forms we must refer to the Dictionary and to §§ 53—55.

Form II.—(*Participial Mood.*)

Singular.

zâni-dawóyowa, 'I am going to return, or on the point of returning.'
zaka-kâmawa, 'thou art going to catch, or on the point of catching.'
zâki rubutuwa, 'thou art going to write, or on the point of writing.'
zâši-taffia, 'he is going, or on the point of going.'
zâta-goddawa, 'she is going to show, or on the point of showing.'

Plural.

zâmu-fittowa, 'we are coming out, or on the point of coming out.'
zaku-kaššiewa, 'ye are going to kill, or are on the point of killing.'
zasu-hadiewa, 'they are going to swallow, or are on the point of swallowing.'

The Second Future.

§ 80. The Hausa language has not developed a separate form for the Second, or Future Perfect Tense. In sentences where such a form is expected, the Aorist seems invariably used with the temporal Adverb *kadan*, 'when;' as, *kadan na-taffi*, 'when I have gone=shall have gone.' *Kadan ka-rufe kofa, kada ka-bude*, 'when thou shalt have closed the door, thou must not open it again.' *Kadan ka tši nama nan dûka ba ka-id ši-n-yuṅwa*, 'when thou shalt have eaten all this meat, thou wilt not be hungry.'

Formation of the Passive.

§ 81. From all transitive verbs, and consequently also from all transitive forms of intransitive verbs, a passive may be formed, although passive constructions are, on the whole, not very frequent. The Hausas, like other African nations prefer speaking in the active, and avoid passive constructions by the use of the third person plural, active, so that instead of saying aṅkamani, 'I was caught,' they will say, sunkamani, 'they caught me.' In Ibo, Nupe, Gã, and probably also in the Yoruba, the passive consists merely in this kind of circumlocution.

The Passive Voice is formed in a very simple manner. The verbal particles *na*, *n*, and *ka*, are preceded by *a*; as, *anabani*, 'I am given;' (*mir ist gegeben*,) *ambani*, 'I was given;' (*mir ward gegeben*, or *man gab mir*,) *akabani*, 'I have been given;' (*man hat mir gegeben*,) *aṅbani*, 'I had been given;' (*man hatte mir gegeben*,) *ābani*, *und*, *zāabāni*, 'I shall be given;' (*man mird mir geben*.)

Conjugation of the Passive.

Aorist.

Singular.

Radical.	Form II.	III.	IV.	V.
a-búni	a-bádá mani	a-bašie garéni	a-bayes garéni	a-bayesda mani
a-búka	a-bada maka	a-bašie garéka	a bayes garéka	a-bayesda maka
a-baki	a-bada maki	a-bašie gareki	a-bayes gareki	a-bayesda naki
a-baši	a-bada masa	a-bašie garéši, or a-basasa garasa	a-bayes garésa	a-bayesda masa
a-bata	a-bada mata	a-bašie gareta, or a-basata	a-bayes gareta	a-bayesda mata

Plural.

a-bamu	a-bada mamu or muna	a-bašiemu	a-bayes garemu	a-bayesda mamu
a-baku	a-bada maku	a-bašiēku	a-bayes gareku	a-bayesda maku
a-basu	a-bada nasu	a-bašiesu	a-bayes garesu	a-bayesda masu

THE TENSES.

Radical.	Form II.	III. *Imperfect Tense.*	IV.	V.
aṅ-bani (for aṅ-bani)	aṅ-bada mani	am-bašiéni	am-bayes mani	am-bayesda mani

Like the preceding Form.

Present Tense.

Radical.	Form II.	III.	IV.	V.
ana-bani / ake-bani, &c / ana-yi-n-rua, 'it is raining,' &c.	ana-bada mani	ana-bašiéni	ana-bayesua gareni / ake-bayesua	ana-bayesda mani

Perfect Tense.

| aka-bani | aka-bada mani | aka-bašiéni | aka-bayes gareni | aka-bayesda mani |

Future Tense.

| ā-bāni | a-bādá | ā-bašié | ā-bāyes | ā-bāyésla |

Future Tense, (Participial Form.)

| zā-a-bāni | za-a-bada | za-a-bašie | za-a-bayesua. | za-a-bayesda |

Indefinite (Participle.)

| añ or añka-bani añbada | | añ or añka-bušie | añ or añka bayes | añ or añka-bayes da |

añka-haiféni, a very few forms of this class in our collection.

§ 82. In a language in which there is so little *internal* inflection of the verb itself, it is plain that we cannot speak of *irregular*, but only of *defective* verbs. Most of the verbs occur only in the *radical* form, and of those from which others are derived there are, comparatively speaking, few of which all the forms possible are found. A list of some of those collected may prove of some service here, though their full illustration must be reserved for the Dictionary.

III. *Aŝie*, (trans.) 'to lay aside;' passive, *a-āŝie*, 'to be laid or put aside, preserved, kept.'

Ba (trans.) 'to give as a present.' II. *bada*, 'to give up, deliver, hand over.' III. *baŝie*, 'to cause to give, give, give up;' *a-bāŝiëni, mir ist gegeben*. IV. *bayes*, 'give, give up.' V. *bayesda*, 'to give up freely, willingly;' *Bada gaskia*, to give one right,' *i.e.* ' to acquit, or justify one;' *bada laifi*, 'to give one wrong, *i.e.* to condemn.'

Beritŝi, (intr.) 'to sleep.' III. *beritŝie*, (causative,) 'to make sleep; to accommodate or entertain for a night.'

Berikitŝe, 'to upset, to overthrow.' II. *birikida*, 'to go back;' *biriki*, ' to come back.'

Daka, ' to beat or thrash,' so likewise *doke*. III. *dakie*, and *dokie*.

Dambe, ' to box.' III. *dambatŝie*, 'to be engaged in boxing.'

Dsaye, (intr.) ' to stand.' II. *dsaida*, (tr. and refl.) to 'place oneself, to stand on.' III. *dsaiŝie* (causative), 'to make to stand, to stop one=detain, prevent, hinder.' IV. *dsayes*, 'to stop.' V. *dsayesda*, 'to detain by force;' *kowane zaŝi-dsayesda wonnan mutum za-a-kaŝŝieŝi*, 'any one who shall detain this man shall be killed.'

Fitta or *futta*, ' to go out of something;' II. *fitta*, ' to depart, to break out,' used of the guinea-worm breaking out in the skin; *fiŝie* or *fuŝie*, ' to make to go out, to pull out by force; to extricate, discharge, dismiss, to ferry across a river;' IV. *fitas,* ' to take out;' V. *fitasda,* ' to take off, as garments, to undress, to adduce arguments.'

II. *Gaida,* ' to salute, to thank;' III. *gaišie,* ' to send salutations.'

Gamma, ' to meet, to join together ;' III. *gamšie,* ' to meet so as to fit, to suit, as garments.'

Gaše, (intr.) ' to be tired ;' III, *gašie,* ' to make one tired.'

Gbatše, (intr.) ' to be spoiled ;' II. *gbata,* (tr.) ' to spoil or destroy, to waste ;' III. *gbatšie,* ' to cause to be ruined or lost.' IV. *gbatas,* ' to spend, as money, dispose of something ;' V. *gbatasda,* ' to lose.'

Ia, ' to be able, can ;' II. *issa,* ' to be sufficient, to arrive at a place ;' III. *išie,* to meet, pervade, saturate ;' IV. *iyes,* ' to be able, equal to, to succeed ;' V. *iyesda,* to accomplish.'

Kada, ' to condemn, beat, strike, chastise ;' III. *kašie,* to pass sentence on one, to inflict punishment, to cause to be punished ;' IV. *kayes, kayesua,* ' condemnation ;' *kayes ga šeria,* ' to fall in judgment or court, to lose one's cause ;' *masuša-n-gia a-kašiesu,* ' those who drink fermented liquors are condemned.'

Kao, or *kawo,* ' to bring ;' II. *kauda,* ' to take away, to turn away, to abrogate a law, to diminish the value, as of money ;' *kaušie,* ' to remove, to take away ;' IV. *kawas.* V. *kawasda,* ' to remove something, disperse, dispel.'

Kai, ' to carry ;' III. *kašie, überführen,* ' to convince.'

Kwantše, (intr.) ' to lie down ;' II. *kwanta,* (tr. and refl.) ' to lay down, to sleep.'

II. *Maida,* ' to turn round, to give something back ;' III. *maišie,* ' to compare, to reduce to something ;' IV. *mayes,* 'to throw back, push back, to restore something;' V. *mayesda*, ' to turn into something, to change oneself, to restore.'

II. *Murda*, ' to gripe, to wind up as a watch;' III. *muršie*, ' to rub, to grind.'

Samna, 'to sit down;' III. *samšie*, 'to cause to sit down.'

Saye, ' to buy;' II. *saida*, ' to sell;' III. *saišie*, ' to sell;' IV. *sayes*, *sayesua*, ' selling;' V. *sayesda*, ' to be dealing in, or trading in something.'

Suba, (tr.) ' to pour out;' (intr.) ' to gush out;' IV. *sabas*, ' to pour out;' *subu*, (intr.) V. *subasda*, ' to drive out, to spit.'

Šiefa, to cast, to throw;' II. *šiepta*, *šiebda*, and *šiefta* ; III. *šiefšie* ; IV. *šiefas* ; V. *šiefasda*.

Tara, ' to gather, collect;' II. *tarda*, ' to overtake;' III. *taršie*, or *tarišie*, *taru*, (intr. passive, or causative); IV. *taras*, ' to reach to, to arrive at ;' V. *tarasda*, ' to overtake, to outrun one.'

Taši, (intr.) ' to rise ;' II. *tada*, ' to raise, to lift up ;' III. *tašie*, (causative), ' to make to rise ;' IV. *taras*, ' to waken one;' V. *tayesda*, ' to rise up.'

Tši, ' to eat ;' II. *tšida*, (tr.) ' to feed ;' III. *tšišie*, (caus.) ' cause to eat, feed, maintain.'

Yes, ' to throw;' V. *yesda*, or II. form, ' to throw away.'

Wohalla, ' to be in trouble ;' *wohalda*, ' to trouble;' III. *wohalšie*, ' to cause trouble, vex, annoy.'

CHAPTER VII.

PREPOSITIONS.

§ 83. IN the Hausa, as in many other African languages, the same word occurs, according to its use and connection, sometimes as an adverb, *i.e.* completing the notion of the verb; sometimes as a preposition, *i.e.* referring to a substantive, and sometimes as a conjunction, *i.e.* being connected with a sentence.

1. Simple Prepositions.

There are but three *original* Prepositions in the Hausa language, viz.: *da, ga,* and *ma. Daga* is in form a compound, though now used as a simple preposition, and *gare,* or *gara,* must be regarded as originally a substantive, meaning 'place, side, part,' &c., because it is invariably accompanied by a preposition, though it appears at present merely as a preposition having reference to a person or thing; as, *daga garēni* or *garēka, garēki, garēsa* or *garása garēta* or *garáta, garēmu, garēku, garēsu,* ' to me, to him,' &c.,; *ya-dauka kušiéra ya-dsaya bissa garéta,* ' he took a chair, (and) he stood on it.'

Da and *ma* likewise take the personal pronouns and suffixes; as,

Dani (נִי) and *mani,* ' to me, for me, with me,' &c.; as, *ya-taffo gidda da sañfo,* ' he came home with the basket.'
Dakai (ךָ) *maka,* ' to thee.'
Daki, (ךְ) (כִי) *maki,* ' to thee.'
Daši, masa, ' to him.'

Daita, (אָתָה) *mata*, 'to her.'
Damu, (נָי) *mamu*, 'to us.'
Daku, (אָתְכֶם) *maku*, 'to you,' forming the plural of
k=ה̄= כ in כֶם.
Dasu, masu, 'to them.'

2. In the Hausa language substantives supply, to a considerable extent, the place of prepositions, more especially: *báya*, 'back;' *bissa*, 'top, summit, what is above;' *dzakka* or *dzakkani*, 'middle, midst;' *gaba*, 'bosom, chest, front, before;' *fuska*, 'face;' *kalikási*, 'bottom, the lower part of any thing;' *kassa*, 'ground, earth, land, down,' &c.; *tšiki*, 'inside, hence belly, in.' But such nouns are sometimes preceded or followed by one of the few *original* prepositions (or postpositions;) as, *daga tšiki-n-giddamu*, 'in our house; *kada ya-šigga tšiki-n-giddana*, 'lest he enter my house;' *ya-kwanta bissa ga gadó*, 'he lays himself on the bed;' *ta šigga ga-kalikaši-n-gadó*, 'she went under the bed;' *kussa ga gidda*, 'near the house;' *baya-m birni* or *baya ga birni*, 'outside the town;' *ya-fádo daga samma*, 'it fell from the sky.' To construe these sentences literally, we must render them: 'in the *inside* of our house;' 'he laid on the *top* of the bed;' 'she entered at the *bottom* of (=under) the bed;' 'near to the house;' 'at the back of the town (=outside the town,' &c.)

NOTE.—Something analogous to this twofold or threefold use of prepositions, or rather of prepositions and nouns, is found in some English expressions; as, 'up-on,' 'in-to,' 'within,' 'far-from,' 'near-to,' 'from-within,' 'from-without,' 'from-on-high.'

3. Substantives being used in the place of prepositions, it is but natural to suppose that they should be treated as such; that is, take the *n* as the sign of the Genitive; as, *daga tšiki-n-gíddamu*, 'in the inside *of* our house;' *daia tšikinsu* 'one *of* them;' and the nominal suffixes *dagá bayansa*, 'at his back=behind him.' And this is also the reason why we

connect the Suffixes with the few original prepositions, as in Hebrew בְּ, מִן, אֵת, כְּ and אֶל are treated; and this arrangement need neither offend nor surprise any one. For further explanation we must refer to the Dictionary.

CHAPTER VIII.

ADVERBS.

§ 84. The necessity of some adverbs is superseded in the Hausa language by the use of certain verbs, § 58, which involve the force of what is often expressed in other languages by the use of some adverbs; thus for instance: *ya-kussa mutua*, 'he was near to death=he almost died;' *Ráni ya-kussa zakkua*, 'the dry season is nigh coming=will soon come;' *aikinsa ya-kussa karewa*, 'his work is nearly finished;' *ya kussa fadua*, 'he almost fell.' But these instances too may be called prepositional combinations, verbal substantives being combined with the verb; but not so in

Ya-samna, 'he sat down;' *ya-táši*, 'he got up, arose;' *Ya-kekaše*, 'it is dried up.'

§ 85. Adverbs of Place. These are either *Simple* or *Compounds*. Some demonstrative pronouns are used as adverbs by themselves, or combined with prepositions; as,

Nan, 'here.'
Tšan, 'there.'
Daganan, 'here, at this place,' and 'whence.'
Dagatšan, 'there, at that place, yonder.'
Wurinan, 'this place,' and 'here.'
Wurinda, 'the place which.'
Nana, 'here.'
Kussa, 'near, nigh, at hand.'

M

Nésa, 'far, at a distance.'
Gaba, ' before, in front.'
Baya, 'behind.'
Bissa, ' above, upon, on, over.'
Kassa, ' below, beneath, under, down.'
Kalkas, or *kalikaši*, ' under, below, underneath.'
Wośe, ' out, outside.'
Dzakkani, ' between, in the midst, among.'
Tare, ' together.'
Gabadai, ' together.'
Tsïki, ' in, within.'
Énna, ' where, whence.'
Kōénna, 'anywhere, wheresoever.'

§ 86. *Adverbs of Time.*

a) Simple.

Abbada, 'ever,' *hal abbada*, ' for ever.'
Baya ya, ' after that.'
Dādaí, ' heretofore, never, never before.'
Haryao, ' again, not until now.'
Kadai, ' once, alone, only.'
Duka, ' all, whole ;' *rana dúka*, ' the whole day.'
Gaba, ' before.'
Hal, or *har*, ' till, until,' (conj. ' so that.')
Kána, ' before, then.'
Kulum, ' always.'
Nada, ' before, above.'
Sammasamma, ' by and by.'
Tun, ' since.'
Tunda, ' before, while, while as yet.'
Yansu, ' now.'
Yaúśe, ' when.'
Kuma, ' again.'
Da, ' when ;' *da ya gannéni*, ' when he saw me.'

ADVERBS. 83

b) Compounded with nouns and the demonstrative pronoun *nan;* as,

Lottu nan, 'that time, at that time, then.'
Lokatši nan, ' then, at that time.'
Saanan, ' then, at that time.'

c) Compounded with *kō*, intensive; as,

Kōyansu, ' even now, just now, immediately.'
Kōyaüše, ' any time, at any time, always, constantly.'

d) Adverbs are derived from nouns and adjectives, by the prefix *da:*

Dafari, ' at first, long ago, before this.'
Dasáfe, ' early in the morning;' *dasasafe,* ' very early.'
Dasáfia, ' in the morning.'
Da maraětšie, ' in the evening.'
Da baya, ' after, last, secondly.'

e) Substantives are used adverbially; as,

Badi, ' next year.'
Yao, ' to-day.'
Gobe, ' to-morrow.'
Šia, ' yesterday.'
Banna, ' this year.'
Šiékaranšia, ' the day before yesterday.'
Šíbi, ' the day after to-morrow,' and
Gáta, ' the day following, the day after to-morrow, or the fourth day.'

f) Adverbs of Time are formed from *saa,* ' time;' as, *saanan,* ' that time,' and the *Ordinal* Adverbs:

Saodaia, ' once.'
Saobiu, ' twice.'
Saouku, ' three times,' &c.

§ 87. *Adverbs of Manner.*

a) Simple.

Ai, ' verily, truly, really.'
Ašie, ' verily, truly.'

Bansa, 'for nothing, good for nothing, vain, foolishly, to no purpose.'

Bissai, 'erect;' *wuzia bissai,* 'the tail erect.'

Dabam, and *dabamdadam,* 'different, not the same, separately, by itself.'

Daídai, or *deidei,* 'properly, correctly, equally, justly, fitly, lawfully, becomingly.'

Hakka, 'so, thus;' *ba hakka ba,* 'not so.'

Hakkanan, 'so, in this way;' *hakkanan ši ke,* 'so it is.'

Kamma, (כְּמָה) 'as, like as, as it were, like to, equal to.'

Kua, 'too, likewise;' *ni kua,* 'I too.'

Ma, 'too, likewise.'

Kwarai, or *korei,* 'well, properly.'

Massa, 'quickly:' *massa massa,* 'very quickly, suddenly, hastily.'

Sanu, 'slowly;' *sanusanu,* 'very slowly, gently.'

Compounds—

b) with *da*; as,

Dadádi, 'sweetly, agreeably.'

Dagaskia, 'with truth=truly, certainly, of a truth.'

Dakarifi, 'with power=powerfully.'

Damasifa, 'in mischief=mischievously.'

c) with *kō*; as,

Kokakka, 'any how, in any way.'

Kohakka, 'so, even so.'

§ 88. Specific Adverbs. These are very few, and occur only in the examples here mentioned:

Sai, 'quite;' *sai láfia,* 'quite well.'

Lau, lafia lau, 'pretty well, quite well.'

Kerin, 'very;' *bakki kerin,* 'very black.'

Wur, 'very;' *ša wur,* 'very red.'

Fet, 'very;' *farifet,* 'very white.'

Dakat, 'with difficulty.'

When a higher degree is to be expressed, the Adverb is

repeated; as, *farifari*, 'very white;' *massamassa*, 'very quickly;' *sannusanu*, 'very gently.'

§ 89. *Interrogative Adverbs.*

Mi? 'what?' *Mi ya-saméka?* 'what is the matter with thee?'
Domi? 'why?' *Domi ka-tše hakka?* 'why dost thou say so?'
Nawa? 'how much?' *Nawa kurdínša?* 'how much money for it?'
Kaka? 'how? in what way?'
Dagaénna? 'where? whither?' *Dagaénna ši-ke?* 'where is he?' *dagaénna ka-fitto?* 'whence comest thou?'
Dagayaúše? 'when? at what time?' *dagayaúše abokimu záši taffia?* 'when is our friend coming?'

CHAPTER IX.

CONJUNCTIONS.

§ 90. Conjunctions are not very numerous in the Hausa language. There are, in fact, but few words which are exclusively used as such; and some words classed with conjunctions, are, as was observed above, also used as adverbs or pronouns, *i.e.* they are sometimes used to qualify verbs, and sometimes to connect propositions.

The Conjunctions are either *Simple* or *Compound*.

§ 91. Simple Conjunctions are:

Amma, 'but, further,'

Da, 'if, when, of, with;' *daydwa sunka-mutu da yuñwa*, 'many were dying of hunger.' *Da... da..* correspond to the English expression, 'both ... and,' as: *da ni da obana*, 'both I and my father;' or, 'neither ... nor,' after a negative sentence; as, *ba mu-soka ba da kaí da gōnánka*, 'we do not like thee, neither thee nor thy farm.' *Da ni da ši mu dúka, muna taffia, tšiki-n-káya*, 'both I and he were walking upon thorns.'

Don or *doṅ,* 'because, for, in order that, that, to, stating the ground or the reason of anything, and expressing a purpose or intention;' *don ba ka-ši ba,* 'because thou dost not hear.'
Amma máta-n-Hausa suna-so-n sa Kolli ga ĭdănúnsu don ši-sa idănúnsu šiúni, 'but Hausa women are fond of putting Kolli to their eyes, that it may make their eyes blue.'
Domi (contraction for *doṅmi,*) 'why, wherefore.'
En, 'that, in order that, for, to.' § 59 *b,* and § 62 Note.
Ga, 'for, to, in order to.' § 59, *a.*
Ko, 'if, or, about, even; whether . . . or whether; neither . . nor; though, although.' *Amma ban ši-ba ko daía ya-mutu, ko wonni ya-halba kíbia,* 'but I have not heard whether any one died, or whether any one shot an arrow.' *Ko ya-koréta, ko yáki ya-rabasu, ban sanni ba,* 'whether he drove her away, or whether war separated them, I do not know.' *Hario mutume nan, ko obánta ya-zakka, ya-maišiéta,* 'again the same man, or (=*i.e.*) 'her father came, and caused her to return.' *Ina-tamaha kanena šiékarūnsa šídda ko bokoi* 'I think the years of my brother were six or seven=he was six or seven years old.' *Da muka samma ko šiékára daía,* 'having remained there *about* one year.' *Da babu raírai ko kadán,* 'there was no sand there, not *even* a little.' *Da kasuansu ba mu-so mu-kara dubata, don ta-samu ruá-n-ído, ko, so-n-abubua dayawa,* 'and as regards their market, we did not wish to see it any longer, because it made our eyes water; or, (=*i.e.*) to long for many things.'

§ 92. COMPOUND CONJUNCTIONS.

Kada, Negative Conjunction, 'that, not;' *kada su-mutu* 'that they should not die.' *Kada kówa ya-táffi ga baki-n-rua nan*, 'let no one go to the mouth of that water.' *Na támbayẹ́su domi mutane kada su-taffi*, 'I asked them why the people should not go.'

Kada en, " that not, that I not=lest I . . .'

Donkadá, ' so that not, that not, lest.'

Don en, ' that I might,' &c.

Donwónnan, and *donhakka*, ' because of, for the sake of, for this reason, therefore, on that account.'

Kadán, 'if, when.'

Kamma, ' as, like as.'

Kammāda, 'as soon as, as, like as, like to, according to.'

Kóda, composed of *kō*, intensive particle, and *da*, Adverb of time, ' when, if=even if, though, although.' *Kóda ya mutu ši yi rai*, ' though he should die, he shall live.' *Koda ba su-ši ba tšiwukin gaiwa sunaganni enda ta-kwánta*, ' although they do not hear the chewing of the mud-fish, they see where it lies.'

Kuá, ' too, likewise.'

Bamda, ' besides.'

Bamda wonnan, ' besides this.'

Sabbaba, ' because, for the sake of, on account of.'

Sabbada wonnan, ' for this reason, therefore.'

Hakkanan kua, ' so likewise, therefore.'

Wotakíla, ' perhaps.'

Hakkana, ' so, thus;' *hakkana ši-ke*, ' so it is.'

CHAPTER X.

INTERJECTIONS.

§ 93. There are but a few; as, *ó*, ' of surprise and astonishment,' and *kai*, *a*; *a mugum bára*, ' o wicked servant.'

88

PART III.

SYNTAX.

CHAPTER XI.

§ 94. Syntax treats of the construction of sentences; it points out the different parts of which a sentence is composed, and the relation which each part bears to the whole.

§ 95. A sentence consists of the *subject* and the *predicate;* as, *dóki ya-mutu,* 'the horse died.'

The subject is the word of which something is affirmed; the predicate is that which is affirmed of the subject: *dóki ya-mutu,* ' the horse *died.*' Comp. § 107.

The Subject.

§ 96. The subject is either *grammatical* or *logical.*

1. The *grammatical* subject is either a noun, or some word occupying the place of a noun, as a *pronoun*, or *adjective* used substantively ; as,

Yáro ya-kúka, ' the boy cries.'
Matše ta-fádi, ' the women fell.'
Saríki ya-mutu, ' the king died.'
Ya mutu, ' he died.'
Maikúnu da rua-n-saínyi góni ne, '*he who* boils gruel in cold water is clever.'

Talakáwa ba su-da abokai, amma masudukia suna-da dayáwa, '*the poor* have no friends, but *the rich* have many.'

2. The *logical* subject consists of the grammatical subject with its various modifications.

The grammatical subject is modified and transformed into the logical subject by,

a) Demonstrative pronouns; as,
Wonnan mutum, or *mutume nan,* 'this man.'
Wogga mátše, 'this woman.'
Wonnan rua babu keáo, 'this water is not good.'
Wonni mākájo, 'a certain blind man.'

b) By possessive pronouns; thus, *kurdina ya-gbatše,* 'my money is lost;' *bindigansa ya-tšikka,* 'his gun is loaded.'

c) By *adjectives*:
Mutum babá ba ši-šin-dsóro, 'a great man does not fear.'
Zunzua maikéáo tana-waka, 'the beautiful bird is singing.'
Kurdinsa duka ya-gbatše, 'all his money was lost,' or, 'he lost all his money;' the subject becoming the predicate.
Mutane mainya sun-taffi ga wári-n-saríki, 'respectable persons went to the king's place=to the king.'

d) By *numerals*; as,
Yára biu suka-samna, 'two boys sat down.'
Kwáná iširin sun-káre, 'twenty days are over.'

e) By substantives either in apposition or in the genitive case; as,
Gaiwa, wonni iri-n-kífi, 'gaiwa, (mud-fish,) *i.e.* some kind of fish.'
Malka, rua šina-zakkua kassa har kwānáki šidda, 'malka, *i.e.* rain which falls for six days in succession.'

Naíno, fádáwá-n-Saríki, 'Naino, the minister of the king.'

Kūrége, bara-n-mallami, 'the fox, the servant of the priest.'

Tāróko, kānuáta, ba ta-da láfia, 'Tāróko, my sister, was not well.'

f) An infinitive, or an entire relative sentence, may be the logical subject; as,

Sāmu-n-magana ba dawūya ba, 'it is not difficult to find words;' or, 'the finding of words is not difficult.'

Mutum da ya-yi masu dāriá ya-fádi tšiki-n rámi, 'the man who laughed at them fell into the hole.'

§ 97. The subject is also either *simple* or *compound*.

A *simple* subject is a single noun, or word standing for a noun, either alone or variously modified; as,

Yáro ya-worigi, 'the boy plays.'

Nabíssa ya-tše, 'the one above said.'

Nakalkas ya-fadi kassa, 'the one below fell down.'

Tūmáki-n-abōkimu woddanda sun-ša rua dadaffi sun-mutu, 'the sheep of our friend which drank the poisoned water are dead.'

Gōnansa kārami ne, 'his farm is small.'

§ 98. A *compound* subject consists of two or more simple subjects, to which *one* predicate belongs; as,

Yáro da ōbánsa suna-da bindiga sun-taffi faraúta, 'the boy and his father, having guns, went hunting.'

Fuskanta, da sanninta, da hanunta dúka sun-tšikka da tagbo, 'her face, her dress, her hands were all full of mud.'

The Predicate.

§ 99. The Predicate, like the subject, is either *grammatical* or *logical*.

1. The grammatical Predicate is either a verb alone, as,

Aiki ya-kăre, 'the work is finished;' or, the copula *ke, ne, tše,* ' to be,' and *da,* ' to have,' or ' to be ;' and *mai,* pl. *masu,* ' one who is,' or ' which is,' with a noun or adjective ; as,

Yăro karami ne, ' the boy is little.'
Yărinia tăgari tše, ' the girl is good.'
Timbuktu gari karami ne, ' Timbuctoo is a small town.'
Aiki da wuya, ' labour is hard.'
Gari mainĕsa, ' the country is distant=which is at a distance.'

2. The *logical* Predicate consists of the grammatical predicate with its various modifications; as,

Yăro ya-ša magani maidŏatši, ' the boy drank the bitter medicine,' or relative sentence, ' the medicine which was bitter.'
Ta-taffi ga gidda-n-maimagani, ' she went to the house of the doctor.'
Ya-dauki woddansu măgani daga tšiki-n-alšifunsa, ' he took some medicines out of his pocket.'

§ 100. The Predicate also, like the subject, is either *simple* or *compound.*

1. Simple Predicate:

Kanua ba ta-da karifi, ' the sister was not strong.'
Ina-sonsa kwarai, ' I like him much.'
Mišinta šine maisaida-n-sinăria, ' her husband was one who was trading in gold=gold-merchant.'

2. A compound Predicate consists of two or more simple Predicates belonging to the same subject; as,

Yăro ya-guddu, ya-fădi tšiki-n-rămi, ' the boy run, and fell into a hole.'
Zūnzua ta-tăši, ta-taffi, ta-samna bissa itatše, ' the bird got up, went, sat down on a tree.'

Different kinds of Sentences.

§ 101. In simple sentences the subject stands generally first, the predicate next, and the copula, if it be one of the substantive verbs, *ke, ne,* or *tše,* last; but in negative sentences, the copula may precede or follow the predicate; as,

Yáro-nan karami ne, 'this boy is little.'
Yārínia mūgūniá tše, 'the girl is bad.'
Bardo mugu-n-mutum ši-ke, 'a thief is a bad man.'

Negative Sentences.

Yaro nan ba ši-ke karami ba, 'this boy is not little.'
Mátše ba ta-ke mugunia ba, 'the woman is not bad.'
Bardo ba ši-ke mutum nāgarí ba, 'a thief is not a good man.'

§ 102. When *da,* ' to be,' and ' to have,' is used as a copula, it generally, but not always, precedes the predicate;

Wúka da kaifi, ' the knife is sharp (lit. has an edge).'
Yaro nun šina-da wáyo, 'this boy is cunning=is possessed of cunning.'
Magana-n-Engliz da wúya-n-kóya, ' the English language is difficult to learn.'

Negative Sentences

Wuka nan ba ta-da kaifi ba, ' this knife is not sharp.'
Magana-n-Engliz ba da wuya ban koya ta-ke, ' the English language is not hard to learn.'
Akoí, ' there is, there are,' and ' they have,' stands before the subject:
Akoi mutane dayawa, ' there are many people.'
Akoi Alla, ' there is a God.'
Akoi záki tšiki-n-giddamu, ' there is a lion in our house.'
Akoi woddansu, ' there are some.'
Akoi bareyí dayawa daga tšan, ' there are many deer there.'

Interrogative Sentences.

§ 103. Interrogative sentences are distinguished from Indicative Propositions; *a)*, by the accent or stress of the voice; as,

Kaí ka ke yi maní magana hakka? 'dost thou speak to me in this manner?'

Ba ka rubuta wotíka ga Abbega? 'dost thou not write a letter to Abbega?'

Kaí ka kašśie matśiśi nan? 'hast thou killed the serpen?'

b) Interrogative *pronouns* are used; as (See § 32.)

Wanéne ka-ke kírra biri? 'whom dost thou call a monkey?'

Énna kánka? 'where is thy head?'

Domi ya-kirrāwota Hava? 'why did he call her Eve?'

Minéne zāsu-yi daganan? 'what are they going to do there?'

Kaka ka-sanní wonnan? 'how dost thou know this?'

Mi zāmu-yi daśi? 'what shall we do with it?'

c) In indirect questions, *ko,* 'whether,' is often used; as,

Ta-tše, ko daganan rua Madína śi-ke or, *na-taffo ko nan ne rua Madína?* 'she said, whether the water of Medina was there?' or, 'I came (to see) whether that is the water of Medina.'

Imperative Sentences.

§ 104. Imperative Sentences take the subject before the predicate. The subject is rarely omitted, only in sentences and connections where gender and person are sufficiently clear from the connection: *Ga śi,* 'see it, look at it;' where the person is directly addressed: *Ta-tše máta : taffi,* 'she said to her, go;' but *ta-tše, ki kuntśiesu,* she said, (thou, f.) *ki kuntśiesu,* 'let them loose, untie them.' *Na-*

tše mḁsa: bắni rua, ' I said to him, give me water;' or *natše ka-bắni rua.* *Ban sanni ba, faddá mani en ši,* ' I do not know, tell me, that I may know (hear).' § 69.

Compound Sentences.

§ 105. When two or more simple sentences or propositions are connected together, they are called a compound sentence.

a) Some sentences are connected by means of conjunctions; as,

Kadán ka-bắni kurdi nan nī-baka tagia, 'if thou give me the money, I shall give thee the cap.'

Kadan dere ya yi šɨ́ kaššieka, 'when the night has come he will kill thee=he will kill thee in the night.'

b) The conjunction is often repeated in conditional sentences, where other languages would use a copulative conjunction; thus,

Kadan na-taffi, kadan ka-rufe kofa, kadan wonni ya zakka, kada ka-bude, 'when I have gone, when thou hast shut the door, if any one should come, thou must not open it.'

c) Two sentences may be so arranged and connected that the one denotes the cause or reason of what is expressed in the other:

Rairai ya-šigga ga idanumu, don hiska ta-busa da karifi, 'sand got into our eyes, because there was a strong wind.'

Amma ka-ša rua nan da tilass, don ba ka-sắmu ba ya-fi wonnan, 'but you drink that water, being forced, because you get none that is better.'

d) In the Hausa language both subject and object are sometimes accompanied by sentences or short propositions, as they appear at first sight; but which are, in fact, participles in the form of finite verbs, *i.e.* indicating Person, Tense, and Gender, and must be construed as such: *e.g.*

Kurítšia ta-zakka tana-yi-n-kúka, tana-tšewa ga matše : yi-kununki ki ša, 'a dove came crying, saying to the woman, make thy gruel, drink thou.'

Sunka-taffi ga báki-n-ríšia, ya-tše masu,' when they had gone to the mouth of the well, he said to them.'

Dzakka-n-dere mayia tana-daúki wuka tana-wazawa tana-tšewa : ki-tši náma, ki tši náma,' in the middle of the night the witch took a knife, sharpening it, and saying to it, eat thou flesh, eat thou flesh.'

Gísso šina-da sanda ta karifi, ya ašie kussa ga kánsa, 'the spider having an iron stick, laid it close to his head.'

Yaro šina-taffia ya-gammu da abokínsa gísso,' as the boy was going he met his friend, the spider;' *ya-tše mása, záni en ganni mákára-n-dúnia,* 'he said to him, I am going to see the end of the world.'

Askake sunka-yenka hānuánta ta-berí, ta-dsaya tana-lašiewa šinninta, ' the razors having cut her hand, she left (them), she (and) stood still licking the blood.'

Wonni ya-táffo ya-hawa rakumi sunka-baši búlála ya-yi-sukua; ' the one came, mounted the camel, when they had given him a whip, he galloped;' *ya-fádi,* 'he fell down.'

CHAPTER XII.

SUBSTANTIVES.

§ 106. To substantives belong Cases, Number, and Gender. There are, in fact, no cases in the sense in which the word is used in the Latin or in the Greek, but rather in the sense in which we speak of them in the Hebrew, that is, the case of a noun is marked, as in English, either by the relation which it sustains to the sentence (as subject, object, &c.) or its relation to some specific part of it, or by prepositions connected with it, either expressed or understood.

§ 107. The Concordance of a *real* nominative with its verb is that of a Subject with its Predicate. By the *real* nominative we mean the verbal pronouns (§ 69) always connected with the verb when in a state of conjugation. What, therefore, is usually taken for the nominative is, in fact, either a noun or a pronoun put in apposition with the real nominative, and is regarded more as the subject of discourse than the grammatical subject—hence nouns, and pronouns at the beginning of a sentence must be treated as absolute nominatives; and to avoid obscurity, nouns and pronouns of this kind must be rendered into English by some such words as, *in respect of, as regards, with regard to, as to,* &c. (Lee's Hebrew Grammar, § 216.)

Examples:

Máta-n-Bornu aikinsu daia ke nan, wonda na-sanni, 'women of Bornu work their one, is this which I know,' *i.e.* 'as regards the women of Bornu, there is one thing they do which I know.'

Kurdi-n dokina sai da nono n-matše anasayensa, 'as

regards the price of my horse, it can be sold only for the breast of a woman.'

Namíši ya-taffi faraúta, amma matše tana-yin aiki-n-gídda, 'as to the man, he goes hunting, but the woman is doing the work of the house.'

Ni ína-taffia tšiki-n daši, 'as for me, I am going into the forest.'

Ši dakansa ya-fadda mani hakka, 'he himself told me the same.'

Sunka-tše: wonnan, múriánsa kamma na matše, woddansu sunka-tše: wonnan, muriansa namiši, 'some were saying, as to this (person), his voice is like that of a woman, others said, as to this (person), his voice is that of a man.'

Wonnan da-n-sariki ne, 'as to this (person), he is the son of the king.'

The Genitive Case.

§ 108. It is not necessary to repeat here what has been said respecting the formation of the Genitive case in § 28. We shall therefore only add a few instances of its occurrence and use, not noticed there:

a) The Genitive is sometimes expressed by *ga;* as,

Ga mi? 'of what?'

Ga hakkarikari na šikki-n-Adam, 'of a rib of Adam's body.'

b) By suffixed pronouns, equivalent to our adjective pronouns; as,

Gidda obansa, 'his father's house.'

Busu mišimu, 'our husband's mat.'

c) The Partitive Genitive is expressed by the same pronominal suffixes combined with numeral adjectives or nouns, &c.; as,

Daiansu, 'one of them;' and *daía daga tšikinsu.*

Doki-n-wonni mutum ya-mutu, 'the horse of some one, or some body's horse died.'

Woddansu, 'some of them, some.'

Babu daiansu, ko babu daia tšikinsu, 'not one of them.'

Biunsu, 'two of them.' *Ba kowansu,* 'not one of them.'

Kānénsu ya-taffi, 'the younger (brother) of them went.'

Wotše ga tšikimu, 'which of us.' With *kamma,* 'as, like as, like to;' thus,

Dadaí ban ganni ba wuri da mamaki kamma-n-kassa mutane farufaru, 'I have never seen a place so wonderful as (=the likeness of) the country of white people.'

Rua kuá ši samma kamma-n-dusi, 'the water, too, will become the likeness of, *i.e.* like a stone.'

d) Sometimes the genitive form is used with adjectives These forms are most conveniently translated as compound substantives, or as pure adjectives.

Tšiwo-n-kai 'head-ache.'

Rua-n-zafi, 'hot water.'

Šaši-n-garína záni-báši, 'half of my country I shall give him.'

Dunia akoi sabo-n-wata, 'there was new moon in the sky;' or 'the world had a new moon.'

Sariki, Alla ši-baka yawa-n-rai, 'O king, may God give thee length of=long life.'

Sabo-n ríga, 'new dress.'

Kogo-n-ītatše, 'hollow tree.'

A mugu-m-bara, 'O bad servant.'

e) The Genitive is frequently formed by the infinitive of verbs:

Na-mantše faddi-n-matansu, 'I forgot to speak of their women.'

Ba na-dsóro-n-matšiši, 'I am not afraid *of* the serpent.'

We must sometimes use other prepositions than *of;* as:

Ba ni-iansa ba, ' I am not equal to it;' and, *muna-iansa*, ' we are able to do it.'

Ba na-ši-n-dsōrónsa, ' I am not afraid of him.'

En taffi ša-n-rua, ' that I may go to draw water.'

Máta sunka-taffi rišia ga dauka-n-rua, sun-ši, ' the women having gone to the well, in order to get water, heard . . .'

Šina-bínsu daga baya, ' he follows after them.'

Ba záka-kára ganni-n-gari ba kammansa har ga wata, ' you are not going to add the sight of a town in its likeness for a month=you do not see a town like it again for a whole month.'

Mutane nan ba su-tši-n-kómi sai nama-n-daši, ' those people eat nothing except the meat of the desert=venison.'

f) One Genitive is dependant upon another; as,

Da muka-zakka ga kofa-n-gidda-n obansa ya bude kofa-n-karussa, ya šigga tšiki-n-gidda da guddu, ' having arrived at the door of the house of his father, he opened the door of the carriage, and went to the house running.'

The Dative Case.

§ 109. This case is marked by prepositions, especially by *ya, gare, ma, da*, and *daga*.

a) When the object to or for which any thing is done is a personal pronoun, the pronoun is combined with the preposition, and when it is a noun, it stands before it; as,

Yaúše ka-aike wotíka gárésa, or *mása?* ' when hast thou sent a letter to him?'

Ya-bayes rua ga dokinsa, ' he gave water to his horse.'

Ya-tše masa, mata, ' he said to him, to her.'

Ya-issa dani, ' it is sufficient for me;' or, *ya-išiéni*.

Ba ka yi mani amsa ba? ' dost thou not answer me?'

b) These prepositions are used to express motion or direction to a place, where in other languages the Dative would be employed; e.g.

Sun-taffi ga wonni garí, 'they went to some town.'
Da sunka-dawoyo sunka-taffo ga báki-n-gulbi, 'as they were returning, they came to the bank of a river.'
En mun-issa ga wonni wuri enda akoi tšiawa mu-kan yenka mu-dora ga baya-n-rakuma, 'when we arrived at a place where there was grass, we used to cut some, and to put it on the camels.'

c) The price for which any thing is bought or sold may be said to be in the dative case with *da*; as:

Sai da nono-n-matše anasayensa, 'only for the breast of a woman it is sold.'
Uwata! ki-saya mani doki nan da nononki.
Dokina wonnan ba na-sayensa ba da kurdi, 'as to this my horse, I shall not sell it for money.'

d) The Dative also indicates the person or thing for whose benefit or injury any thing is done; as,

Mu-yi addóa masa, 'let us pray for him.'
Ya-mutu damu duka, 'he died for all of us.'

e) The Dative may be called the instrumental case, being expressed by the same prepositions:

Ya-buga dokinsa da bulala, 'he beat his horse with the whip.'
Ya-yenkeši da wuka, 'he cut it with the knife.'
Ka-tšikkaši da rua, 'fill it with water;'

But *da* has also a connective meaning, and then it is coupled with *tare*:

Mu-taffi tare daši, 'let us go with him=together with him.'

f) The relation of time is indicated by this case; as,

Gulbi nan ši-kan kaffé ga ráni, ko ga basara, lottu nda babu rua, ' this river generally gets dry in the dry season, or in the season in which there is no rain.'

The Accusative Case.

§ 110. The Accusative denotes, as in other languages, the object of a transitive verb; and is, as such, sufficiently known by its position after the subject:

Ya-faddí ga mutane maganganu-n-Obangiši duka, ' he told the people *all the words of* the Lord.'
Da akoi šagaba tare damu wonda ya-sanni wuri, ' and there was a guide with us, who knew *the place.*'
Kana-ganni dari suna-taffia gabadai, ' you see *hundreds* walking together.'

The Accusative forms in a great many cases adverbial designations:

a) Of place:
Ya-taffi dáši, ' he went in the desert;' *ta-taffi garí,* ' she went in the field, or country.'
Ta-ašie dánta kalikáši-n-ītatše, ' she laid her child under a tree.'
Ya-samna wuri-n-sariki, ' he resides with the king.'
Ya-samna kassa, ' he sits the ground=down.'
Ta-šigga wuri enda diánta su-ke, ' she entered the place where her brood was.'

b) Of time; as,
Saanan Musa ya-taffo, ' at that time=then Moses came.'
Lotu nda na-táši ba na-ši láfia ba, ' the time at which= when I rose I did not feel well.' So also,
Da safe, ' in the morning;' *da maraetšie,* ' in the evening.'
Ya-samna bissa ga tudu kwanaki arbain, da dere arbain, ' he remained on the mountain forty days and forty nights.'

Ina-tamaha kwanaki šidda daga nan zua ga Bornu, ' I think it is six days' journey from there to Bornu.'

Saodaia obansa ya-kaiši tšiki-n-masallatši ga rana alšima, ' on one occasion his father took him to a place of worship on a Sunday.'

Akoi wonni yaro šiekarunsa šabial, ' there was a boy whose years were fourteen=of the age of fourteen.'

The Vocative.

§ 111. The *Vocative* is expressed by personal pronouns; as, *Kai yáro,* ' thou boy=O boy.' *Kai mutane,* ' O people.' *Ke kúra,* ' O hyena.'

The Ablative.

§ 112. The *Ablative* is indicated by the prepositions *daga* and *gare;* thus,

Daga enna ka-fitto? ' whence comest thou?' *Na-fitto daga Bornu,* ' I come from Bornu.'

Yauše ka-samu wotika garésa? ' when didst thou *receive* a letter *from* him?'

Yauše ka-aike wotika garesa? ' when didst thou *send* a letter *to* him?' or *yauše ka-aike masa wotika?*

Especially with passive verbs: *a-néma dayawa garesa,* ' much will be required from him.'

The Number of Nouns.

§ 113. There is a strong tendency in the Hausa people to use the singular where we should expect the plural. To point out all the instances, or to give definite rules, is more than the present state of our knowledge of the language enables us to do; we shall therefore only point out some cases where the plural form is *never,* and some where it is but *seldom* used.

a) Nouns denoting a mass can form no plural; as,

Sinária, ' gold.'
Azurufa, ' silver.'
Karifi, ' iron.'
Šinkaffa, ' rice.'
Hazi, ' corn.'
Alkamma, ' wheat.'
Zumua, ' honey;' or, rua-n-zumua.
Nono, ' milk.'
Kúra, ' dust.'

b) Several members of the body; as,

Sútšia, ' heart;' the plural, sutotši, occurs in a few instances.
Kurua, ' soul, echo.'
Šínni, ' blood.'
Gaši, ' hair;' the plural, gasusuka, occurs once for ' feathers of fowls.'
Náma, ' flesh.'

c) Several faculties of the mind; as,

Yírda, ' will, belief, faith.'
Murna, ' joy.'
Dsóro, ' fear.'
Tamaha, ' hope, thought.'

d) Most abstract nouns cannot form a plural:

Tšiwuta, ' illness.'
Mugunta, ' badness.'
Madsāworáta, ' cowardice.'

e) Words denoting weights and measures are seldom used in the plural:

Zaka, ' measure.'
Mudu, ' measure.'
Káma, ' cubit.'

Sánda, 'stick;' German, 'stab;' English, 'yard.'

f) Certain designations of time seldom make use of the plural number.

Rána, 'sun, day;' when used for the latter its plural is *kwanaki.*
S ífia, 'morning.'
Maractšie, 'evening.'
Šiĕkara, 'age, year;' when it signifies the latter it forms its plural *šiĕkarú,* as: *šiĕkaránsa goma ša bokoí,* 'his age is seventeen;' and *šiekarunsa šidda,* 'he is six years old=his years six.'

g) The Hausas often employ nouns in the singular in a *collective* sense, especially when modified by numeral adjectives, where other languages use the plural form; Examples,

Zaki ya-tangana ga ītatše kafansa biú bíssa, kafansa biu kassa, 'the lion was leaning against a tree, two of his legs upwards, and two of his legs downwards.'

In cases where nouns are used as collectives, the predicate is mostly in the plural number:

Ta-ganni wuri-enda dianta su-ke, 'she saw the place where her brood *they were.*'

Gender.

§ 114. There are but two Genders in the Hausa language, the masculine and the feminine. In § 20 we pointed out the general rules by which gender is distinguished and known; here we ought to treat of the laws according to which the distinction of Gender is made; but at present we can do no more than notice a few features, and leave the rest for further inquiries.

1) Masculine are the names of

Alla, ' God ;' *Obangiši*, ' Lord ;' *Malaiki*, ' Angel ;' *Ebilis*,
' Devil ;' *Isa*, ' Jesus ;' *Gabrielu*, ' Gabriel ;' *Saitan*,
' Satan ;' *Balarabe*, ' an Arab ;' *mutum*, ' man ;' *zaki*,
' lion ;' *dodo*, ' evil spirit.'
And of all male animals; as,
Sa, ' bull ;' *bunsuru*, ' ram, he-goat ;' *kurége*, ' fox ;' *gado*.
' pig ;' *karre*, ' dog ;' *masuru*, ' wild cat ;' *babé*, ' locust ;'
matšiši, ' serpent.'
b) The names of stars, ranks and offices of men, trees, &c.

Tamraro, ' star ;' *sariki*, ' king ;' *galladima*, ' governor ;'
fadáwa, ' counsellor ;' *bara*, ' servant ; *oba*, ' father ;'
itatše, ' tree.'

2 Feminine are,
a) The names of women and female animals, the sun
the earth, the world, wind, and countries; the names of
female ranks and offices:

Matše, ' woman ;' *yarinia*, ' girl.'
Uworigída, ' mistress of the house.'
Akwia, ' goat ;' *kura*, ' hyena.'
Dumkiu, ' sheep.'
Dunia, ' world ;' *hiska*, ' wind.'
Kassa, ' earth, land, country ;' *rami*, ' hole, cavity.'
Sáfia, ' morning ;' *addóa*, ' prayer.'
Rana, ' sun ;' *waka*, ' song.'
Zunsua, ' bird.'

b) *Abstract Substantives:*
Magana, ' word.' When used for language it is chiefly
construed as a masculine.
Murna, ' joy.'
Makaranta, ' school.'
Tšiwuta, ' illness.'
Bauta, ' slavery.'
Makafta, ' blindness.'
Kuturta, ' leprosy.'
Abuta, ' friendship.'

CHAPTER XIII.

THE PRONOUNS.

A.—*Personal Pronouns.*

§ 115. The Personal Pronoun of the Hausa language is used not only as a substitute for a noun, but also *invariably* as a complement to it. (§§ 69-107.) As a substitute, it is only required when the substantive is omitted; but as a complement, it is *necessary*, whether the substantives be omitted or not, and serves, besides its pronominal use, to indicate the gender of the noun, and, combined with verbal particles (§ 69), the tense of the verb. To translate the pronoun in English would render it harsh and pleonastic, though it cannot be regarded as a pleonasm in Hausa.

1. The pronoun agrees with its subject in person, number, and gender; thus,

Yaro ya-zakka, 'the boy he comes;' *yara ba su-zakka ba,* 'the boys they do not come.'

Matše ta-tắffo, 'the woman she comes;' *Mata ba su-taffo ba,* 'the women do not come.'

2. The same rule is observed when there are two or more predicates belonging to the same subject; thus,

Kúra ta-taffó, ta-kawo náma, ta-báyés ga diánta, da ita kua ta-taba kadán, 'the hyena she came, she brought meat, she gave to her brood, and she, too, she tasted a little.'

Namiši ya-kāma babe, ya-darimeši, ya-ašíe, 'the man caught a locust, tied it up, laid it aside.'

THE PRONOUNS. 107

3. Two or more nouns take the plural form of the pronoun:

Yaro da obansa suna-zua farauta, 'the boy and his father they go hunting.'

Yaro da obansa suna-da bindiga, ni ina-da dási tšiki-n-alšifu, 'the boy and his father they had guns, I had stones in the pocket.'

Yárinia da ūwáta, su-duka biú, sutšiansu ta-gbatše, lit. 'the girl and her mother, they all two, the heart of them it was broken.'

4. The pronoun is used in its simple or emphatic form, as the subject of a proposition: *e.g.*

Ko ni da kaina sai ina-taffia ga kafata, ' even I myself, I travelled only on foot.'

Su da kansu ba su-so su ša-n-rua nan, 'they themselves, they did not like they (to) drink of that water.'

Na-sonsa, ' I love him.'

Ši kua šina-sona, ' he, too, he loves me.'

Ta-taffi, ' she went.'

Mu-samna daganan, ' we remained there.'

B.—*Possessive Pronoun.*

§ 116. The possessive pronoun, in its simple form, follows the noun which it qualifies in the form of a suffix; the compound form is separated from the noun; thus,

Abokimu, ' our friend.'

Garinsu ba da girima ba, ' their town was not large.'

Sutšiata ba ta-so ba wári-n-rua, ' my heart, *i.e.* I did not like the smell of the water.'

Ka-bani nawa, ' give me my own;' *nī-baka náka,* ' I shall give thee thine.'

Kíbia namu su-kaššie dayawa, amma násu kua suna-da dafji, su-kaššie mutanemu dayawa, ' our arrows killed many, but theirs, too, were poisoned, and killed many of our people.'

Suka-tše, nawane ne, ' they said, whose is it, or for whom is it?'

Ta-tše masu naku dúka, ' she said to them, for all of you.'

Matše ta-tše yarinia tata tana-da kedo, táki ba ta-da keao ba, ' the woman said, my girl is beautiful, thine is not beautiful.'

C.—Objective Pronouns.

§ 117. The verbal suffixes are appended to the last letter of the verb as objective pronouns: *ya-bani,* ' he gave me,' *ka-bani dána,* ' give me my child;' *na-baka,* ' I gave thee.'

a) The Infinitive and the Participial form, being considered as verbal nouns, take the nominal suffixes; as,

Gannínsa da kedo, ' it is beautiful to see.'

Muna-kamansa, ' we are catching him,' with the finite verb.

Mu-kamaši, ' we caught him.'

Kura tana-binsa, ' the hyena following him;' finite form, *ta-biši,* ' she followed him.'

Rana duka ína-nēmánsa ban samésa ba, ' all day long I am seeking him, but do not find him.'

Na-samu wonni abu da kamši tšinsa babu dádi, amma woddansu sun-so tšinsa, ' I received something which has a sweet smell (the eating of it is not nice)=it is not nice to eat, but some persons like to eat it.'

The possessive pronouns convey sometimes the sense which other languages express by prepositions; as, ' for,' ' of,' ' with,' &c. *Ka-aiko muna wotika kaka suna-yi-n gerdamanka, da kai kana-gerdamansu har ka kašiesu,* ' send us a letter (to say) how they argue with thee, and how thou dost argue with them, till thou convince them.'

b) The Objective Pronoun is often omitted where it can be easily understood from the connection; as,

> Matše ta-mantše ˙danta tšiki-n-dáši; kura ta-ganni, ta-daúka, ta-kai, ta-gboye, 'the woman forgot her child in the forest: a hyena saw (it), took (it) up, carried (it) away, hid (it).
>
> Gísso ya-daúka sandasa, ya-ašie kussa kánsa, 'the spider took his stick, laid (it) close to his head.'

c) The separable form of the Objective Pronoun is more frequently used with derived verbs of the 2nd, 4th, and 5th form.

> Ya-bada mani, 'he gave me.'
> Su-bayes garesa, 'they gave to him.'
> Ya fittasda daga garesa, 'he threw it from him.'

D.—*Demonstrative Pronouns.*

§ 118. The Demonstrative Pronoun *wonnan*, 'this,' can be used separately as a substantive, and in an absolute sense; as,

> a) *Wonnan ya-kare,* 'this is finished.'
>
> *Wonnan ba na-soši ba,* 'as to this (man) I do not like him.'
>
> *Wonnan ne wáyo da na-baki,* 'this is the advice which I give thee.'
>
> *Wonnan bardo ne,* 'this (person) is a thief.'
>
> *Wonnan namiši ba matše ba ne,* 'this (person) is a man, not a woman.'

b) *Wonnan,* 'this,' is applied to those persons or things which are nearer to the speaker in point of *time* or *place*; *nan,* 'that,' on the other hand, to those persons or things which are more distant from the speaker . . . *wonnan ba nan ba ni-ke so,* 'this, not that, I want;' referring to things, and : *wonnan mutum ba nan ba ni ke so,* ' this man, not that one, I like.' These two demonstratives appear to be the only ones which *can* be used absolutely and separately ; the rest partake more of the nature of adjectives, for which reason we designate them:

E.—*Adjective Demonstrative Pronouns.*

§ 119, 1. The Demonstrative Pronouns, which are employed to define other words, like adjectives, are the following:

Nan, ' this or that;' plural, *woddanan.*
Nga, ' this or that.'
Wonnan, ' this or that.'
Woṅga, m., *wogga,* f., pl. *woddanga,* ' this, these.'
Wontšan, m., *wotšan,* f., ' the one, the other, the former, the latter ; this side, that side.' *Obansa sariki ne, wontšan mutum ši kua sariki ne,* ' his father was a king, the other man (before mentioned) was also a king.'

2. These Demonstrative Pronouns are placed before the noun which they qualify whenever the emphasis falls on them ; as,

Duba, wonnan mutum da ši-ke bayanka, ' beware of that man who is inferior to thee (in rank or position).'
Šinni na woṅga mutum, ' the blood of this man.'
Wonnan mutum talaka ne, ' this man is poor.'

Otherwise they may follow the noun; as,

Ki-koya mani waka nan, ' teach me that song.'
Doki nga naka ba na-ia-sayinsa, ' this thy horse I cannot buy.'
Ba na-son-tši tuo nan, ' I do not like to eat this food.'

3. Gender is not regarded of much importance in the use of demonstratives, and is only distinguished in those cases above mentioned; hence it comes that Hausas say; *Mutume nan*, 'this man;' and *yarinia nan*, 'this or that girl:' and also, *wonga mutum* and *wogga budurua*.

4. The same observation must also be made with regard to number; for, contrary to what might be expected, the singular number of the pronoun is frequently used to define substantives in the plural form; as,

Yaro nga, ' this boy;' and *yara nga*, ' these boys.'
Yaro nga koyause šina-yin fadda, ' this boy is always fighting.'
Yara nga koyause suna yin fadda, ' these boys are always fighting.'
Mutume nga, ' this man;' *mutane nga*, ' these persons.'
Abin nan, ' this thing;' *abubua nan*, ' these things.'
Mutane nga da mutane ntšan, ' these persons and those (yonder).'

5. In many instances it may be said that the pronouns have lost their demonstrative force, and can, therefore, only be translated by one of the articles in English. In this way some compensation is made for an apparent deficiency in the language. We mention but a few instances:

Mutume nan da ya-mantše sandansa ya-dawoyo, ' the man who had forgotten his stick came back.'
Ta-dauki hazi nan, ' she took the millet.'
Labari nga ke nan, ' the news is this,' or, ' this is the news.'

6. While treating on the Demonstrative Pronouns, it is necessary to notice a few words which are often used with a demonstrative meaning; as for instance,

Šine, lit. ' it is he=the same;' *šine na-fadda maka*, ' the same I told thee.'

Šine oba na yara goma, 'the same is the father of ten children.'

Kōwané ya-hawa bissa rakumi nan ba fádi ba, šine mišina, 'whosoever shall mount this camel and not fall down, the same shall be my husband.'

Šine, sariki ya-aiko ya-wutše gaba garemu, 'the same (*i.e.* the slave before-mentioned) the king sent to go before us.'

Hakka, 'so=such a, in such a manner.'

Domi kana-tambayana hakka? 'Why dost thou ask me such a question?' and also like *šine,* 'the same.'

Yaro ya-ši hakka magana-n-zakkara, 'the boy heard the same word of the cock.'

Kai ka-ke yi mani magana hakka? 'dost thou talk to me in this manner?'

Da kasa ta-ši hakka ta yi fuši, 'when the fowl heard the same she was vexed.'

Nana, 'here,' and *nan* and *tšan,* 'there,' must be regarded as Demonstrative *Adverbs* of place; as,

Mi ga-ki yi nana? 'what wilt thou do here?'

7. Among these, the use made of *mutume nan da,* and *abin nan da,* 'for he who,' and 'that which=what,' must be mentioned; as,

Mutume nan da ši yi hakka, ban soši ba, 'the man who= him who will act in this manner I do not like.'

Abin da su-ke faddi ban yirda ba, 'the thing which= that which=what they say I do not believe.'

8. So likewise *kamma,* 'for such a one;' as,

Mutume kamma-n-wonnan dadai ban ganni ba, 'a man of the likeness of this=like this=such a man I have never before seen.'

F.—*The Interrogative Pronouns.*

§ 120. Most Interrogative Pronouns can be used substantively, or in the absolute sense. They are the following:

Wa, pl. *sua,* ' who ?' referring to persons only.
Wane, m., *watše,* f., ' who ?' referring to persons only.
Wanéne, pl. *suane* and *suanene,* ' who ?' referring to persons.
Wonne, ' which ?' referring to persons and things.
Mi? ' what?' in a few instances it occurs for ' who?' referring to persons.
Mine? ' what ?'
Minéne? ' what ?' or, ' what is it that ?'
Kaka? ' how ;' *kaka mutum ši-kan sanni magana-n-gari kadan ši báko?* ' how can a man understand the language of a country if he be a stranger?'
Domi? ' why ?' *domi ana-bada mágani ga masutšiwo?* ' why is medicine given to the sick ?'
Domi ba ka-zakka ba kassa? ' why dost thou not come down?'
Domi tana-yi-n-káka? ' what is she crying for ?'
Wa ya-baka wonnan hankali? ' who gave thee this understanding.'
Wa ya-fadda maka labari nan? ' who told thee this news?'
Wane maikiddi? ' who is playing ?'
Mutum maidukia wotše iri-n-riga ši-kan sa? ' as regards a rich man, what kind of dress does he put on ?'
Mi ya-faru? ' what is the matter? what has happened?'
Wanene šina-ía sayansa? ' who is able to buy it ?'
Wanene ya-kaššie matšiši nan? ' who killed that serpent ?'
Mi kuna-so ya fi wonnan? ' what do you want better than this ?'

Q

Tagía-n-wa ke nan? (genitive) 'whose cap is this?'
Tumaki-n wa su-ke? 'whose sheep are they?'
Ga wa kuna-bada kurdinku? 'to whom do you give your money?'
Mi záni-yi yao? 'what shall I do to-day.'
Mi na-yi? 'what have I done?'
Da mi zani-tši en ka-debe hakkorina duka? 'with what shall I eat if you draw all my teeth?'
Watše tše matše tafári? 'who was the first woman?'
Wanene ka-ke kírra bíri? 'whom dost thou call a monkey?'
Suanene suka-tšiétu dagá tšitšikowa? 'who were those who were saved in the flood.'
Domi mutane India suna-kaššiewa farufaru mutane? 'why do the people of India kill the white people?'
Mišina! mi ya saméka, 'O my husband! what has happened to thee?

Adverbial interrogative pronouns are:

Enna, 'where? where to? whither?' *enna záka-taffia?* 'where art thou going to?'
Dagaenna? 'whence?' *dagaenna ka fitto?* 'whence dost thou come from?'

G.—*The Relative Pronouns.*

§ 121, *a*) The Relative Pronoun includes frequently the Demonstrative; as,

Wonda ya dumke násà dafári ši-ne míši diata, 'he who sows his own (cloth) first, the same is the husband of my daughter.'
Ina-so wonda ūwáka ta-baka, 'I want that which thy mother gave thee.'
Ba ni-da wonda uwaka ta-baka, sai ina-da wonda wánn

ya-bani, 'I have not that which thy mother gave thee, I have only that which my elder brother gave me.'

b) The relative pronoun introduces a clause which defines an individual *simply,* and sometimes a clause that refers it to a particular class or kind; as,

Ba su-kašsie mutume nan wonda ya-satše dóki, 'they do not kill that man who stole the horse.'

Dambária ya-tšainye gutšiata, wodda ni-ke so-n-tši gobe, 'the mouse has eaten my nuts, which I wanted to eat to-morrow.'

Ba mutume-n-da ka-ganni ga hainya, 'it is not the man whom thou hast seen in the street.'

Matšiši wonda ke tšiki-n-rišia ya-mutu, 'the serpent which was in the well is dead.'

Ríga-n-da ka-bani ta-zúfa, 'the coat which thou gavest me is old.'

Wonni gari ne da uwaka záta-kaika? 'which is the country to which thy mother is going to take thee?'

Su-godda masa bayi-n-da suka-káma, 'they showed him the slaves which they had caught.'

c) The form *da* is always used after the personal pronoun, and the personal pronoun is repeated after the relative; as,

Ni da ni-ke karami ba ši-ši taúsaina,—'*Ich der ich klein bin fur mich fühlt er kein Mitleiden,*' 'for me who am little, he feels no compassion.'

Kai da ka faddi hakka,—*du der du solches sagst,* 'thou who dost say such things.'

H.—*Indefinite Pronouns.*

§ 122. The Indefinite Pronouns are (§ 33) for the most part formed from the interrogative forms, by means of the intensive adverb *kō*; as, *mi?* 'what?' *kómi,* 'any thing, some thing, every thing, all.' *Wa*, 'who?' *kṓwa*, 'any one, every one, any person, whoever, whosoever.'

a) The same is the case with the compound forms of *mı́ne* and *wáne*, as: *kōminé* and *kōwané*, the former referring to things, and the latter to persons; while *kōwonni* and *kōwotše* may refer to persons or things; and *wonni* and *wṓta*, and their pl. *woddansu*, signifying, ' some, some one, a certain,' and sometimes merely the indefinite article in English; and as correlatives, 'the one,—the other,' ' some—some one,' and ' another,' are still more indefinite.

b) Gender and Number are but of secondary consideration in the indefinite pronouns, especially when used as substantives; and *woddansu* alone requires the verb in the plural.

c) The Negatives, as, ' no one, nobody, nothing, not any one,' &c., have no corresponding words in Hausa; and the negative is expressed much as in English, ' not any one, not any thing.' *Ba su-tše ba kṓmi*, ' they did not say any thing;' *Ina tamaha ban tše ba kṓmi*, ' I think I did not say any thing;' *ba kṓwa*, ' not any one;' *babu kṓmi* and *ba kṓmi*, ' no matter, nothing.'

A few examples will best explain the use made of them:

Kṓmi da ka-bani ni-ke so, 'any thing which thou mayest give me, I like.'

Komine ta-roka Alla, Alla ya-bata abu duka da tana-so, ' whatever she asked of God, God gave her what she wanted.'

Ba ya-berí komi sai gasusuka, ' he left nothing but the feathers.'

Mu-rubuta magana-n wonni mutum da na-ši daga Bornu, ' let us write the story of a man, which I heard in Bornu.'

Wóta kuritšia ta-taffo, ' another dove came.'

Zurukia, igia karama, wonni ana-yi da fata-n-sania,

wonni ana-yi da šišia, 'zurukia, *i.e.* small strings, some are made of cow-skins, some of the guts.'

Wonni ya-taffo, ya-hawa bissa, ya-fádi, wonni ya-taffo, 'one came mounted, fell down, another came . . .'

Kada ka-faddi ga kowa, kadan na-ši ka-faddi ga wonni ina buganka, 'thou must not tell it to any body, if I hear that thou hast told it to any one, I shall beat thee.'

d) *Mutum,* 'man,' and *mai,* 'one who,' are sometimes employed like indefinite pronouns; as,

Mutum ya-taffi tšiki-n-dáši, ya kaššie mutum; wonni ya-šígga tsíki-n-gari, ya-yi sáta, da wonni ya-taffi ya-kama bayi, ya-sayes, ya-tši kurdinsu, wonnan ba daídai ba ši-ke, 'one goes in the forest and kills some person; another enters a town, and commits theft; and another goes to make slaves, sells them, and (eats) keeps the money, and (all) this is not proper.'

e) When the indefinite pronouns are used as adjectives, they generally precede the noun which they modify; as,

Kowonne da šina da nása sána, 'every child having its own name.'

Kowotše safia ya-yi hakka, 'every morning he did the same.'

Wonni yaro ya-taffo, 'a certain boy came.'

Wonni mutum šina-da yaya biú, 'a certain man having two sons.'

f) Adverbial pronouns of place and time, see § 33, 9.

CHAPTER XIV.

ADJECTIVES.

§ 123. 1. When the Adjective is used as an Attribute, it *generally* follows the substantive which it modifies, and agrees with it in Gender; *e.g.*

Mutum nāgari ba ši-ši-n-dsóro mutua, 'a good man is not afraid of death.'

Matše tágari tana-kula da iyálinta, 'a good woman is taking care of her family.'

Ke dia takwarai tše, 'thou art a good daughter.'

Ta-suba rua kadan, 'she poured out a little water.'

Dáki karami, 'a small room.'

Igia karama, 'a small string.'

Suka sáta tšiki-n wonni dáki babu keáo, 'they put her into an uncomfortable room.'

2. The adjective precedes the substantive whenever it is intended that the quality should be prominently pointed out; as,

Ya-kaisu ga dógo n-dáši, 'he led them into a *large* forest.'

Ta-tambayi wonní gašiĕri-n-dóki, 'she asked another, *i.e.* a *little* horse.'

Záfi mútane ba su-yi fádda ba, 'old people do not fight.'

Mugu diyaútši ke nan, 'this is a bad kind of liberty.'

Ya-kaššie baba-n-bunsuru, 'he killed a large he-goat.'

Suka-dumka mani sabo-n-ríga ta alkamura, 'they made me a new shirt of white linen.'

Karifi-n-matše sai yawa-n-magana, 'the strength of women consists in talking much.'

3. A substantive in the plural, or a collective noun, may be defined by an adjective in the singular, and whenever that is the case, the masculine form of the Adjective is used in preference to the feminine; *e.g.*

Mutane nāgari ba su-kaššie ba mīágu. ' good people do not kill the bad.'

Iri nāgari ana-šipkasu, ' good seeds are sown.'

Dianta duka sai rami su-ke, ' her whole brood was altogether lean.'

But sometimes the qualifying adjective agrees in form with its plural substantive :

Dia-n-ītatše ninanu an-tširesu, ' the fruit of the tree, the ripe ones, they are plucked.'

Ki-basu dia-n-durumi ninanu, ' give them the fruit of the durumi tree, *i.e.* the ripe ones.'

Karre da kurege rāmámu su-ke, ' the dog and the fox were lean.'

4. The adjective, as attributive, cannot take the possessive or any other pronouns; all such qualifications or modifications are appended to the substantive ; as,

Ta-tafji ga wurinta dafari enda ta-fitto, ' she went to her place the first (=first place) from which she had come.'

Ya-tše ga diasa baba, ' he said to his daughter, the eldest=to his eldest. . .'

5. Words formed by the prefix *mai*, pl. *masu*, are always placed after the substantive, as it were in apposition to it—or they correspond in meaning with participial nouns, and chiefly in an active sense :

Ta-ganni gídda maikeao ta-šigga, babu komi tšikinsa, ' she saw a house, a beautiful one, went in, there was nothing in it.'

Karre maidsáro šina-yi-n-hapši,— *Ein wachsamer Hund*
— 'a dog that keeps watch, barks.'

Kai mutum maigaskia ne, 'thou art a man of truth.'

Na saka maidukia, ka-sani talaka, 'I have made thee rich, thou hast made me poor.'

Ta-sa sanné maisindria? 'does she put on garments of gold?'

b) The prefix *da* is employed to form a class of adjectives which indicate that a person or thing *has*, or is what the word with which it is combined implies; as,

Ši-ke da ši, 'he has it.'

Mutum da sanda, 'a man having a stick.'

Ba ni-da yunwa, 'I have no hunger=I am not hungry.'

Mutum da karifi, 'a man having strength=strong man.'

Rišia da-dsáwo, 'a deep well.'

Doki-maiguddu-šina-da anfani kwarai, 'a horse which runs well is of great use.'

7. The Adjective is used as a substantive, but not as frequently as in other languages:

Baba, 'the great,' is used for 'father,' and 'chief,' both masculine and feminine of the latter.

Babansu ya-taffi gaba da su sun-bíši, 'their chief went before, and as for them, they followed him.'

Nabíssa ya-tše ga nakalkas, 'the one above said to the one beneath.'

Nafari, 'the first,' *nabaya,* 'the one after, the second, the last, the one inferior as regards rank or position, or the latter as regards time.'

Zofua, 'the old woman,' is used for *Zofua matše,* an expression of contempt for a witch.

Comparison of Adjectives.

§ 124. The Hausa language has not developed any distinguishing forms to express the different degrees in the adjective itself, and is therefore obliged to have recourse to circumlocution of various kinds, as they may happen to be most suitable.

But before we mention in what manner the comparative and superlative are expressed, it may be proper to notice the emphatic repetition of adjectives; the force of which must sometimes be rendered by the comparative, and sometimes by the adverbs, 'much, or very much, very, and many, very many;' as,

Akoi rana kadan kadan, 'there was still a very little sun,' *i.e.* it was not yet quite night.

Aya wonni abu karami karami da dádin tši, 'aya is a very little thing (nut) nice to eat.'

Ta-basu rua da faraufarau, 'she gave them water which was very clear.'

1. The Comparative.

A.) We would here notice the use made of some words which must be translated into English by the comparative:

a) Kári, 'more,' *ba-na-so kári, ya-issa,* 'I do not want more, it is enough.'

Da Alla ši-koya muna kári, 'and may God teach us more.' From *kára,* 'to add;' hence *kari,* 'as much as,' 'an addition.'

Ni ba na-so kari ba, 'I do not want any more.'

b) Goŭma, in the sense of 'rather,' 'it is better,' 'more advisable;' as,

Kadan ku-'áši ši yaro ne šína-gbatasua, goŭma ku-bašiéta ga Tebíb, 'if you give it to him, he being a boy, will destroy (or lose) it, it is better to give it to Tebib.

c) *Dáma,* signifying (with or without *hanu*), the right hand, we may, perhaps, think of the idea of strength connected with it; as,

Ka-ši dáma kadan? 'dost thou feel a little better?'
Ka-ši dama ya-fi šia? 'dost thou feel better than yesterday?'

d) *Rongomi* is used in the same sense; as,

Na-ši rongomi yao, 'I feel better to-day.'

B) The comparative is expressed by verbs; as,

a) *Fáye,* 'to abound in something, to be very fond of something, to be addicted to,' &c. *e. g.*

Yara sun-fáye da worigi, 'the boys were very fond of play.'
Abin da faye masu, 'that is beyond them, above their power and capacity, more than they are equal to.'
Sun-fayemu da wáyo, 'they were more cunning than we;' or, 'surpassed us in cunningness.'

b) *Faskare* is used in the same way; as, *babu abin da ya faskare mutane, Engliz,* 'there is nothing too difficult for the English.' *Ya-faskaréni dauka, don da nauyi,* 'it is more than I am able to take up, because of its weight.'

c) The comparative is also, and principally, expressed by the verb *fi,* 'to surpass, to excel,' with or without *da,* in that in which it takes place; *e. g.*

Ya-fi kurége da wáyó, 'he surpasses the fox in cunningness=he is more cunning than a fox.'

Náma na kurege ya-fi náta dayawa, 'the flesh which the fox had was much more than her own.'

Minéne kana-so ya-fi wonnan? 'what dost thou want better than this?'

Naki ya-fi nawa da naúyi, 'thine surpasses mine in weight=is heavier than mine.'

Ina-fiki da keáo, ' I am more beautiful than thou.'

Abin nan ya fini da wáya, 'this thing is too difficult for me.'

Gaiwa, woddansu da girima kamma-n-kobri-n-mutum, em ba ta-fi ba, ' as regards the mud-fish, some large ones are as thick as a man, if not thicker.'

Mnn-ša rua nan da tilass, don ba mu-samu ba ya-fi wonnan, ' we drank the water from necessity, because we found none better.'

The Superlative.

§ 125. The Superlative is expressed by *fi,* ' to surpass,' and *dúka,* 'all,' for one that surpasses all must be the greatest.'

Alla šina-fi duka da girima, 'God does excel all in greatness;' or, ' is the highest of all.'

Wanene tšikinsu duka ya-fisu da karifi? 'which of them is the strongest of all?' or, ' surpasses all in strength.'

Sariki ya-fisu duka, 'the king surpasses them all=is the highest.'

In a few instances the word *gaba* is used with *duka* in the same sense ; as,

Amma Tebib šina-da bara ši-ne baba gabá ga baruansa duka, ' but Tebib had a servant who was great before,' *i.e.* the chief of all his servants.

CHAPTER XV.

THE NUMERALS.

§ 126. The Hausas count as we do up to ten, and not like the Sherbros or Mampas, Bulloms, Ibos, (see my Vocabulary of the Sherbro, published anonymously, and Ibo Grammar), and many other nations, to the number of five, and then repeating and saying, five one, five two, &c.

The number *ten* is *gôma*, and the cardinals from ten to twenty are either *šadaia*, *šabiu*, 11, 12, &c., or *goma šadaia*, *goma sabiu*, &c. The meaning of *ša* in this combination is doubtful; and the question whether it be the verb 'to draw=draw one to it,' &c., must be left undecided.

It may be as well to mention here what has been omitted in Chapter V., that, besides the decades from 20 to 90, according to the system of the Arabs, there occurs a form which is probably the ancient idiomatic Hausa (though not known to all who speak the Hausa language), which forms the Cardinals from 20 to 90 by what may be regarded as a plural form of *goma*, 'ten,' and the units up to 9; as,

10 *goma*.   60 *gomia šidda*.
20 *gomia biù*.   70 *gomia bokoi*.
30 *gomia uku*.   80 *gomia tokos*.
40 *gomia fudu*.   90 *gomia tara*.
50 *gomia bial*.

Another peculiarity as regards the form may be noticed in this place. Some will say, *iširin babu biu* or *babu daía*, and *tallatin babu biú*, and *babu daía*, that is, twenty, two less=18, one less=19; and so before each decade numeral up to 100. A few instances also occur in which *gaíra* is thus used with numerals; as, *settin gaíra uku=hamsin da bokoi*, 57; and *aširin=iširin gaira daía=goma ša tara*, 19; literally, sixty, less three; twenty, less one. This method of counting is insisted on as the only correct one by a native of Gobir, though ridiculed by others. It is given for what it is worth, and with a view to arrest the attention of travellers and linguists, to ascertain how far it is in use.

There is no distinction of Gender observed in the Cardinal Numerals; hence we say, *mutum daía*, and *matše daía*.

§ 127. The Cardinals are also employed, (*a*) as adverbs, like the Ordinals, compounded with *saa;* as,

Kadán ka-ši na-yi kúka daía na-mutu; kadan ka-ši na-yi kuka biú, ba na-mutu ba. Záki ya-taffi tšiki-n-dáši, ya-yi kuka saodaía, ba ši kára ba ya-mutu. Su duka biú su-mutu, 'if thou shalt hear me cry once, I die; if thou hear me cry twice, I do not die. (Then) the lion went into the forest, he cried once, he added no more, and died. They all two=both of them, died (*kúka*, however, being a noun after *yi*, the rule in this instance is not applicable).

b) The Cardinal Number *daía*, 'one,' when used correlatively, corresponds with our expression, ' one, another ; the one, the other; the former, the latter;' *e. g.*

Matše daía tana-da dukia dayawa, matše daía tana-da dukia kadan, ' the one had much property, the other had but a little.'

Mutane biu suna-yin tšatša: daía ya-tše: kadan na-tšíka ka-bani kurdi dari, daia ya tše: ni kuá, kadan na-

tšika ka-bani kurdi kammada ka-fadda mani; yatše dakedo. Suna-yin tšatša. Daia ya-tši daia. Hario sunka-kóma suna-yi, daia ya-kaššie daia. Da suka-yi tšatša nan mutum daia ya-daúki báši dubu bial na kurdi; daia ši kuá ya-daúka dubu bial kanima na wóntšan. 'Two persons were playing (cards); the one said, if I win (lit. eat thee) thou must give me a hundred pieces of money; the other said, and as to me, if I win, thou must give me as much as thou hast said to me; he answered, very well. As they were playing, the one got the better over the other. Again coming back, they played; the one beat the other. And when they had finished their play, the former took a sum of five thousand heads of money: the latter took as much as the former.'

c) *Daia* is also used for 'the same;' as,

Da ni da ke ba daia ba tše, 'as regards me and thee = both I and thou, are not the same.'

Mu duka muka-samna ga wuri daia, 'we all sat together at the same place.'

Su duka daia ne, 'they are all the same = alike.'

d) When *daia* is combined with *mutum*, 'person, man,' it must frequently be translated as though *mutum* were not in the text; as,

Mutum daia šina-kora mutum biu, 'one is driving two before him.'

e) The units of the Cardinal numbers can take the suffixes of the plural; as,

Daiamu, 'one of us;' *daianku,* 'one of you;' *daiansu,* 'one of them.'

§ 128. When Cardinal Numerals are connected with substantives, they occupy the same position as the adjective, *i.e.* they follow the noun; thus,

Šína-da bindiga da baki biú, 'he has a gun with two barrels.'

Ka-bani bayi tallatín, 'give me thirty slaves.'

Ina-tamaha mutane da suka-káma tare dani, ba su-fi ba dari biú, ko dari uku, 'I think the people who were caught with me were not more than two or three hundred.'

Na-ganni taguaye biu an-yašiesu bissa haínya suna-kuka, 'I saw two twin children thrown on the road, crying.'

§ 129. When the noun is qualified by an adjective and a cardinal numeral, the numeral is placed immediately after the noun, and the adjective follows it, as it were, in apposition to it; *e. g.*

Idonsa daía, maigírima, ga dzakka-n-hantši, 'one of his eyes, a large one, was on the middle of the nose.'

Muka-taffi da barua-n-Tebib biú, da bara-n-sariki tare da bawansa daía, kuruma, 'we went with two of Tebib's servants, and with the king's servant, together with a slave, who was dumb.'

The Ordinal Numerals.

§ 130. We shall do no more at this place than refer to Chapter V., and to what we said there on the *Ordinal, Distributive,* and *Fractional* Numerals, and only add a few examples of the Ordinals:

Na-samna ga wurina nafári, ' I sat down to my place the first=the former.'

Da muka-taši dagá Kanum muka-zakka ga haínyamu tafári, wodda ta-ke kaimu ga Kukawa, ' when we had started from Kanum, we came to our first=former road, which brought us to Kukawa.'

Yao na-ganni abin mumaki uku; nafari: gādó šina-da kafafu šidda, fudu ga baya, da wuziasa kussa ga hakarikari, da kafafunsa biú agabá, da idonsa daía, maigirima, ga dzakka-n hantši, da halšinsa kamma na kífi: nabiú kéaṅwa da kafafu bokoi; nauku: zunzua da kafafu fudú, da fukafukaí fudu. ' To-day I have seen three wonderful things: the first was a pig with six legs, four behind, and its tail close to its ribs, and two legs in front, and one eye, a large one, on the midst of the nose, and its tongue was like that of a fish; the second was a cat with seven legs; the third was a bird with four legs and four wings.'

129

CHAPTER XVI.

THE VERB.

§ 131. The Verb of the Hausa language presents a great contrast to other parts of speech. It is, comparatively speaking, poor and meagre, while other parts of speech abound in forms, and contain the elements for a still greater development by means of derivation and combination in conformity with those already in existence.

It may, in fact, be said that the same word is used as a substantive, and, to a limited extent, as an adjective (*girima*, 'great,' and 'to grow,) or a verb; and that the possessive pronouns suffixed make it a noun, its predicative position an adjective, and the verbal pronouns or particles before it a verb. Hence it comes that we may say : *Da ya-káre faddinsa,* ' when he had finished his saying;' and, *ya-kare faddi,* ' when he had finished to speak;' and, *da ya-fara yin magana,* 'when he began making words=to speak;' *da sunka-kare gerdamansu*=or *gerdama,* ' when they had finished their disputes, or to dispute.' And the changes which the verb undergoes in the present and future tenses are by no means in contradiction with this assumption, since the form there used may be regarded as abstract, and those of preterite tenses, as concrete nouns. This appearance in the language accounts, in a great measure, for the total absence of internal inflections, by means of which other languages indicate Persons, Moods, and Tenses, and shows at the same time the necessity of assigning those offices to particles, pronouns, adverbs, and conjunctions.

s

THE TENSES.

§ 132. To distinguish the tenses in the Hausa language, regard must be paid to the various forms of the personal, and as we have styled them (§ 69), Verbal Pronouns in connection with the verb, this being the only means by which different relations of time are indicated.

THE PRESENT TENSE.

§ 133. The characteristic of this tense with regard to its *form* (see § 74), consists in the particle *na*, combined with the substantive pronouns; as, *ina, kana*, &c., and the use of the auxiliary verb *ke*; as, *ni-ke, ka-ke*, &c., and the syllable *wa* annexed to the verb, as *suna-kaššiewa*, 'they are killing,' &c. The forms compounded with *na* may be regarded as the finite verb in the Indicative mood, and those with *wa*, as a kind of *participial form*, though regularly inflected through all the persons and numbers like the finite verb. But it will often be found convenient to construe the forms with *na* in the same way as participles, *i.e.* by '*while, während, when, als, indem, da*,' &c., or by a relative sentence. But if any thing is to be represented as being in the act of performance, the forms in *wa* or *ke* are *chiefly* used, and must be translated like the forms, 'am reading,' 'do read,' 'was thinking,' 'did think,' &c., in English; as,

Mi kana-kaowa? 'what art thou bringing?'
Gata, tana-taffowa, 'see her, she is coming.'
Tana-wazawa wukanta, 'she is sharpening her knife.'
Domi ba ki-šidowa? 'why dost thou not come down?'
Rana duka ina-nemansa, 'all the day long I am search-
    ing for him.'
Kada ka-ši dsóro, don Alla šina tare dakai, 'thou must
    not be afraid, for God is with thee.'

Kowotše safia tana-duba fuskanka, amma ita kua tana-tamaha, kana-duba táta kuá, 'every morning she looks at thy likeness, but she hopes also that thou dost look at hers too.'

Sai lafia ši-ke, 'he is quite well.'

Muna-da abu duka da mu-ke so, 'we have all we want.'

Suna-tšewa: wonnan dá-n-bawa ne, ba dā-n-sariki ba ne, 'they were saying, this is the son of a slave, it is not the son of a king.'

Da muna-dawoyowa ga Kukawa, 'as we were returning to Kuka.'

Tana-waka hakka, kura ta-ši, ta-taffo, 'as she was singing in this manner, the hyena heard it and came.'

§ 134. The present tense is employed in *all its forms* in such cases as are expressed in other languages by active participles or relative sentences, and can therefore follow preterite tenses; *e.g.*

Na-ganni mutane suna-taffia, suna-yi-n-wákansu, suna-dāriá sabbada murna, 'I saw persons walking, singing their songs, laughing for joy.'

Ta-gammu da kudá suna-daffa kansu, 'she met some flies (=who were) cooking for themselves.'

Ta-ši túkúnia tana-tafassa, 'she heard that the kettle was boiling.'

Mu duka muku-samna ga zofo-n-gídda muna-širánsu, 'we all remained in the old house waiting for them.'

Muka-samu mutane dayawa suna-yi-n-yawa-n-magana, suna-yi-n-dummí sabbadamu, 'we found many persons talking very much, and making (noise) disturbance about us.'

§ 135. This tense likewise expresses capability, continuation and repetition of an action; as,

Šina-ia yínsa, 'he can do it;' *Kana-ia kainí?* 'canst

thou carry me?' *ína-íd kaíki, ba na-ía kawoki,* ' I can carry thee thither, but I cannot bring thee back.'

Šina-awuna kurdi har kurdi ya-kare, ' he was measuring money till it was finished.'

Kowotše safia kurege šina-daukà kaší-n-tumaki, da na áwáki.

Da safe har maraetšíe ya yi tana-gerta kašia, tana-kawo, tana-ašíewa, ' from morning till evening she prepared hay, carrying it and laying it down.'

NOTE.—This form can never be used with the negative.

§ 136. This Tense is employed for the future when a future event is considered as certain; and especially when the future is indicated by another word in the sentence; as, *gobe,* ' to-morrow.'

Kadan ban kaššie yaro nan da gisso suna-kai labari nan tšiki-n-garinsu, ' if I do not kill the boy and the spider they will carry the news to their own country.'

Zunsua ta-tše ga káza, kadan ba ki-so ki-ší maganata gobe mutane suna-kamaki su-kaššieki, su-tši namaki. ' the bird said to the hen, if thou dost not like to listen to my advice, to-morrow the people will come, catch thee, kill and eat thee.'

Kadan na-fušieta kuna-bani íta en yi-arime? ' if I draw her out (of the water), will you give her to me in marriage?'

Kadan ni-šído dianki suna-tšainyéni, ' if I come down, thy younglings will eat me.'

The Imperfect Tense.

§ 137. This tense is designated the Imperfect, because it expresses an action or a state, as it existed or took place at a time specified by some past tense in the sentence. It is, moreover, also used as a definite past tense, and without any reference to another event. With regard to the form by which it is indicated (§ 73), it may be said, that it lays aside the *a* of the present tense; as, *mun*, instead of *muna*, &c. In the singular, it is only the second person fem. which retains the *n*, as *kín*, in the other persons there is no tense-distinction left, but merely that of person. So,

Yao da na-taffi ga makaranta na-ganni abu mamaki uku, 'to-day when I went to school I saw three wonderful things.'

Da mun-gannési ya-gúddu ya-šigga tšíki-n saria-n-šiúri, 'when we saw him he ran, and entered into an ant-hill.'

Da mun-daúka káyamu, da mun-gode ga sariki, mun-taffi ga Kukawa, 'when we had taken up our goods, and thanked the king, we went to Kuka.'

Kun-taffi makaranta yao, ko ba kun-taffi ba? 'did you go to school to-day, or did you not go?'

Yao ba mu-taffi ba ga makaranta sai mun-taffi mun-yi worigi, 'we did not go to school to-day, we only went, we played.'

Domi kin-faddi hakka? 'why dost thou say so?'

Kadan kin-šigga tšíki-n tšiáwa kada ki-mósi, 'when thou hast gone under the grass thou must not move.'

Past Participial form, or, Indefinite Past Tense.

§ 138. In § 78, the form of this tense has been explained, and a few remarks of its use have been added; still it is necessary to add a few observations here to illustrate its use.

It is called the Past Participial, or Indefinite Past Tense, because it is *generally* used in connection with past tenses, and but very rarely independently as an historical tense. It may be said that its prominent character is *descriptive*, grouping several events together without any precise regard to time, and that the time can only be ascertained from the connection, and from the tense of the concluding verb, which is either the aorist or the perfect. It may be said to bear the same relation to a past tense, as the forms compounded with *na* bear to the present, and is, therefore, most conveniently rendered into English by a past participle, or the forms, 'was saying,' 'were eating,' 'having said, done,' &c.

A few examples in addition to those already given will best illustrate the use of this tense :

Kanua ta-tše da keao, sunka-yi- širi sunka taffi, ' her sister said to her, very well : having made ready, having gone=when they had made ready, they went.'

Da sunka-taffi ga wonni gari sunka-tše ga mutane : watše ta-ke da keao ga tšikimu ? wodda ta-ke da keao ku-bata dukia. Woddansu mutane sunka-so kanuata, woddansu mutane sunka-so ta, sunka-basu dukia daga gari nan, sunka-wutše, suka taffi ga wonni gari, ' having gone to some town, said to the people, which of us is most beautiful ? to her which is most beautiful you must give some goods. Some persons preferring one of the sisters, some preferring the other, were giving them money at that town, (and) having started, they went to another town.'

Da sunka-ša rua sunka-kóši, kanuata ta-taffi ta-ša rua, ' when they (oxen, sheep) had drunk water, when they were satisfied, her sister said she would go to drink water.'

Da sunka-taffi wuri-n-kíwo tare da ūwán yaro-da obansa sunka-sawoya tumaki, ya taffo, ya-samna, ' having gone to the field together with the boy's father and mother, (they having) turned into sheep, he came and sat down.'

Mutane sunka-ganni rua ya-samma farifari—sunka-šima kadan, sunka ganni rua ya-sawoya bakki kirin suka-fara kúka, ' the people seeing the water turn very white

—and, waiting a little while, saw the water turn very black—began to scream.'
Iayenta sunka-ganneta suna-murna da káka, ' her parents seeing her, rejoiced and wept.'

THE AORIST TENSE.

§ 139. (Compare § 70). The Aorist is used much in the same way as the Imperfect in German, *i.e*, in narrations, but is not confined in its meaning to a past tense; as, *ta-taffi, ta-dauko rua, ta-kawo mata ta-bata,* ' she went, took water, brought, gave it to her.' *Hario gobe ya-tafji, ya-samna nan šina-kíwo, šina-wākánsa, ta-fitto, ta-taffo garesa, ta-gaisasa, ya-karigbe gaisuata,* ' again the following day he went, sat down there watching his herd, and singing his song, she came out of the water, walked to him, saluted him, and he received her salutation.'

Even the future, and the second future, is expressed by this tense, when futurity is sufficiently indicated in some other way; as, *kadan na-fušiēta daga rua ?* 'if I draw= when I shall have drawn her out of the water;' *kuna-bani ita en yi arime?* ' will you give her to me in marriage?' So again, *kadan na-šigga ga tšiki-n-rua, kadan ku-ganni rua ya samma bakki ku-yi káka, kada ku-yi murna,* ' when I shall have entered into the water, when you see the water turning black, you must cry, you must not rejoice.'

Verbs in this tense frequently express conditions and qualities, and must be rendered in English by adjectives; as, *ya-mutu,* ' he died=is dead;' *ya-tšikka,* ' it is full;' *rana ta-bada haske,* ' the sun shines;' *su-kussa garemu,* ' they are near to us;' *ya-yi girima,* ' he is great or grows;' *diansa ta nína,* ' its fruit is ripe;' *aiki ya-káre,* ' the work is finished.'

§ 140. The Aorist is also employed when an idea is to be expressed as a general truth, without any limitation to a certain time; and when this is the case, it is most suitably rendered by the indefinite *man* in German, or '*one*,' 'you,' as, one saith, goes, &c., in English.

Rāgó-n-laíya : kadan ka-sāyésa ba ši-da kíbba, ka-saši ga tšiki-n-dáki, ka-dārimési, ka-suba rua kadan ga tšiki-n dúsa ka-baši ya-tši. Kadan mātáka tana-da dsirāre ta-baši ya-ša; ka-baši hazi, da dáwa ya-tši, kóda tšiáwa kadan; ka-ríkéši wata biú ko daía. Kādán salla-n-laíya ta-zakka ka-taffi ka-wānkéši ga tšíki-n-rua har ya-yi fári. A-kāwóši ga gídda, a-kaššieši dasáfe. Kadan ana-fide fatansa saí tana-fítta da-kise, a-daffa náma-n-rágo nan, a-yi tuo maídádi, ko tuo-n-salla, sunansa gūdá : a-suba romua rāgo bissa garesa, da a-kaí tuo da nama gaba ga maínya mútané, násu dabám, na yára dabám, da na mātása dabám; salla-n-laíya hakka-ta-ke. Daga rana nan ana-sukuá-n-dóki, da ana-buga bindiga. 'The paschal lamb: when you buy it, it is not fat; you put it in a room, and tie it, you pour a little water upon some bran, you give it to the ram to eat. If thy wife has some wash, she gives it to the ram to drink; you give it millet, and corn to eat, and even a little grass, you keep it two months or one. When the time of the Passover has come, you go and wash the ram in water till it becomes clean. It is then taken in the house, and killed early in the morning; when it is flayed the skin comes off, and much fat; the flesh of the ram is cooked, and a good dinner is made of it; or, the passover feast, which is called *gūdá, i.e.* some kind of pudding. A little broth is poured over it, the dish and the meat are brought before the great people, their portion by itself, that of the children by itself, and that of the women by itself; in this way the passover is observed. They gallop about on horses during the day, and there is much firing of guns.'

The Perfect Tense.

§ 141. The Perfect Tense (§ 69 and 77) expresses past time fully completed; *nina-fadda maki*, 'I have told thee.' *Yao muka-taffi farauta*, 'to-day we have been hunting.' *Da suka-wutše nama nina-gannéši*, ' when they had passed by the creature, I saw it.' *Da muka-taffi baya kadan, ya halba da bíndiga, ya-kaššiéši*, 'having gone a little backwards, he fired, and killed it.' *Daga tšiki-n šírigi nan muka kwana dere daía*, ' we slept one night in that vessel.'

The Future Tense (Subjunctive Future).

§ 142. Two forms are given in § 69 and in § 79 by means of which the future tense is expressed in the Hausa language. The first is in form almost the same with the subjunctive as exhibited in § 62, and only distinguished by the doubling or lengthening of the end vowel of the verbal pronoun; but as that doubling or lengthening of the end vowel itself is not always very distinctly heard, it is doubtful whether a distinction between a *tempus* and *modus* form ought to be introduced in a grammar on such slender grounds. Yet it is necessary to state the case as it presents itself in the language, although the final and precise definition must be left open for further inquiries. It may, however, be observed, that the Hausa is not the only language in which this apparent uncertainty prevails, (and that the Hebrew and other languages use the future for the subjunctive mood,) more especially when it is preceded by the particles *don* and *kada*, ' that,' and ' that not;' as, *don su-kawo mata kári*, ' that they should bring her more;' *kada su-mutu*, ' that they should not die.' *Kada ka-tše ga mutane záni en kawo maku wonni abu*, ' thou must

not say to the people, I am going to bring you something.'
When *don* signifies 'because, for,' it is generally construed
with other tenses; as, *don ba ka-sanni ba kana dawoyowa
darai*, 'because thou dost not know whether thou shalt
return alive.' To illustrate the use of this form more
fully, we add a few examples:

Kadan na-baši takarda ši-tšagéta, 'if I give him the paper,
he will tear it.'

Ina-tamaha ši-báni kurdinsa duka, 'I thought he would
give me all his money;' or 'I hope he will give, &c.'

Kadan wuta ta-taba kwoi ši-búga kamma-n-kara-n bindiga,
'when the fire touches the egg, it will burst like the
sound of a gun.'

Kĕanwa ta-kī kama danbaria, don ba ta-da yunwa, 'the
cat will not (lit. refuses to) catch the mouse, because
it is not hungry.'

Yi hankali ši-búgéka, 'take heed, he will (may) strike thee.'

Gobe mu-tši saura, 'to-morrow we shall eat the remainder.'

Gobe dasáfe su-tašiesu, 'they will wake them early to-
morrow.'

Kadan ba ka-kaffa ba lemánka kwarai, hiska ši-tširéta,
'if thou dost not fasten thy tent well, the wind will
tear it.'

Fulane ba zásu-faddamu ba, 'the Phulas will not fight
with us.'

Kadan ba ka-suba mai tšiki-n-fatilla ta-mutu, 'if you do
not put oil in your lamp, it will (die) go out.'

Kadan na-yi šíri nī-kirrawoka, 'I will call thee when I
am ready.'

Kadan ba ka-guddu ba su-kaššieka, 'if thou dost not
run they will kill thee.'

Kadan ba ka-guddu ba zasu-kūmaka su-kaššieka, 'if thou
dost not run they will catch thee, they will kill thee.'

§ 143. The second form employed to express the future is that compounded with the verb *za* (*zua*) 'to go.' The form of the predicate is that of the present tense; as, *taffia, samne, kaowa,* &c., corresponding with the English expression *about to go, going to, to be on the point of,* and is therefore not always indicating absolute futurity, but also the immediate presence, and even a past tense, as the connection in a sentence may require it. Thus is *záni-taffia,* 'I am about to go, going, and I shall go,' and *da zata-mutua,* 'when she *was* going to die, or about to die.' In some sentences it is difficult to assign any definite meaning to it; *e. g. Babu abin da záši-ía rábásu daga wonnan abuta,* 'nothing could disturb their friendship;' while in *babu abin da zaši-samunka,* 'nothing shall happen to thee,' it expresses a plain future. *En ka-ganni suna-yin abin nān ba zaka-ía rīke darianka,* 'when you see them do that, you cannot help laughing.' *Ba zaka-ia daukanta massa,* 'you can not take it up quickly.' *Da báki suka-zakka ga gíddamu, ba mu-sanni ba enda zamu-sasu,* 'when the strangers had come to our house, we did not know where we (shall) should put them.' *En zasu-tši-n-tuonsu suna-buga baba-n-kubé,* 'when they are going to eat their dinner they ring a large bell.' *Da komi zaka-tambayansu ka-tše, kadan ka-yirda,* 'and whatever you ask them for, you say: if you please.' *Kuma, wota rana da zamu-taffia ga gona ta kanensa,* 'again on another occasion, as we were going to his brother's farm.'

Pluperfect and Second Future Tense.

§ 144. The Hausa language has not developed any forms for these tenses; any past tense, with the temporal adverb *da,* 'when,' may express them. *Da suka-zakka ga gíddamu,* 'when they had come to our house.' *Da suka-taffi wonni gari suka-śída ga gídda-n-wonni mutum, maidukia,* 'when they had gone to a certain town they alighted at the house of a rich man.' *Na-yi murna don kun-fadda mani gaskia, kadan ba ku-fadda mani gaskia, kadan na-taffi na-tambaya maimakaranta, kadan ya-fadda mani ba ku-taffi ba ga makaranta, ína-buganku,* 'I rejoice, because you told me the truth, if you had not told me the truth (lit.) when I had gone, and asked the schoolmaster, and he should have told me, that you had not been, I should have punished you.' *Kadan na-kaššic kaza nan ni-daffata da albassa,* 'when I shall have killed this fowl, I shall cook it with onions.'

MOODS.

§ 145. Having discussed the manner in which the *Moods* of the Hausa language are expressed, and given many examples of their uses, and likewise interspersed some observations, properly belonging to the Syntax, in the First Part of this Grammar, it will not be necessary to do more at this place than to refer the reader to what has been said in §§ 59, 60, 61, and 62, 63, 64.

Government of Verbs.

§ 146. Transitive Verbs govern, to use the common phraseology, an accusative; thus,

Ya-ši mosimu, ' he heard our motion=us move.'
Ya-tšíka bindiga, ' he loaded the gun.'
Na-dauka dusi, 'I took up a stone.'
Na-kirrawo oba-n-yaro, 'I called the boy's father.'

a) Some transitive, as well as intransitive verbs, are followed by prepositions; as,

Gáši da, 'to be tired of, or with something.'
Na-gaši-da sukua bissa rakumi, 'I was tired riding on a camel.'
Har yansu hanunka bai (instead of *ba ši*) *gáši ba da rubutu?* ' is thy hand not yet tired by writing?'

Tuna da, 'remember;' as, *ta-tuna da mišinta,* 'she thought of her husband.'

Ta-mutu da yuṅwa, 'she died of hunger.'

Yirda da, 'to believe, believe in;' *ni ban yirda da ba daši,* 'as for me, I do not believe in him.'

Obana ya-fadda mani, kada en yirda da komine da ni-ši, 'my father told me that I should not believe every thing I hear.'

b.) The radical and the causative form of transitive verbs is *generally* followed by the simple form of the objective, while the compound forms of the verb are followed by the compound forms of the pronouns; thus,

Ya-bani, 'he gave me;' *abašieni,* 'I am given;' *ya-saišiéni,* 'he sold me.'

Ya-bada mani, 'he gave me;' *ya-bayes garesu,* 'he gave them;' *ya-sayesda masu doki,* 'he sold them the horse.'

c.) Many verbs are accompanied by prepositions (govern a Dative) which do not require them in English; as,

Ya-faddi ga makéri ya-kíra mani haiwa, 'he told (to) the blacksmith to make me a hoe.'

Ina-son koya masu abin da Isa ya-tše, 'I wish to teach them what Jesus says.'

Don ina-son koya ga mutane-n-kassamu, 'because I wish to teach the people in our country.'

§ 147. Many transitive verbs take two accusatives, generally the one of the person and the other of the thing; *e.g.*

Sariki ya-bamu šanu biu, 'the king gave us two cows.'

Ba ina-tamaha ba ši-bani abin da ni-ke so, 'I do not think that he will give me the thing=what I want.'

Ši-kan šimfuda mani taberma daga dákinsa, 'he used to spread a mat for me in his room.'

§ 148. *Verba sentiendi et declarandi* generally introduce direct speech, and are not followed by any conjunction; thus,

Na-sanní ka-bani abin da ni-ke so, 'I know thou wilt give me what I want.'

Ba-ta-sanní ba kurege šína-tšíkin rámi, 'she did not know that the fox was in the hole.'

Ba-ta sanní ba suna-n-kurege Nakuduka ne, 'she did not know that the name of the fox was Nakuduka.'

Ina-tamaha šína-da rai har yansu, 'I hope he is still alive.'

Da muka-samna na-ši suna-so-n-taffia yáki, 'when we were sitting down, I heard that they wished to go to war.'

Da suka-ganní garí nan da girima, da suka-ganní mutane sun-fitto woše suka-tše masu : ba mu zakka ba fadda da garinku, 'when they saw that the town was large, and (when they saw) the people coming out, they said to them, we have not come to fight with your town.'

Da muna-ganní suna-guddu, zakkua garemu, muka-tše : mu taši, mu-guddu, sun-korosu, 'when we saw them running, coming towards us, we said, let us get up, and run, they are pursuing them.'

Ban yírda ba mutane-n-garí nan suna-saída bayi kammada su-ke yi daga garímu, 'I do not believe that the people of this country deal in slaves, as they do in our country.'

§ 149. It has been observed above, § 69, that the *Participle* appears in the form of a finite verb ; as, *ina-taffia,* 'I am going ;' *suna-kaššiewa,* 'they are killing;' *šína-sámu-n-kári,* 'he is receiving more;' *sunka-samna,* 'they were sitting.' But there is this difference in the use of these forms, that they do not represent an action as emanating from a person or thing, but represent the person or thing as that to which the action is attributed or ascribed, and is, therefore, *chiefly* used, as it were, in apposition to a substantive, and also contains in itself the idea of a verb used as a relative word of description *with* or *without* the relative conjunctions *da*, 'when, as;' *kamma*, 'as;' *tun* or *tunda*, 'while;' *e.g.*

Ni kua ína-kallonsa šína-taffiá sannusannu, 'I too, I was looking at him, as he was walking very softly.'

Da muna-samne ga dzakka-n-gídda, na-ganní dógo-n-mutum ya-fítta, fuskansa, da hanunsa duka fari kamma-n-takarda, da ša tágiá bissa ga kánsa, da dsawo-n-géme, da šína-da ríga fara, šína-dubina, ína-ši-ndsóro kamman záši-tšína, 'as we were sitting in the house, I saw a tall man coming, his face and his hands quite white, like paper, and a red cap on his head, and a long beard; being dressed in white, looking at me, I was afraid, as though he was going to eat me.'

Muka-dsaya muna-ganninsa har ya-taffi ga wonni wuri ya-gbáya, 'we stopped looking at him, till he went to another place to hide himself.'

Ya-karigbe daga hanunsa suna-santše, 'he snatched it from his hands as they were conversing.'

Daiansu šína-tšewa wonnan náma da kibba, 'one of them was saying this venison is fat.'

Muka-šigga tšíki-n-gídda, muka-samna kussa ga wuta muna-santše da murna, muna yin dáriá, 'we went in the house, sat down near the fire conversing cheerfully and laughing.'

Da na-tšíka tuluna da rua ga dawoyowata na-sámëši á-túnsure, 'having filled my jug with water, on my return I found it upset.'

Na-sámu yaro šína-worigi da širiginsa karami, ya-tše maní: ka-ganní širigina šína-taffia bissa ga rua? 'I met a boy playing with his little boat, he said to me, dost thou see my boat going on the water?'

Šatau ya-yi mafalki, Naino šína-baši kurdi fudu, da ya bayes ga matasa. Da gari ya waye Šatau ya-wanke fuskansa šína-murna šina-tamaha suna da sinária su saye gurassa, 'Shatau had a dream that Naino had given him four pieces of money, which he gave to his wife. When it began to dawn, Shatau washed his face, rejoicing and thinking that they had gold to buy bread.'

Da Šatau šina-kwantše ga kassa ya-ši magana-n-matasa 'and Shatau, lying on the ground, heard the word of his wife.'

Da suka ši šina-daria sun sanní ya-ša gia, 'when they heard him laugh, they knew that he had drunk wine.'

Da ina-io wonni yaro ya-bíni, muna-yin io gabadai, da hiska šina-búsá šina-so ya-yi io da baya, amma da ya ša rua dayawa, ya-fadda mani mu-dawoi, 'as I was swimming, a certain boy followed me, we were swimming together, as the wind was blowing the water, he (was wishing) wished to swim on his back, but having swallowed much water, he said to me, let us return.'

Idiomatic use of some Verbs.

§ 150. *Ya kussa,* 'he is near,' or, neuter, 'it is near;' is used as an adverb, *nearly, almost, about to, on the point of;* e. g.

Ya-kussa fadua, ' he *nearly* fell.'

Ta-kussa mutua da dáriá, ' she almost died with laughing.'

Da maraetšie ya-yi rana ta-kussa fadua kassa, 'in the evening when the sun was about to set.'

Ya-kussa káréši, 'he has nearly finished it,' or, 'it is nearly finished.'

Kára (=יָסַף), ' to add,' instead of ' more, again;' as,

Ba ya-kara ba tšéwa, ' he did not add speaking=he said no more.'

Záki ya-yi káka saodaia ba ši-kara ba, ya-mútu, 'the lion cried once, no more, and died.'

Ba ši-kara ganninsa, 'he saw him no more.'
Ba zăka kara ganni gari ba har, 'thou wilt not see another town until.'
Gúddu, 'to run,' to be rendered by *quickly*; *taffo da gúddu*, 'come and run, or come with running = come quickly.'

CHAPTER XVII.

THE PARTICLES.

§ 151. In the first part of this Grammar, §§ 83 to 89, the *particles* of the language have been exhibited under different heads, as *prepositions, adverbs, conjunctions,* and *interjections*; and it has there been shown that in the Hausa, as in other languages, the different classes of particles often blend with each other in their use, and that the context alone can decide as to which class the respective word belongs; and this being more especially the case as regards adverbs and prepositions, the latter will henceforth find a full illustration, though indirectly under the head of Adverbs, and the various combinations with prepositions, and substantives in which adverbial notions are expressed. To the examples already given we shall add a few more; and, at least in some instances, explain more fully the laws in operation in *propositions* and *connected* sentences.

Adverbs, Adverbial Combinations, and the various methods employed to express Adverbial relations.

§ 152. *Simple* adverbs, merely completing the notion of the verb, are placed immediately after the verb; thus,

Doki šina-guddu kwarai, 'the horse is running well.'

Ya taffi sannu, 'he went softly.'
Ya zakka massa, 'he came quickly.'
Ta táši sannu, 'he rose up softly.'
Ya yi hakka, 'he did so.'
Na ši dádi, 'I feel pleased.'

§ 153. Verbs, both transitive and intransitive, include in themselves the notion of adverbs, and are therefore used *with*, or more frequently *without*, prepositions expressing locality or motion, and direction *to* or *from* an object. Such are,

Fádi, 'to fall;' *Wonni ya-taffo, ya-yi sukua, ya-fádi,* 'another came, galloped, and fell down.'

Taffi, 'to go to;' *ko yao na-taffi London,* 'this very day I go to London;' *na-taffi bírni,* 'I go into the town;' *ya-taffi Bornu,* 'he went to Bornu.' Proper names of countries and towns seldom take prepositions.

Taffo, 'come from, come to;' *ta-taffo garesa,* 'she came to him.'

Fítta, 'to go out,' (intr.) *fitas* and *fišie* (trans.) 'to take out, to pull out, to extricate from;' *ya fitasda rīgása,* 'he took off his clothes.'

Fitto, 'to come out;' *ya-ganni ta-fitto daga tšiki-n-rua,* 'he saw her coming out of the water;' *rana-ta fitto,* 'the sun came out.'

Šída, 'to ascend, as a mountain, to alight at a place;' *muka-šída ga tšíki-n-mašídi,* 'we took up our quarters in an inn.'

Šído, 'to descend, come down;' *ka-šído,* and *ka-šído kassa,* 'come down, come down (ground). *Ya-šído daga bissa itatše,* 'he came down from the tree.'

Suba, 'to spill, to gush out, as water;' and (trans.) 'to pour out.'

Yi kussa, 'to draw near;' *ya-kussa*, 'to be near.'
Yawo, 'to walk about.'
Samna, 'to remain, to sit down;' *ya samna*, 'he sat down;' *ina samna ga dandali-n-sariki*, 'I reside at the king's palace.'
Sa, 'to place, to put;' *dsaya*, 'to place, to put oneself, or something, down,' &c.; and *dsaya*, 'to stand still, near, far,' and many more, which need not be mentioned.

§ 154. Locality is expressed by adverbs of *place; ya-samna nan*, 'he sits here;' *šina-dsaya tšan*, 'he is standing there;' or in an abstract way, *ya-taffi gídda*, 'he went home;' *ya-fáddi gaskia*, 'he speaks truth;' *ya-yi murna*, 'he makes joy=rejoices;' *muka samna kassa*, 'we sat ground=down;' or, by a substantive with a preposition; as, *ya-samna ga wuri-n-sariki*, 'he resides at the king's place=with the king.' *Muka-santše da murna*, 'we conversed with joy=cheerfully.' *Ši-ne daga bayana*, 'he is at my back=behind me.'

§ 155. The use of substantives such as *tšiki*, 'inside=in,' *baya*, 'back=behind;' *gaba*, 'front=before;' *da karifi*, 'with power=powerfully;' *da murna*, 'with joy=cheerfully;' to express adverbial relations of place, time, instrument, and manner, is very common in the Hausa language. These substantives, however, do not in themselves *generally* express place or time, like adverbs, but form, as it were, the central points from which an action emanates, or to which it reverts, hence the necessity of prepositions to indicate the relation the action bears to its centre, and in this way prepositions and substantives are employed to express adverbial notions.

The place itself can be conceived of, as: *in, out, on, above, over, below, under, before, behind, within, without, far, near, here, there, where, whence.* And these relations again are conceived of, either as a state of rest, or a state of motion *in a place*, and motion again as direction *towards* or from the person speaking, or the thing spoken of. These various relations, and the means employed to indicate them, will be illustrated in the following examples:

§ 156. Adverbs of *place* are, for the most part, substantives, or substantives combined with the prepositions *ga* and *daia*.

Tšiki, ' inside=in, within ;' as,

Tšiki-n-garinsu duka babu budurua da ta-fíta kedo, ' in all their country there was no maid that surpassed her in beauty.'

Ši-ne daga tšiki-n-dākinsa, he is in his room=in the inside of=*i.e.*—*Im Innern seines zimmers.*

Daga tšiki-n-garinku na ganni oban Tebib, ' in your country I saw Tebib's father.'

Ki-taffo, ki-sāmna tšiki-n-gíddana, ' come thou, sit down, live, reside in my house.'

Uwasa tana-daga tšiki-n-gídda-n sariki kaka fuskansa kamma-n-bawa ? ' his mother being in the king's house, how is it that his face is like that of a slave ?'

Ta-fitto daga tšiki-n-rua, ' she came out of the water.'

Zani-taffia tšiki-n-rua, ' I shall go in the water.'

Mun-šigga tšiki-n-širigi, ' we went into a boat=on board.'

Muka-samu yara suna worigi daga tšiki, ' we found some boys playing within.'

Woše, ' out,' (*wošie* occurs as a substantive, meaning, ' part,' and ' side' in a few instances).

Ya-fitta woše, ' he went out ;' (*woše* as it were pleonastically.)

Ta-fitas šinkaffa da nama, ' she took out the rice and the meat (from the pot);' *ya-fitto woše,* ' he came out.'

Bíssa, 'what is above, on, up;' ši-ne daga bíssa, ni-ne daga kalkas, ' he is above, I am below.'
Yara duka sun-túma bíssa kušiérinsu, 'all the boys jumped upon their chairs.'
Na-ganneši šina-yawo bíssa dáki, ' I saw him walking on the house.' Ya šído daga bíssa, ' he came down.' Ya-hawa bissa dóki, ' he mounted the horse.' Kadan ka-kaiši bíssa ka-kawoši kassa, ' when thou hast carried it up, bring it down (again).' Watše bíssa zaka-kai bíssa? ' what creature art thou going to take up?'
Kalkaši, ' the lower part of a thing, bottom=under, below, beneath, underneath;' thus,
Ita ta-šigga ga kalikaši-n-gádo, ' she crept under the bed.' Dasáfe ta-fítto daga kalikaši-n-gádo, ' early in the morning she came out from under the bed.'
Gaba, ' front, chest, bosom=before, forwards;' suna-taffia gaba ina-binsu daga baya, ' they walked before, I behind, lit. I following them from behind.' Ki-wutše gaba rua-n-Madina ba kussa ba, 'pass on (forwards), the water of Medina is not near.' Mu-dsaya gaba ga gídda, ' we stood before the house.' Ši-ne gaba gareni da ni ga bayansa, ' he is before me, and I am behind him;' or, ' he is above me and I am inferior to him.'
Baya, ' back, behind;' see gaba.
Kussa, ' near, nigh, at hand;' ši-ne kússa gareni, ' he is near me;' ba ka-ganni ba ya-kussa gareka? ' dost thou not see he is near thee?' Ya-kussa tšikka da rua, ' it is nearly full of water.' Muka-zakka ga wota baba-n-hainya dagá kussa gareta akoi masallatši, ' we came to another large street, close to it is a church.'
Nésa, ' far, far away, at a distance;' ya-dsaya daga nésa, ' he stood at a distance.' Sun-gannéta daga nésa,

'they saw her from a distance.' *Kadan ku taffi nèsa daga garemu kada ku-šída nesa daga obanenku*, 'when you go far away from us, you must not encamp far from your parents.'

Nan and *nana*, 'here, at *this* place;' *ba ši-ne daga nan*, 'he is not at this (*wuri*) place=here.' *Tumaki duka suna-nan?* 'are all the sheep here?' *Ba su duka ke nan ba*, 'not all are here.' *Mi zaki yi-nana?* 'what wilt thou do here?'

Tšan, 'there, yonder, at *that* place.' *Daga tšan na-ganni abin mamaki*, 'there I saw a wonderful thing.' *Daga nan muka-taši, muka-íssa nana*, 'from thence we started, and reached this place.' Sentences with *nan* and *tšan* are elliptical, *wuri*, 'place,' being left out; as, *daga wuri nan*, or *tšan*, 'from this or that place.'

Enna and *enda*, 'where, whence.' *Kōénna*, 'any where, from any place.' *Suka-tambayéta enna abukiaki?* 'they asked here where is thy friend?' *Ta tše masu, ta-gbata; sunka-tambayéta daga enna? Ta tše: ga tšiki-n-gulbi*, 'she said to them, she is lost. They were asking her where? She said, in the lake.'

Ku-tambayesa enna uwasa, 'ask him where his mother is.' *Suka-tambayesa enda (wurin· da) uwasa ta ke.* 'they asked him where his mother was.' *Daga enna ka-fitto? Na-fitto daga Bornu,* 'where dost thou come from, or whence comest thou—from Bornu?' *Daga enna ka-taffo?* 'whence comest thou?'

The four quarters of heaven may be mentioned in connection with the adverbs of place: *Ariéwa*, 'north,' *gabaz*, 'east,' *gussum*, 'south,' and *yamma*, 'west.' (יָם יְמָהִין *nach westen*) *Rana ta-taši daga gabaz tana-íssa-dzakka, tana-fadua yamma*, 'the sun rises in the east, reaches the middle (south), sets in the west.'

Adverbs of Time. Adverbial Combinations to express Time.

§ 157. The form of the object of time is either a simple adverb, as *kulum,* 'always,' and *yansu,* 'now,' or an adverb compounded with the preposition *da,* which is likewise an adverb of time, 'when;' as, *dasafe=*'when morning, in the morning, early;' and, *daga, e.g. daga yansu,* 'from henceforth,' and *daga gaba nan,* 'from henceforth;' or with the intensive particle *kō,* as in *kōyánsu,* 'any time, at any time, always, constantly;' and *kōyánsu,* 'even now, just now,' *e.g. kōyánsu na-taffi London,* 'just now I go to London;' or a substantive, as *yao,* 'to-day;' *yao na-ganni abu mamaki,* 'to-day I have seen wonderful things;' *yao ba mu taffi ba ga makaranta,* 'to-day we did not go to school;' or a substantive with the adverb *da*; as, *da maraetsie ya-yi,* 'when the evening arrived=in the evening;' and the postposition *ga* (sometimes instead of *nga,* 'this, that'); as, *baya ga,* 'after;' *daga baya ga wonnan,* 'in the back of this=after this,' *e.g. baya ga beri-n-giddansa,* 'after leaving his house;' or, the substantive expressing time is followed by the demonstrative pronoun *nan;* as, *lottu nan,* and *saanan,* 'that, or at that time=then.'

§ 158. Adverbial forms and combinations, whether expressing time, *simple* or *compound,* denote —*a*) either the time *when* the action takes place, or *b*) the *length* of time it occupies. In answer to the question *when?* the *point,* and in answer to the question *how long?* the *duration,* of time is expressed.

a) When the object of time denotes a *point of time,* it is *generally* put at the beginning of the sentence; *e.g.*

Yao na-ganni abin mamaki uku, 'to-day I have seen three wonderful things.'

Wonni lottu si-kan kawo labari nāgari, da wonni lottu

mugu, 'sometimes he used to bring good, and sometimes bad news.'

Gobe dasafe mu-táši mu-taffi ga˙ gonansa, 'to-morrow early in the morning we shall start and go to his farm.'

Šia na-ši labari da ni-ke so, 'yesterday I heard the news I like.'

The expressions: *da safia ta yi,* 'when the morning came (had come);' *da gari Alla ya-waye,* 'when the country of God (=the sky) was dawning;' *da maraetšie ya-yi,* 'when the evening arrived (had come);' *da dere ya-yi,* 'when night had come;' are all employed in the same way as simple adverbs (=in the evening, morning, &c.) of time, in answer to the question *when;*

Da gari ya-waye muka-táši, muka-taffi dasafe ga góna 'at daybreak we got up, and went early to the farm.'

Da maraetšie ya-yi, da muka-dawoyo daga abduga-n-gona, na ganni kānéna daga bíssa tudu, 'in the evening, as we were returning from the cotton-farm, I saw my younger brother on a hill.'

Da muka samna, īna-tamaha daga tšiki-n-šiekara nan muka-ši mutane-n-Bornu sun-šigga tšiki-n-Kantše, 'having remained there some time, I think it was in the same year, we heard that the Bornu people had entered Kantshe.'

Baya ga mutua-n-kānuata na ši labari n-yaki, 'after the death of my younger sister I heard rumours of war.'

Kána, before, or *then,* is sometimes used between two propositions, so that it may be rendered *before,* being construed with the first, or by *then,* being construed with the second part. *Obana ya-zakka šina-némana daga tšiki-n-tšiáwa, ya-kirrani, ina-šinsa, amma ban amsa ba; hario ya-kirrani saobiu kána na-amsa,* 'my father came looking for me in the grass, he called me, I heard him, but I did not answer him; again he called me the second time *before*=then I answered him.'

Lottu nan ina-tamaha šiekarata ša daia, ' I think I was eleven years of age then.'

The object of time is sometimes put after the predicate:

Muka-taši da dere, ' we got up in the night.'

Ina-tamaha sun-aike woddansu daga tšiki-n-dere nan, ' I think they sent some persons away during the night.'

Sao daia da na-taffi garesu da maraetšie ya-kirraní, ' on one occasion, as I was going to them in the evening he called me.'

b) When the adverb, or adverbial combination, expresses a duration of time, in answer to the question *how long?* it takes its place generally after the predicate; *e.g.*

Ya-šíra har ruaye su-suba kassa, ' he waits until it rains, lit. waters pour down.'

Su-yi masa aiki kwana šídda ko uku, ' they worked for him six, or three, days.'

Kadan sun-kwāna dere uku ko fudu, ' when they had slept three or four nights.'

Kada ka-maída mani dána har na-gammu da kai daga tšiki-n lāhirá, ' thou need not return my child to me until I meet thee in the sheol.'

Muka-samna daga nan kwanaki dayawa, ' we remained there many days.'

c) Adverbial accessory sentences of time take the conjunctions *da,* ' when, as ;' *kadan,* ' if, when ;' *tunda,* ' while, while as yet ;' *har,* ' till, until.'

Da ta-ganneni ta tambayeni : enna obanka? ' when she saw me she asked me, where is thy father ?'

Da suna-yin magana-m-Bornu ban sanni ba abin da su-ke tšéwa, ' as they were talking Bornu, I did not know what they were saying.'

Da suka daúka abu duka daga tšiki n-gari sun-sa wuta,

x

'when they had taken every thing in the town they set fire to it.'

Kadan, 'if, when,' is used when the time refers to some indefinite past event, or to some event in the present and future time, and consequently most frequently in conditional sentences; as,

Kadan mu-sanni zasu-kámamu mu-yi fadda kamma-n-wuta, 'if we had known that they were going to catch us, we should have fought like fire.'

Kadan na-ši ka-faddi ga kowa ína-buganka, 'if I hear that thou dost tell it to any body, I shall beat thee.'

Tunda expresses simultaneousness of action:

Na-kuntše darime nan tunda tana-yin magana-m-Bornu na guddu, 'while she was talking Bornu, I untied the chain and ran.'

Tunda suna-tšikka bindigansu dorina ta-taffi nésa, 'while they were loading their guns, the hippopotamus went away.'

Har, 'till, until;' *na rike asiri nan har ga yansu,* 'I kept the secret until now.'

Ina tare daku har ga makarin dunia, 'I am with you to the end of the world.'

Adverbs and Adverbial Combinations of manner.

§ 159. The prepositions *da* and *babu,* and the adverbs *kamma,* or *kammada,* and *hakka,* are employed to express the adverbial object of manner; thus,

Ya-taffi da kaffa, 'he went on foot.'
Ya-taffo da guddu, 'he came running.'
Ya-yi magana da Hausa, 'he spoke Hausa.'
Sun-kirráni da sunana, 'they called me by name.'

Da, 'with,' and *babu,* 'without,' denote both the manner in which a thing is done, and the instrument by which an action is performed; as,

Ya-sokēši da maši, 'he pierced him with a spear.'
Ba ka ía-sayensa babu kurdi? 'canst thou not buy it without money?'
Da nono-n-ūwata na-sayēka, 'for the breast of my mother I have bought thee=with,' &c.
Ya buge dokinsa da būlála, 'he beat the horse with the whip.'

By *kamma,* or *kammada,* and *hakka, kaka*:
Ina-fadda maka kaṃmada a-ke-yíši, 'I tell thee in what way it is done;' *kammada ši-ke-yi,* 'how it is.'
Muka·ši abu daga tšiki-n rua kamma-n širigi na-zakkua garḗmu, 'we heard something in the water like a canoe coming towards us.'
Ya-tše hakka, 'he said so;' *ina-fadda maka hakka ši-ke,* 'I tell you how it is.'
Da kaka zaka-taffia yíki babu fadáwa? 'and how wilt thou go to war without officers?'

Negative Particles, and the way in which Negation is expressed.

§ 160. There are three Negative Particles in the Hausa language; as *babu, (ba) ba—ba,* and *kada,* and this seems to be the proper place to explain the use made of them.

1. *Ba—ba* forms, properly speaking, the Negative Indicative Mood, and negatives an *action* absolutely; as,

Ban sanni ba, 'I do not know.'
Ban tše ba hakka, 'I did not say so.'
Ba su-kamaši ba, 'they did not catch him.'
Ban yirda ba wonnan magana, 'I do not believe this word.'

2. *Ba,* single, and *babu* express negation of *existence* absolutely. In English they must generally be translated by 'there is,' or, 'was not.' They cannot, like *ba,* be connected

with the finite verb, but stand before nouns, pronouns, and numeral adjectives, which they negative; as,

Babu kowa da ya-yírda daši, (lit.) 'not any one who, *i.e.* there was no one who believed in him.'

Babu mutum da ya-taya masa, 'no man helped him.'

Babu abin da kana-ia yi, 'there is nothing that thou canst do.'

Amma ši ba ia sannina ga šaušawa, 'but he cannot know me by the marks in my face.'

Ba ni-da komi da ni-ke basu, 'I have not any thing to give them.'

Babu bawa ko daia sai ni, 'there was no slave there, not even one, except myself.'

Ba kowa da ya-zakka nána? 'has no one come here?'

Ba kowa da ši-ke nāgari, 'there is no one that is good.'

Ba daia da kíbba, 'not one was fat.'

3. *Kada* is prohibitive (and dissuasive, and as a conjunction is used like פֶּן in Hebrew), 'that not, lest.' See § 92.

Kada su-taffi su-yi abin da ši-ke ba daidai ba, 'lest they go to do something which is not proper.'

Kada su-mutu, 'that they might not die.'

Kada ka-tše ga yaranka zani kawo maku wonni abu, 'thou must not say to thy children, I shall bring you something.'

4. Adverbs of intensity and frequency, as well as the comparisons formed with adverbs, have been illustrated in § 86.

§ 161. The signification and use of prepositions has been fully explained in Chap. VII, § 83 and § 108—112, on the cases of the language, and incidentally treated in other parts of the Grammar; it is, therefore, not necessary to say more about them here.

CHAPTER XVIII.

CONJUNCTIONS.

§ 162. Conjunctions are words which serve to connect words and sentences, and to bring them into a certain relation with each other. With regard to their form, they are either radical words, such as, *da, don, kadan;* or words derived from others, such as *nafari, nabaya,* &c.; or compound words (conjunctional combinations), such as, *don wonnan; hakkanan; bamda wonnan,* &c.

Conjunctions may be divided into as many classes as there are connections and relations effected by them; as, *copulative, adversative, causative, concessive, exceptive, exclusive, comparative, conclusive,* &c.

1. Copulative conjunctions. These are, *da,* 'and,' *kuá,* 'also, likewise,' *ko,* 'even.'

Da ni da kai, 'I and thou;' *oba da uwa,* 'the father and the mother.'

Da connects two propositions, when each proposition has its own subject; as, *ni-zani-taffia ya kasua, da kai kua zaka-taffia ga kasua,* 'I shall go to the market, and thou also shalt go too;' but also, *ina-tši, ina-ša,* 'I eat, I drink,' and not 'I eat and drink.'

Ni-taffi ga sariki, da ni tše masa, 'I shall go to the king, and I shall say to him.'

Two or more predicates of the same subject are generally not connected by the copulative conjunction; *e.g.*

Mutum ya-taši, ya-dauka sanda, ya-guddu, ya-taffo ga wuri-n enda matšiši ši-ke, ya kaššieši, 'the man rose, took a stick, came to the place where the serpent was, killed it.'

Da is used correlatively, like 'both,'—'and'; as, *da ní da kai,* 'both I and thou.'

Da obansa da uwansa su-duka biu, ba su-soši ba, 'both his father and his mother, all two, did not like him.'

Da is sometimes at the beginning of a sentence merely a connective particle, like 'but, now,' &c.

Da kaka zaka-yaki babu faddwa? 'but how wilt thou go to war without officers?'

Kuá, 'also, too, likewise;' *Ina-sonsa, da ši kua šina-sona,* 'I love him, and he also loves me.'

Ko, 'even;' *ko ni dakuína ina-taffia da kaffa,* 'even I myself was travelling on foot.'

Ko kua mu ya-n-Africa muna-tši-n-nama daínye, 'even we Africans eat raw meat.'

Ko-ko, correlatively used as 'whether, or;' as, *amma ban ši ba ko daía ya-mutu na garimu, ko wonní ya-halba kibiá,* 'but I have not heard whether any one of our country died, or whether any shot an arrow.'

Amma ban sanni ba ko káya ta-sokéni, ko ba ta-sokeni ba, 'but I did not know whether the thorns had pricked me or not.'

2. Adversative conjunctions are, *amma,* 'but, yet, however, nevertheless.'

Ina-dubensa, amma ban gannéši ba, 'I looked for him but did not find him.'

Da uwata kua tana-kúka, amma kánéna ba ši-sanni ba kómi, 'and my mother *also* was crying, but my younger brother did not know any thing (what it meant).

3. Conjunctions expressing a cause, as well as ground, purpose, and motive; *doñ,* and *don (en)* 'for, because, in order that, to;' and *kada,* negatively, ' that not.'

Ina-tamaha kai ba ba-haŭse ba ka-ke, don halšinka ba kamma namu, ' I think thou art no Hausa man, because thy tongue is not like ours;' *na-tše masa, nasanni Hausa kwarai, don ni dā-n-Tuntume ne,* ' I said to him, I understand Hausa very well, because I am a native of Tuntume.'

Yao na-taffi ga makaranta, don en ganni abin da zasu-godda ga ya-n-makaranta, ' I went to school to-day to see what they were going to show to the school-children.'

Don ya-sanni wuri enda mutané su-ke wutšewa koyaŭse tšiawa ba ta-dzira daganan, ' for he knew that at a place over which people were constantly passing no grass could grow.'

Ya-aiko maní wota budurua, kada en taffi har ya-n-makaranta-su-fitta, ' he sent a girl after me (to say) that I should not leave until the school-children left.'

Don wonnan, ' for this reason;' *sabbada* and *sabbada wonnan,* ' on that account, for the sake of,' &c.

Ya-bani duka don wonnan na-yi murna, ' he gave me all, therefore I am glad.'

Ya-kī zakkua don wonnan ya-saši tīlass, ' he refused to come, for which reason he forced him.'

Ni kua ina-yi-n-kúka sabbada gašia, ' I was crying too on account of fatigue.'

4. *Koda* is concessive, meaning, ' though, although;' as,

Koda ta-ke kĕāokĕāwa ba ta-da dukia, 'though she is very beautiful, she is not rich.'

Koda na-sanni ba zaši-bani kurdina na-yi masa aiki, 'although I knew that he would not give me my wages I did his work.'

Koda akoi dzamki dzakkanina, da ši, ba ši fušieni ba daga gíddansa, 'although there is a dispute between me and him, he does not drive me out of his house.'

Koda ka-gannesu suna-radda ba don su-kaššieka, 'though you see them whispering together, it is not to kill you.'

5. Exceptive and exclusive conjunctions. These are: *bamda,* 'besides,' and 'except;' and *sai,* or *saidaí.*

Mi kana-so en sawo maka bamda šinkaffa, 'what dost thou wish me to buy and bring to thee, besides rice?'

Ban ši ba abin da sun-tše bamda wonnan, da na-fadda maka, 'I did not hear any thing they said, except that which I told thee.'

Bamda kaí ba na-ši-n dsóro kowa, 'I do not feel afraid of any one except of thee.'

Sai, saidai, 'except;' but it has a great many meanings besides this, and as it occurs so often, a few examples will be given under this heading of its use in general.'

Sai, 'except,' *babu bawa ko daía daga tšiki-n-gidda sai ni,* 'there was no slave in the house, not even one, except myself.'

Sai, 'but;' *sai obana ya-tše mani,* 'but my father said to me;' *mun-kirráka saidai ba ka-šimu ba,* 'we called thee, but thou didst not hear us.'

Sai, 'nothing but,' *sai hayaki muna-ganni ga tšiki-n-gari,* 'we saw nothing but smoke in the town;' *kafata duka sai šinni,* ' my feet were nothing but=full of blood.'

Sai, ' only ;' *sai mutume daía a-ke-saši, ya-hawa bissa itatše,* ' only one man was made to ascend a tree.'

Sai is sometimes used like 'all is right, or well, or quite well.'

Ya-tše mani babu kŏmi, sai láfia, ' he said to me, there is nothing the matter, all is well.'

6. Comparatives. *Kamma,* and *kammada,* 'as, like as,' and *hakka,* and *hakkanan,* ' so, in this way, or manner.'

Hakkanan ši-ke, ' so it is ;' *ba hakka ba,* ' not so.'

Ki-faddi hakka, ' say so.'

Ina-fadda maka kammada a-ke-yi-n-tuo, ' I am telling thee how the food is made.'

Kamma, ' as though ;' *da rana ta-fara taši ina-ganninta kamma-n-tana-fitta daga tšiki-n-gulbi,* ' when the sun was about the rise, I saw it was as though it came out of the sea.'

Fuskanta fara kamma-n-alli, ' her face was as white as chalk.'

Kaka, ' how, in what manner ;' *mutane n-kassa nga gonai su-ke, ka-ganni kaka-su-yi ginna ga kalikaši-n-kassa kamma-n-kurege?* ' the people of this country are very clever, you see how they dig under the earth like foxes.'

7. Temporal or consecutive conjunctions, indicating certain relations of time ; as, *har, kána, en, kadane.*

Har, ' till, until ;' *ka-širáni har en zakka,* ' wait for me till I come.'

Har, ' whilst ;' *ka-rike wakata har en taffi en tši*

tuona, har en dowoyo, ' hold my song whilst I go to eat my food, and until I return.'

En, ' when ;' *amma en lottu-n-tši-n-tuo ya-zakka, su-kan kirramu, mu kaššie káši kammada mu-ke-yi ga áda-n-musulmi,* ' but at dinner time they used to call us, that we might kill fowls according to the custom of Mohammedans.'

Da en ya-dúbeni ši-sata kaṇsa kassa, ' and when he had looked at me, he would incline his head down.

Kána, ' before=then ;' *ga šimawa kadan muka-ši mosi ga kalikašimu kána muka-fara taffia,* ' after a little while we felt some thing move under us, before (then) we began travelling' (often strictly conjunctional, as it might be rendered here) ' we felt something move under us before we started.'

Da kadan mutane su-zakka ga salla suna-taru ga šiére daia ; da mutum daia ne ši-ke-yi-n-addáwa (addowa) ; sú wanke kansu dafári kána enda zasu-yi-n-addawa su-dauke hanunsu bissa kána su-ašie ; da su-sunkwia, kadan su-dsaya daidai kuma, su-durugussa har góšinsu ya-taba kassa; sú-yi hakka saobial kána su káre, ' and when the people come to worship, they are placed in a line ; and there is one man who is offering up a prayer ; they lift up their hands, then they take them down, and kneel-down, and stand up straight again, they bow down till their foreheads touch the ground; they do the same five times, before it is finished.'

Tunda, ' while ;' *tunda mu-ke-samne daga tšiki-n-giddansa,* ' while we were residing in his house.'

Amma tunda suna-tšikka bindigansu dorina ta taffi nésa, ' but while they were loading their guns the hippopotamus went far away.'

Tunda muna nan na-ši aka-tše : kada kowa ya-taffi ga baki-n-rua nan gobe dasafe ! Na-tambayesu : domi, mutane kada su-taffi ? Suka-tše : en ka ganni yaya-n-rua nan ka-mutu, ' while we were there I heard it said, let no one go to the bank of the water early to-morrow morning! I asked them why is nobody to go there? They said, if you should see the children of the water you would die.'

Tunda dewa, ' long since.' *Ya-mutu tunda dewa,* ' he died long since.'

8) Conditional. *Kadan,* ' if,' *en,* ' if;' *kadan ban tše ba karia,* ' if I am not telling a story.'

APPENDIX.

CONTAINING SPECIMENS OF A HAUSA LITERATURE, TAKEN FROM THE NATIVES IN THEIR OWN TONGUE, AND ACCOMPANIED WITH AN ENGLISH TRANSLATION.

1. *Narrative of a Hunting Match.*

Yáo muka táffi faraúta, mu úku. Yaro da obansa suna da bindiga, ni ina da dusi tšikin alšifu. Da muka taffi tšikin dáši babu karre tare da mu; amma oban yaro ya sanni enda náma ši ke. Da muka taffi ya gannéši, ya godda ga dansa, amma dansa ba ši ganni ba. Hario ya godda masa, da ya ganni, amma ni ban ganni ba, don na dsaya baya gárésu, don kada mu taffi wuri daía, kada nama ya taší, kadan ya ši mósimu; amma suka kirrani, na taffi kussa dasu. Amma dafari oban yaro ya tše ga dansa: kadan nina halba dafari, kai ka yi guddu ka halba, ya tše dakeao.

"To-day we went hunting, three of us. The boy and his father had a gun (each), I had stones in my pockets When we went into the forest there was no dog with us, but the boy's father knew where the game was. As we were going along, he saw it, and showed it to his son, but his son could not see it. Again he pointed it out to him, and he saw it, but I could not see it, because I was standing behind them, that we might not go to the same place, lest the creature should start when it heard us move, but they called me, and I went to them. But the father of the boy had previously told his son: When I have shot first, then run thou, and fire. So he said, Very well."

Da muka gewoya ga wonni wošĕ kadan, muka dsaya, obansa ya halba, da nama ya tumá bíssa, ya fádi, ya fara guddu, kána dansa ya halba; ni kua na šiĕfa da dusi, kána muka fara ǵuddu, muna binsa, ši kua šína guddu kána muka dsáya, ši kua ya yi guddu ya šigga tšikin sansámi.

Da muka ganni ya šígga, muka dsaya wuri daía; dansa ya tšika bíndiga; da šína tšikawa, na ganni nama nan, ya fitta daga tšikin sansámi, na tšĕ, gaši, šína fittá. Da ya fitta ya fara guddu, ba ya ia guddu massa, don bindiga ta halbésa dafari. Muka dsaya muna ganninsa, har ya taffi ga wonni wuri ya gbóya. Na dauka dusi, kána muka fara guddu; da muna guddu muka dsaya muna taffia. Du suka wutšĕ nama nī na ganní, ina son šiefesa da dusi, amma ban šiefa ba. Na dsaya, na kirráwo oban yaro, na tšĕ: gaši kun wútšĕ, ya tšĕ; enna? na tšĕ: gaši kussa da mu.

"When we had turned round a little to the other side we stopped; the father fired, the creature jumped up, fell down, and began to run, and then the son fired; I too was throwing stones at it, and then we began to run after it; it was running too, then we stopped, it ran on, and entered under some dry leaves."

"When we saw it going in, we remained standing at the same place; the son loaded his gun; while he was loading it, I saw the creature coming out from under the leaves, and said, see there, it is coming out. When it had come out, it began to run, but it could not run fast, because the gun had wounded it before. We stopped, looking at it until it went to another place and hid itself; I took up stones, and then we began to run; when we had been running some distance we stood still and then walked about stealthily. When they were passing by the creature, I saw it, and wanted to throw stones at it, but I did not throw any. I stopped, and called the boy's father, and said, See it there, you passed it. He said, Where? I said, See there, close to us."

Da muka taffi báya kadan, ya halba da bindiga, ya kaššieši, ba ya ia táši, sai šina šiúri da kaffa. Oban yaro ya tše ga dansa: ka dauka, ba ši sanni ba kammada zaši daukansa, sai sína so ya káma kunua; obansa ya tše: ba hakka ba. Da obansa ya sa hanu, ya kama kaffafun baya biú, ya murde wuyansa, kána ya daúka, ya godda ga wonni mutum daga nésa.

Mutume nan ba ši ganni ba. Hario ya nuna masa, ya ganni, ya dsaya har muka išieši. Ya karigba daga hanunsa suna yin sɐntše. Daiansu šina tšéwa: wonnan nama šina da kibba. Maaikatšinsa ya tše: ina guddu da nama nan; na tše, kadan mutume nan ya guddu ina kamaši. Har muka zakka ga gidda, ya karigba, ya sa wuka, ya tšage dzakkankané dāgará (šišiá) ya sa wotšan kaffa daga enda ya kéta, ya rataye ga bíssa itatše.

"Having walked a little way back, he fired his gun, and killed it (the creature), it could not get up again, but only kicked. The father of the boy said to his son, Take it up,' but he did not know how to take it up, he wanted to lay hold of its ears; his father said, not so. And the father, putting his hand on it, seized it by both its hind legs, wrung its neck, then took it up and showed it to a man who stood some distance from us."

"The man could not see it; so he showed it to him again, and he saw it then, and stood still until we met him. He snatched it from his hands as they were conversing together. One of them said, This creature is very fat. And his servant said, I shall run away with this game. I replied, If this man runs away, I will catch him. When we had reached home he took it, put a knife to it, cut it open in the middle, and put the other leg in the place where he had made a cut, and hung it on a tree."

Ya tše : kana so ka halba bindiga? Na tše : í; kadan na taffi garina ina dauka daia. Muka fitta; ya kaššie zunsaye biú kanana; ni kuá na halba saouku, ban kaššie ba kōmi, sai sansamin itatua suna fádi kassa. Muka šigga tšikin gídda, muka samna kussa ga wuta, muna santše da murna, muna yin daria. Ši ke nan ya kare; na kawo maka labari yao.

"He said to me, would you like to fire a gun? I answered, Yes, when I return to my country I shall take one with me.' So we went out; he killed two birds, little ones; I too, fired three times, but killed nothing, only leaves fell down from the trees. We went into the house, sat down near the fire, talking cheerfully, and laughing. This is it, it is finished; I have brought thee some news to-day."

2. *Maganan kura da kurege.*

"The Story of the Hyena and the Fox."

Kura ta haifi diánta, tana kawo masu abintši; ta taffi tšikin dáši, ta dauko kašši, ta kawo, ta bayes ga diánta suna tši. Da dere ya yi ta taffi tana neman kašši. Kurege ya taffo, ya šigga wuri enda dianta su ke; ya šigga kalkas, ya gbúya.

"The hyena having given birth to some young ones, brought them something to eat; she went into the forest picked up bones, brought them and gave them to her children to eat. When it was night, she went again to look for bones."

*Da dere ya yi ta taffi tana neman kašši, ba ta sanni
ba kurege šina tšikin rámi; da ta kawo nama ta bayes ga
dianta sunka tše nawane ne? Kura ta amsa ta tše masu naku
duka. Kurege ya tše : ku bani, namana ne ; suka baši, ya
tšaínye, dianta sunka samna da yuñwa. Hario, da dere
ya yí ta taffi ta samu nama ko kašši, ta kawo, ta
bayes ga dianta. Dianta sunka amsa mata, suka tše : nawane ne ? Uwasu ta tše masu : naku duka, sunka bayes ga kurege,
kurege ya tšainye, ya ber dian kura da yuñwa. Kowonne dere
tana taffia, tana kawo kašši, tana basu ga dianta, tana tšewa:
naku duka.*

"The fox came, and went to the place where the children of the hyæna were, entering underneath and hiding himself. The hyena came, brought home meat and gave it to her children. Now every child had its own name, and the name of the fox was For-all-of-you. When it was night she went to look for bones, not knowing that the fox was in the hole; whenever she brought meat and gave it to her children, they used to say, For whom is it? And the hyena answered and said to them, For all of you. The fox said, Give it to me, it is my meat. They gave it him and he ate it, while the children sat fasting. Again, when night came on, she went, found some meat or bones, brought it, and gave it to her children. Her children answering, said to her, Whose is it? Their mother said to them, For all of you. So they gave it to the fox, and the fox ate it, leaving the children of the hyena hungering. Every night she used to go and bring bones, and give them to her children, saying, For all of you."

Ba ta sanni ba naku duka sunan kurege. Har wata ya yi ta tše ga dianta : ku fitto; kowonne šína fittowa babu kibba; wonnan ya fitto sai da rama, su duka babu daía da kibba tšikinsu. Ta tše masu, enna nama duka da ina kaowa, kuna tši? Suka amsa, suka tše mata : Nakuduka ya tšainye nama duka, ta amsa, ta tše : wānéne Nakuduka, ya tšainye nama? Suka tše mata, sūnan kurege. Ta tše masu, enna ši ke? Sunka tše, šína tšikin rami; ta duba rami, ta gaнncši, ta tše masa: yáka, fitto, yao kariaka ta káre. Ya amsa, ya tše da kedo, ina fittowa. Ya míka kunuansa, ya tše ga kura, ki karigbe takalmina en fitto; ba ta sanni ba šikkinsa ne duka, ya yi kibba? Ta kamu kunuansa, ta yes; ba ta sanni ba ta šiefasda Nakuduka, tana tamaha takalmansa ne.

"She did not know that the name of the fox was For-all-of-you. After a month she said to her children, Come out. Every one on coming out was thin: one came, he was altogether lean—there was not one of them that was fat. She said to them, Where is all the meat which I have brought you to eat? They answered and said to her, The For-all-of-you has eaten all the meat. She answered and said, Who is this For-all-of-you, who has eaten all the meat? They said to her, It is the name of the fox. She said to them, Where is he? They answered, He is in the hole. She looked into the hole and saw him, and said to him, Come, get out, to-day thy deception is at an end. He answered and said, Very well, I am coming out. He stretched up his ears, and said to the hyena, Lay hold on my shoes, that I may come out. She did not know that it was his whole body: he was fat. She laid hold of his ears and threw him aside, not knowing that she was throwing away the For-all-of-you, (but) thinking it was only his shoes."

Tana šira, ya fitto, ta kamaši; ba ta sanni ba šina daga bayanta. Ya tše mata : kura! kura! dubani, na tuffi garimu. Šina guddu, tana binsa ; sai šina tše mata: daia, biú, uku, daia, biú, úku, ya taffi, ba ta kamaši ba ; ta dawoyo, tana tšison hakkora, tana šin haúši. Dianta duka sun rama ; sai ta taffo, tana šin haúši, ta samna. Ši ke nan ya kárc.

"She was waiting for him to come out, that she might eat him, and did not know that he stood behind her. He said to her, Hyena, hyena, look at me, I am going to my own country. So he ran, and she was following him, but he only said to her, One, two, three, one, two, three, and went, and she could not catch him. She returned, gnashing her teeth in vexation. All her children were lean; but she came and sat down, being vexed. This is it; it is finished."

3. *Maganan Mallami da kurege.*

"*The Story of the Priest and the Fox.*"

Mallami šina da dukia dayawa, da šánu, da awaki, da tumaki. Kurege ya zakka garesa, ya tše: Mallami, ina so en yi maka barantaka. Ya tše, da keao. Ya tše: mi záka yi mani? Ya tše, ina yi maka šira garike tumakinka, da awakinka. Ya tše dakeao sunka samna. Kowotše sáfia kurege šina dauka kášin tumaki, šina gerta turiken tumaki da na awaki.

"There was once a certain priest who had much property, cows, goats and sheep. A fox came to him, and said, O priest, I should like to enter into service with thee. He said, Very well; what art thou going to do for me? He answered, I shall prepare and keep clean the place where thy sheep and goats are kept. He replied, Very good. So they laid down. Every morning the fox took up the dung of the sheep, and kept the place of the sheep and of the goats clean."

Samma samma suna nan. Kadan gari Alla ya waye ši kan taffi, ši kan šáre garike na awaki. Mallami ya baši sanfo karami. Kurege ya tše masa, O ka bani baba, ya fi. Mallami ya baši. Sunka kwana, da safe ya yi ya kaššie tumkia, ya sa tšikin sanfo, ya suba kášin awaki bissa gareta, ya daúka ya kai woše, ya taffi tšikin dáši, ya fura wuta, ya gassa, ya tši, ya taffo gidda da sanfo. Ya samna. Da maraetšie ya yi ya darime tumaki da awaki; sunka yi beritši. Hario da safe ya yi hakka kamma na šia. Mallami šina ganni tumaki da awaki suna ragewa, ya tše, minene šina tši tumakina da awakina? Ya faddi hakka, ya taffi, ya samna. Da maraetšie ya yi ya darime tumaki da awaki.

"By-and-bye, as they were there, when the sky began to dawn, he would go and sweep the goats' stall. The priest gave him a basket, a little one. The fox said to him. O, do give me a large one, it will be better. The priest gave him one. They laid down and slept. In the morning. he killed a sheep, put it into his basket, poured some goats' dung over it, took it up, carried it out, went into the forest, lighted a fire, cooked it, and ate it, and returned home with the basket. He sat down. In the evening he tied up the sheep and the goats; and they slept. Again in the morning he did the same as the day before. The priest, seeing his sheep and goats diminishing, said, What is it that destroys my sheep and my goats? Having said so, he went and sat down. In the evening he tied up the sheep and the goats."

Da safe ya yi ya taffi, ya kaššie baba bunsuru, ya nassa tšikin sañfo ; ya suba kašin awaki bissa garesa Šina dauka, ya faskaresa dauka, abu ya ša kansa. Kadan záši dauka, ya faskaresa. Dia mallami ta taffo, ta tše masa : ba ka ia ba dauka kaya nan ? ya tše, taffo, ki tayani dauka. Ta tše : ka rage. Ya tše, aa, ba na ia ragewa. Yarinia ta rage kášin tumaki da na awaki, ta ganni bunsuru tšikin sañfo, ta tše: O, obana! taffo, ka ganni abin da kurege ya yi ; ya tše: mi ya faru ? Ta tše, ya kaššie baban bunsuru. Ya tše, a mugum bara ! Ya tše : ku kamaši ! Sunka kamaši, sunka darimeši tšikin itatše, tunda safe har maraetšie ya yi suna bugansa, har sunka gaší, kamman zaši mutua. Sunka tše, ku berši, da safe mu bugaši; sunka darimeši nan. Da dere ya yi kura ta taffo, ta ganneši, ta tše masa; mi ya saméka, suka darimeka ?

"In the morning he went and killed a large he-goat, and put it in his basket; he put sheeps' dung and goats' dung upon it. When he was going to take it up he could not do so, the weight pulled him down ; when he was going to take it up, it was more than he was able to do. The priest's daughter came, and said to him, Canst thou not take up that load ? He replied, Come, help me to take it up. She said, Diminish it. He answered, No, no, I cannot lessen it. The girl took off some of the sheeps' dung and goats' dung, and saw the he-goat in the basket, and said, O my father ! come, see what the fox has done ! He said, What is the matter ? She replied, He has killed a large he-goat. He said, O thou bad servant ! He said, Catch him. When they had caught him, and tied him to a tree, they beat him from morning till evening, until they were tired, and the fox looked as though he was going to die. So they said Leave him, in the morning we shall beat him again : they tied him up there. In the night there came a hyena : she saw him and said to him, What is the matter with thee, that they have tied thee there ?"

Ya tše, O, sai laifi kadan na yi, sunka darimeni. Ta tše masa : en kuntšieka ? ya tše, kadan kin yirda. Ta tše: en mutum ya yi muku rána ku kan yi masa dere? Ya tše, aa, ba na yi maki dere. Ya tše mata, kadan kin kuntšieni en darimeki daga nan, da safe mutane suna taffo, su baki nama, ki tši. Ta tše dakeáo ; ta kuntšieši ; ta zakka, ta šigga, ya darimeta kwarai; ya taffi, ya berta. Da safe ya yi sunka taffo sunka ganneta, suka tše: kura tše; ku bugata, suna buganta, tana kúka, tana zao; suna buganta kwarai ; ta tšire, ta taffi tšikin daši tana neman kuŕege; ta samésa, ya yi guddu, suna guddu tare ; ba ta kamaši ba ; ya guddu, ya šigga tšikin rami. Kura tana šin hauši, ta taffi giddanta. Ši ke nan, ya káre.

"He said, O, only some little wrong I have done, for which they have tied me up. The hyena said to him, Shall I let thee loose? He said, If thou please. She asked, " If a man makes day for you, do you make night for him ?" He said, O, no, I shall not make night for thee. He said to her, If thou let me loose, so that I may tie thee up in this place, the people, coming in the morning, will give thee meat to eat. So she said, Very good. She untied him ; came, went in, and he made her very fast ; then he went away and left her. When the people came in the morning and saw her, they said, It is a hyena, beat her. They were beating her—she was crying—they were beating her well: she broke loose, and ran into the forest, seeking the fox; she found him, he was running; they were both running together, and she could not catch him ; for he ran and went into his hole. So the hyena felt vexed, and went home. This is it, it is finished."

TASUNIA.

4. *Maganan budurai biú, uwasu daía, obansu daía.*
"*The Story of the Two Girls who had the same Mother and the same Father.*"

Budurua daía ta tše ga kanuata: ni na fíki keáo; kanuata ta tše mata: ni na fiki keao. Wotšan ta tše mata, kadan kin fíni keao taffo, mu taffi tšikin dunia, mu ganní watše ta ke da dukia dayawa. Kanua ta tše dakeao. Sunka širi, sunka taffi. Da sunka taffi ga wonni gari, sunka tše ga mutane: watše ta ke da keao ga tšikinmu? Wodda ta ke da keao ku bata dukia. Woddansu mutane sunka so kanuata, woddansu mutane sunka sota; sunka basu dukia daga gari nan, sunka wutše, sunka taffi ga wonni gari; da sunka issa ya gari nan, hario mutane sunka basu dukia daga gari nan, sunka wutše.

"One of the girls said to her sister, I am more beautiful than thou. Her sister replied, I am more beautiful than thou. The former answered, If thou art more beautiful than I, come, let us go into the world, let us see which is to have most goods. Her sister said, Very well. So when they had made ready they went. Having arrived in some country, they said to the people, Which of us is most beautiful? to her which is the most beautiful you must give some goods. Some persons liked the one of the sisters, some the other, so they gave them both some goods in that country. Then they passed on, going to another country; when they had reached that country, the people again gave them some goods at that place. So they passed on."

Da sunka taffi kanuata ta samu dukia dayawa. Sunka yi yawo garurua dayawa sunka dawoyo. Da suka dawoyo sunka taffo ga bakin gulbi. Šanunsu da awakinsu, da abu duka da suka samu, sunka kawo nan, sunka ša rua. Da sunka ša rua sunka kóši kanuata ta taffi ta ša rua, iyata ta tše mata : ki kawo mani rua, en ša, ta tše da keao; ta taffi, ta daúko rua, ta kawo mata. Iyata ta tše mata: wonnan rua babu keao: awakinki da tumakinki da šanunki sunka ša, ki kawo mani kua en ša; ba na so taffi, ki kawo mani woddansu masukeao; tana šin haúši. Kanuata ta taffi, ta tše: daga nan? iyata ta tše mata: ba daganan ba, taffi gaba. Hario ta taffi wuri dasurufi nan ta fáda, ta gbata. Iyata ta kawo dukiata duka gidda.

" When they had gone on, the younger sister received much property. They travelled through many countries, and then returned. As they were returning home, they came to the shore of a lake. Their cows and their goats, and every thing which they had received, they brought with them to that place; and there they were drinking water. When they had drunk water, and were satisfied, the younger sister went to draw water. The elder sister said to her, Bring me water, that I may drink. She said, Very well; she went, took up some water, and brought it to her. Her elder sister said to her, This water is not good; thy sheep, and thy goats, and thy cows having drunk, bring me also some to drink—I do not want to go myself—bring me some that is good. (She did so because) she was jealous of her sister. The younger sister went, and said, From this? Her elder sister said, Not from that, go further. Again she went to a deep place, there she fell down and perished. The elder sister brought all her goods home."

Sunka tambayeta, sunka tše, enna abokiaki? Ta tše masu ta gbata. Sunka tše daga enna ? Ta tše masu ga tšikin gulbi. Sunka samna, kanenta ya taffi šina kiwon tumaki ga bakin rua nan; šina wakansa sunan kanuasa: zo gidda. Šina daganan šina waka šina kirra iyasa. Ya šima kadan, ya ganni ta fitto daga tšikin rua, ta taffo garesa, ya gaišieta; ta samna, ta gerta masa gašin kansa, ta šafa masa mai, ta tše masa: zani taffia gidda. Ya tše mata, wonne gidda za ki? Ta tše masa, zani taffia tšikin rua; ta taffi ta fáda tšikin rua, ba ši ganneta ba. Da maraetšie ya yi ya dawoyo ga gidda, ya faddi ga mutane: na ganni iyata. Sunka tše karia; don ba su yirda ba. Hario (gobe) ya taffi wata rana, ya samna nan šina kiwo, šina wakansa; ta fitto, ta taffo garesa, ta gaisasa, ya karigba gaisuata.

"When they were asking her, and saying, Where is thy friend? She said to them, She is lost. When they said to her, Where? She said to them, In the sea. As they were sitting down, her younger brother went feeding sheep on the shore of the lake, and singing the name of his sister, he said, Come home! So he was there singing, and calling the name of his sister. When he had waited a little, he saw her coming out of the water, and coming to him; he saluted her; she sat down, combing the hair of his head, and anointing it with oil. Then she said to him, I shall go home. He said to her, To which house art thou going? She said to him, I am going into the water. She went and fell into the water, and he saw her no more. In the evening he returned home, and told the people, I have seen my elder sister. They said, It is not true, because they did not believe it. Again, the next day, he went on another day (?) he sat down there feeding (his flock) and singing his song; she came out, and walked to him, saluted him, and he received her salutation."

Suka samna, suka yini nan. Da maraetšie ya yi, iyata ta tafji ta fáda tšıkin rua. Ši ya taffo gúlda. Hario ya faddi ga mutane, ya tše masu, da gaskia na ganneta. Ya tše masu, kadan kuna so ku ganneta ku samma tumaki, gobe nu taffi, ku ganni. Sunka tše dakeao. Da gari ya waye sunka sawoya tamaki sunka taffi wurin kiwo. Da sunka taffi wurin kiwo tare da uwan yaro da obansa, sunka sawoy ι tumaki, ya taffo ga bakin rua, ya samna šina wakansa; ta fitto daga tšikin rua, ta gai šicsa, sunka samna suna maganansu, ta tše masa. Ai dafari ba ka da tumaki ba da girima hakka! Ya tše mata, ina dasu, ta tše, ban yirda ba, su kua sunka tši tšiawa, suna ganninta. Da maraetšie ya yi ta tše masa, zani taffia gídda; ya tše dakeao. Ta gerta gašin kansa, ta šafa masa mai; ta yi masa dsapka, ta taffi gídda.

"They sat down, and remained there. In the evening his elder sister went and fell in the water, and he went home. Again he told the people and said to them, Verily I have seen her. He also said to them, If you wish to see her you must turn into sheep; to-morrow we shall go, and ye shall see her. They said, Very well. When it began to dawn they turned themselves into sheep, and went to the pasture field. When they had gone to the field, together with his mother and his father, they also having turned themselves into sheep, he came to the mouth of the sea, sat down singing his song; she came out of the water, saluted him; so they sat down, conversing with each other. And she said to him, Verily, before this thou hadst not so many sheep as these. He said to her, I had them. She replied, I do not believe it. They too (the sheep) were eating their grass and looking at her. In the evening she said to him, I am going home: he said, Very well. She combed the hair of his head, anointed it with oil, and made him plaits. Then she went home."

Ya tše masu, kun ganni diaku? *Sunka tše da gaskia mun ganneta, ta gerta gašin kanka, ta šafa maka mai, muna ganninta, dagaskia itatše.* *Sunka tše, kaka sa muyi mu saméta ?* *Akoi wonni yaro, dan sariki, ya tše masu, kadan na fušieta kuna bani ita en yi arime?* *Sunka tše, i, da gaskia muna baka ita ka yi arime.* *Ya tše dakeao.* *Ya samma kuturu, fuskansa duka babu keao, da hanuansa duka akuturtše.* *Mutane ba su sanni ba ya yi dagaṅgan.* *Ya tše masu, kadan na šigga tšikin rua, kadan ku ganni rua ya samma fari, kada ku yi murna; kadan ku ganni rua ya samma bakki, ku yi kika, kada ku yi murna; kadan ku ganni rua ya samma ša, ku yi murna, sunka tše dakeao.* *Ya dauki aska da wukasa, ya šigga tšikin rua, ya gaida mišin yarinia, ya tše: kana lafia sarikin rua?* *Dodo ya tše, sai lafia.* *Ya tše masa, kana so en yi maka aski?*

"He said to them, Have you seen your daughter? They said, Certainly, we have seen her; she combed the hair of thy head, and anointed it with oil; we saw her, certainly it was her. They said, How shall we manage to get her again. There was a certain boy there, the son of a king; and he said to them, If I get her out (of the water) will you give her to me in marriage? They said, Yes, certainly, we will give her to thee, that thou mayest marry her.' He said, Very good. He turned a leper; his whole face was not nice and his hands were full of leprosy. The people did not know that he did it on purpose. He said to them, When I have gone into the water, and you see the water turning white, ye must not rejoice; when ye see the water turning black, you must scream, you must not rejoice; when you see the water turning red, then rejoice. They said, Very good. He took a razor and his knife, and went into the water, and saluting the girl's husband, said, Art thou well, thou king of the water? Dodo answered, Quite well. He said to him, Dost thou wish me to shave thee?"

Dodo ya tše, ina so; ya tše da keao. Ya futasda aska šina askin Dodo. Mutane sunka ganni rua ya samma farifari; sunka šima kadan, sunka ganni rua ya sawoya bakki kirin, suka fara kuka. *Mutum ya yenka kán Dodo.* Sunka šima kadan, sunka ganni rua ya. sawoya ša wur, sunka fara murna, suna kiddi, suna worigi. *Mutum ya futasda yarinia daga tšikin rua. Iayénta* sunka ganneta suna murna da kuka. *Mutum ya dauki matasa, ya kai tšikin giddansa, ya yi amre da ita. Kadan ta yi tuo ta kam baši nasa daga tšikin kasko babu keao, ko kasámi, ba ta sonsa; ba ta wankewa kaskunsa da šina tšin tuo, tana beri hakka dadauda; tana baši rua tšikin kworia babu keao.*

" Dodo said, I do; he said, Very well. He pulled out the razor to shave Dodo. The people saw that the water turned very white. Having waited a little while, they observed that the water turned very black, so they began to cry. The man cut off Dodo's head. They waited a little, and saw that the water turned very red, so they begun to rejoice, beating their drums and playing. The man brought the girl out of the water. Her parents saw her, and rejoiced with tears. The man took his wife, brought her to his house, and married her. When she prepared food, she used to give him his own in a dish, which was not nice, or which was dirty; she did not love him; she did not wash his plates when he had eaten, she left them dirty; she gave him water to drink in a calabash which was not clean."

Wata rana ya tara mutane daga tšikin dandali, ya faddi ga mutane, ya tše: kun ganni tšikin kasko nan babu keao ina tšin tuo, tšikin kworia nan babu keao ina šan rua. Matata ba ta sona, don šikkina babu keao. Yao ina sauya šikkina en taffi tšikin giddana. Sunka tše mun ganni. Ya taffi, ya wanke hanunsa, ya wanke šikkinsa duka, ya sawoya šikkinsa ya samma keao, kuturta duka ta berši. Wota matše ta yi guddu, ta taffo, ta faddi ga budurua, ta tše: mišinki da ba ki so, yao ya gerta šikkinsa: massa ki wanke akošinsa, da kworiasa ta šan rua, ki wanke kwarai! Ta tše da keao; ta taši, ta wanke akoši, ta wanke kworia, ta wanke da keao, ta yi tuo maikeao, ta sa tšikin akoši, ta ašie, ta šima kadan ta ši bušebuše.

"On a certain day he assembled the people in the court, told the people, and said, Ye see from this dish, which is not nice, I am eating my food; from this calabash, which is not clean, I am drinking water. My wife does not love me, because my body is not nice; to-day, when I shall have gone in my house, I shall change my body. They said, We have seen them. He went, washed his hands, washed his whole body, and he changed his body, and it became fine, all his leprosy left him. A certain woman ran, came, told it to the girl, and said, Thy husband, whom thou didst not love, has made his body fine to-day; quickly go, wash his dish and his drinking calabash, wash them well! She said, Very good. She rose, washed the dish, and washed the calabash, and washed them well; she made very good food, and put it in the dish; put it aside, and waited a little till it was dry."

Mišinta ya taffo, ya šigga tšikin gidda ; ya ganni akošinsa, da kworiasa awanke, da tuo nagari. Ya tše ga matasa : ni ba na so en tši daga tšikin akoši nan maikeao, ba na so en ša daga tšikin kworia nan maikeao, ki bani daga tšikin kaskona da babu keao en tši, daga tšikin kworiata da babu keao en ša. Ba na son tši daga tšikin akoši nan maikeao, da kworia nan maikeao, sai kin taffi, kin kawo wuzia n dan zakainya, kin wanke akoši nan, da kworia an, kána en tši, en ša daga tšikinsu. Ta lše da keao. Ta taffi tšikin dākinta, ta samna, ta tše, kaka sani en kawo wuzia dan zakainya ? Ta taffi, ta faddi ga wota matše, ta tše, mišina ba ia so ya tši ya ša daga tšikin kworia nan maikeao, daga tšikin akoši nan maikeao ; ya tše, sai na taffi, na kawo wuzia dan zakainya, na wanke akoši nan da kworia nan kána ya ša daga tšikinsu.

"Her husband came, and went into the house; he saw his dish and his calabash washed, and good food in them. He said to his wife, As for me, I do not want to eat out of this dish, which is clean; I do not want to drink from this calabash, which is now clean; give me in my dish which is dirty, that I may eat, and in my calabash which is not nice, that I may drink. I do not want to eat from this clean dish, and this clean calabash, except thou shalt go, and bring the tail of a young lion, and wash the dish and the calabash with it, and then I shall eat and drink out of them. She said, Very well. She went into her room, sat down, and said, How shall I manage to get the tail of the child of a lion ? She went, told it to another woman, and said, My husband will not eat, he will not drink from the calabash which is clean, nor from the dish which is clean ; he says, that I should go and bring the tail of the child of a lion, that I should wash the plate and the calabash with it, then he would drink out of them."

Matše ta tše mata, abin da kinka yi masa dafari ši ne, šina rama maki yansu. Matše ta tše, ina tayaki, ki taffi, ki gerta hazi, ki wanke, ki beri dzari nan, kūdáše su fáda daga tšikinsa ; ki dauka kudaše nan, ki sōyésu, ki dauka ki taffi tšikin dáši; kadan kin taffi kin ganni uwa yanzakainya ki hawa bíssa itatše, ki samna, kadan uwa yanzakainya ta bude baki, ki suba tšikin bakinta massa, kina samu wuzia danzakainga ; ta tše dakeao. Ta taffi tšikin giddanta ta dauke hazi, ta yi surife, ta wanke-hazi, ta dauke ruan hazi, ta ašie ; kudaše sunka šigga, ta dauki kudaše nan duka, ta soyesu ; ta dauka ta taffi tšikin daši, ta išie uwa yanzakainya ; ta hawa bissa itatše. Uwa yanzakainya tana gerta gášin kura ; ta gaši, ta bude bakinta bissa. Matše ta dauki kudaše massa, ta suba tšikin bakin uwa danzakainya, uwa yanzakainya ta tšainye.

" The woman said to her, This is what thou hast done to him, he now takes vengeance on thee. The woman said, I will help thee ; go, prepare some corn, wash it, and leave the pure corn, that the flies may fall into it ; take the flies, and boil them, take them and go into the forest; when thou hast gone and seen the mother of the young lions climb upon a tree, sit down there ; when the mother of the young lions opens her mouth, pour them into her mouth quickly, and thou wilt get the tail of the child of the lion. So she said, Very good. She went into her house, took corn, soaked it, washed the corn, took the water of the corn, and put it aside. When the flies had got in, she took all the flies, and boiled them ; took them up and went into the forest. There she met the mother of the young lions : she climbed upon a tree."

Hario ta šima kadan, ta bude bakinta bissa; Matše ta suba mata kamma nadá. Uwa yanzakainya ta tše ga kurá, ki taffi giddanki, yao na gáši; ba ta sanni ba uwa yanzakainya tana šin dáda, ta tše na taši. Kura ta taffi. Uwa yanzakainya ta taši, ta dubi bissa itatše, ba ta ganni ba kŏnwa, ta tše, wanéne bíssa itatše nan? Matše ta amsa ta tše mata, ni tše matše; ta tše mata sído kassa, ta tši ba na ia ba. Ta tše, uwa yanzakainya ta tše, domi ba ki šidowa? ta tše, kadan na šido dianki su tšainyéni; ta tše aa, ba zasu tšinki ba, ki taffo kassa. Matše ta šída; ta dauki saurán kudaše, ta bayes ga uwa yanzakainya. Uwa yanzakainya ta tše, mi kina so kin taffo naná? Ta tše mata, ina son wuzia na danki daia; ta tše da keao; ki taffo en rufeki, kada su taffo, su ganneki. Ta tše da keao. Matše ta šigga tšikin rafonia. Uwa danzakainya ta rufeta.

"The mother of the young lions was plaiting the hair of a hyena; when she was tired, she opened her mouth. The woman taking some of the flies quickly and poured them into the mouth of the mother of the young lions, and the mother of the young lions ate them. Again, having waited a little, she opened her mouth; the woman poured something into it as before. The mother of the young lions said to the hyena, Go to thy house, I am tired to-day; she (hyena) did not know that the mother of the young lions felt sweet when she said, I am tired. The hyena went. The mother of the young lions got up, and looked up on the tree, but could not see any body; and said, Who is there on the tree? The woman answered and said to her, It is I, a woman. She said to her, Come down. She answered, I cannot come down. She said, that is, the mother of the young lions said, Why canst thou not come down? She answered, If I come down, thy children will eat me. She said, Oh no, no, they will not eat thee, come down.

Da ta rufeta, da maraetšie ya yi dianta sunka taffo, sunka ši kamšin mutum, sunka tše, uwamu! Yao muna šin warin mutum! Ta tše masu karia, énna kunka ši warin mutum? Tana kuka ta tše, kuna tšewa akoi warin mutum, ni ban ši ba. Baba danzakainya ya taffo, ya tše, ki samna, domi kina kuka? Da suka taffi suka yi beritši, uwa danzakainya ba ta yi ba beritši; ta tše ga mutše, ki fitto, ki taffi, ki yenke wuzia auta danzakainya; ta tše da keao. Ta tše mata, kadan kin ganni dáki šina fari, kada ki taffo, don ba suna beritši ba; kadan kin ganni daki bakki kerin ki šigga suna beritši. Ta tše da keao.

"The woman went down, took the remainder of the flies, and gave it to the mother of the young lions. The mother of the young lions said, What dost thou want, having come to this place? She said to her, I want the tail of one of thy children. She said, Very well; come, let me hide thee, that they cannot see thee when they come home. She said, Very good. The woman went into the store-room, the mother of the young lions covered her over. When she had covered her, and it was evening, her children came, and perceived the smell of a human being, and said, O, our mother! to-day we perceive the smell of a human being! She said to them, It is a lie; where do you perceive the smell of a human being? She was crying, and said, Ye suppose that there is a smell of a human being, and I do not perceive it? The father of the young lions came, and said, Sit down, what art thou crying for? When they went to sleep, the mother of the young lions did not go to sleep; but said to the woman, Come out, go, cut off the tail of the smallest of the young lions. She said, Very well. Then she said to her, When thou seest that the room is light, thou must not come, because they are not asleep; but when thou seest that the room is very dark, go in, they will be asleep. She said, Very good."

APPENDIX. 187

Matše tana dauka wukata karama daga tšikin alšifunta, ta taffi, ta ganni daki fari, ta yi guddu, ta taffo ta gboya, ta tše, ba su yi ba beritši. Sunka taffo wurin uwasu, sunka tše : mun ga mutum ! ta tše masu karia, ta tše ku taffi, ku yi beritši. Sunka taffi sunka yi beritši ; matše ta taffo, ta ganni daki bákki kerin, ta šigga ta taba karami auta dan zakainya, ta yenke wuziansa. Uwa yanzakainya ta tše mata, ki guddu massa, ki taffi tšikin gari. Matše ta tše da keao. Ta taffi tana guddu, ta samu wuzia ta danzakainya. Dasafe dia yanzakainya sunka taši suna tšewa, ina taši da wuziata bissai (bissaye).

Wonnan kua ya tše šina tšewa, ina taši da wuziata bissai Su duka sunka taši da wuziansu, karami ya taši, ya tše, ina da wuziata gundul, (gašiere) ya taši babu wuzia. Sunka dauki guruminsu suna kidde, suna tšewa da baya ! da baya ! wonda ya yenke wuzia danzakainya ši dawoyo ?

"The woman, taking her little knife out of her pocket, went, but saw the room was light; she ran, came, and hid herself, and said, They are not asleep. They came to their mother's place, and said, We have seen a man ! She said to them, It is a lie ! She said to them, Go, lay down and sleep. When they had gone, and had fallen asleep, the woman came, and saw that the room was very dark : she went in, touched the little one, the youngest of the lion's children, and cut off its tail. The mother of the young lions said to the woman, Run quickly, and go into the town. The woman said, Very good. She went running : she had got the tail of the young lion. In the morning the brood of young lions got up, saying, I am rising with my tail erect."

" Another one too got up, saying, I rise with my tail erect. When they had all got up with their tails, the youngest got up, and said, I have but the stump of a tail—for he got up without a tail. They said, Who is it that cut off the tail of the youngest of the lion's children ?"

Matše ta dawoyo baya kadankadan. Uwa danzakainya da ta ganni matše nĕsa tana dawoyowa, ta tše ga dianta, ku bani gurumi ni ina kiddi, tana kiddinta tana tšewa dagaba da gaba! Matše ta taffi gaba tana guddu. Ta taffo tšikin gari; ta kawo wuzia danzakainya, ta taffi tšikin giddanta, ta wanke akoši da wuzia danzakainya, ta wanke kworia da ita. Hario ta darowoye, ta sa tuo tšikin akoši, ta sa rua tšikin kworia, ta kawo tuo gaba ga mišinta, ta kawo rua gaba ga mišinta; kána ya sa hanunsa, ya tši tuo. Daga rana nan ta sanni ši dan sariki ne.

Ši ke nan, ya kare; maganan yamata biu ya kare.

"Having taken their drums, they were drumming, saying, Backwards, backwards, he who cut off the tail of the lion's child, let him return! The woman was turning back a very little. The mother of the young lions, when she saw the woman from a distance returning, said to her children, Give me your drums, I myself will beat the drums; so she was drumming and saying, Forwards, forwards! The woman went forwards running. She came to the town, bringing with her the tail of a young lion, went into her house, washed the dish with the tail of the young lion, and washed the calabash with it. Again she dried them, put food in the dish, and put water into the calabash, brought the food before her husband, and brought water before her husband: then he put his hand to it, and ate his food. From that day she knew that he was the son of a king."

"This is it; it is finished; the story of the Two Girls is at an end."

TASUNIA.

5. *Tasunian uwa da dánta.*
"*The Story of the Mother and her Boy.*"

(This Story was told to some children in English, and related by Dorugu in Hausa.)

Akoi wota matše tana da dū, amma ši marashaṅkali ši ke ; ba šina da wayo ba kammada woddansu yara. Saodaia uwasa ta aikesa ya taffi, don ya sayo mata álúra. Da ya taffi, ya sayi alura, ya gammu da yaro šina da saṅfo tšike da dūsá, ya tše ga yaro, enna zani sa alurata ? Ya tše masa, ka sata ga tšikin dusa. Da ya sa, da ya yi kussa ga gíddansu ya tambayi yaro, enna alurasa ? Yaro ya tše, ka duba ga tšikin dusa. Da ya duba ba ši samu ba alura, ya taffi ga giddansu. Da ya taffo uwasa ta tše masa, enna alura ? Ya tše na gammu da yaro šina da saṅfo tšike da dūsá, da na tše masa, enna zani sa alura ? Ya tše mani, ka sa ga tšikin dusa, amma da mun yi kussa ga gídda, da na duba ga tšikin dusa, ban samu ba.

"There was a certain woman who had a son, but he was a senseless fellow, he had not the good sense as other boys have. On one occasion his mother sent him to go and buy a needle for her. When he had gone to buy the needle, he met a boy who had a basket full of bran: he said to the boy, Where shall I put my needle? He replied, Put it in the basket of bran. So he put it there. When they were near the house, he asked the boy where the needle was: the boy answered, Look for it in the bran. He looked for it, but could not find it, so he went home. When he arrived, his mother said to him, Where is the needle? He answered, I met with a boy who had a basket full of bran, and I said to him, Where shall I put my needle? and he told me to put it in the bran; but as we were coming near to the house, I looked for it in the bran, but could not find it."

Uwasa ta tše masa, kai ba kada wáyo ; domi ba ka sata ba ga hanun riganka, ka kawo mani ? Kadan ka taffi, ka sayín alura, ka sata ga hanun riganka!

Da suka samna ta aikesa, ya taffi, ya sayo mata mai massa, ta tše masa, ka yi guddu. da ka dawoyo da guddu; hakkanan ya taffi da guddu, ya sayi mai, ya sa gu hanun rigasa, ya yi guddu, amma tunda šina guddu mai šina narikewa, šina fadua kassa; amma da ya zakka sai ya kawo mai kadan. Uwasa ta tše masa, enna mai? Ya tše, mai ya narike, sai kadan ga hanuna. Amma uwasa ta yi fuši tana sagensa, ta tše, domi ba ka sa ba ga tšikin tulu, da ka kawo mani? Kadan ka taffi kuma ka sa ga tšikin tulu, da ka rufe tulu kwarai, ka kawo mani!

"His mother said to him, O, thou hast no sense! Why didst thou not put it in the sleeve of thy coat, and bring it to me? Whenever thou goest to buy a needle, put it in the sleeve of thy coat!"

"When they had sat down, she sent him to go and buy some butter for her quickly; she said to him, Go running and return running. So he went running, bought some butter, put it in his sleeve, and run; but as he was running, the butter melted in his sleeve, and dropped down, so when he came home there was only a little butter left. His mother said to him, Where is the butter? He said, The butter is melted, only a little is in my sleeve. But his mother was angry, and scolding him said, Why didst thou not put it into a pot, and bring it to me? When thou dost go again, thou must put it into a pot, cover it well, and bring it to me!"

Da suka samna kwanaki kadan, uwasa ta tše masa, ya taffi, ya kawo dan karre daga giddan abukainsa. Amma da ya taffi, ya gaida masugidda, ya tše masu : uwata ta aikoni, don en dauka dan kuikuyo, sunka tše da keao. Da suka baši ya sa ga tšikin tulu, ya rufe bakin tulu kwarai. Da ya zakka ga gidda, uwasa ta tše, enna karre? Ya tše, šina ga tšikin tulu. Amma uwasa ta tše: ba ši yi kuka ba, da ka saši daga tšiki? Ya tše, í, ya yi kuka, ina tamaha šina šin murna. Da uwasa ta bude tulu ta samu karre amatše! ta tše, kai makelatši ka ke! Amma ya tše, ke kinka fadda mani hakka, kadan na taffi, en kawo wonni abu, ka sa ga tšikin tulu, hakkanan ni kua na yi. Ta tše masa, ya fi ka sa igia ga wuyansa, da ka tše masa: ka taffo, ka taffo!

"When they had sat down a few days, his mother said to him, Go and bring a little dog from the house of his friends. So when he had gone, he saluted the inmates, and said to them, My mother has sent me to fetch a little dog. They said to him, Very well. When they had given it to him, he put it in the pot, and covered the mouth of the pot well. So when he came home, his mother asked, Where is the dog? He replied, He is in the pot. But his mother said, Did he not cry when thou didst put him in? He said, Yes, he cried, I think he was pleased. When his mother opened the pot, she found that the dog was dead! and said, O thou cruel fellow! He said, Thou didst tell me that when I went to fetch something for thee, to put it into a pot, and so I did. She said to him, It would have been better to have tied a string round his neck, and to have said, Come along, come along!"

Hakkanan ga wota safia ya taffi, ya sayo tšinia dan akwia. Amma da ya taffi ya sayi tšinia akwia, ya darime tšinia da igia, ya fara ša šina tšewa : ka taffo! ka taffo! Da karnuka suka ši hakka, suka yi guddu zua garesa, suka tšainye tšinia, sai kašši ya ša zua ga gidda. Uwasa ta tše, enna nama? Ya tše, gaši, ta tše, kai, marashankali ka ke. Ta tše, wonnan ne ka ke kirra nama? Dzafon kašsi. Ya tše, ke kinka aikeni. Da gabá ga wonnan ta tše, ba na kára aikenka!

"Then again he went one morning to buy a leg of mutton. And when he had gone and bought the leg of mutton, he tied a string to the leg of mutton, and began drawing it, and saying, Come along! come along! When the dogs heard it, they ran, came to him, and devoured the mutton, and he dragged nothing home except the bone. His mother said, Where is the meat? He answered, See it there. She said, O, thou senseless fellow! saying, Is this what thou dost call meat? a mere bone! He said, Eh, but thou didst send me! Henceforth, she said, I shall not send thee again!"

6. Maganan mutume Iṅliz da Sandansa.
"*The Story of an Englishman and his Stick.*"

Mu rubutu magana wonni mutum, da na ši daga Bornu. Mutume Iṅliz ya taffi wonni gari, ya samna tšikin garinan, šina da sanda tšikke da azurufa. Rana daia ya fitta woše, ya samna kalikašin wonni itatše; da zaši dawoyowa gidda ya mantše sandansa. Woddansu mutane sunka ganni sanda sunka dauka, sanda da naúyi, suka tše: wotše irin sanda ke nan da nauyi kakka? Daiansu ya daúka bissa kai. Suna taffia mutume nan da ya mantše sandansa, ya ganni mutane sun dauka bissa kai, ya kirrawosu, ya tše, ku saida mani sanda nan? Sunka tše masa : ka sayé, ko nawa ka saye, mu ši? Ya tše masu, ni baku alura duba, da sanda alkamura bokoi, da turare kadan.

"Let us write the story of a certain man, which I heard in Bornu. An Englishman went to a certain town, and sat down in that town : he had a stick filled with silver. One day he went out, and sat down under a tree : when he was returning home he forgot his stick. Some persons saw the stick and picked it up. As the stick was heavy, they said to each other, What sort of stick can this be, being of such a weight ? One of them took it on his head. As they were going along, the man who had forgotten his stick, seeing that the people had taken it up, called upon them, and said, Will you sell me that stick ? They said, Well, buy it, or let us hear for how much thou dost want to buy it ? He said to them, I shall give you one thousand needles, and seven yards of white linen, and a little frankincense."

Sunka tše da keao: suka baši sanda. Bissa sanda nan akoi tagiá karami. Ya dauki makubli, ya būdé, mutane suna ganninsa: ya bude sanda, ya awuna da hanunsa saouku, ya tše, daidai ne. Ya basu alura, ya basu alkamura, ya basu turare, sunka taffi, wonnan ya kare.

"They said, Very well, and gave him the stick. There was a little cap on the stick; he took the key and opened it, while the people were looking at him; he opened the stick, and measured (the money) with his hands three times, and said, It is quite correct. He gave them the needles, he gave them the linen, he gave them the frankincense: they went away. This is finished."

7. Magana yarinia da samari fudu.

"*The Story of the Girl and the Four Bachelors*'.'

Yarinia wonnan tana da keao ; tšikin garinsu duka babu budurua, da ta fita keao. Da samari fuda, suna da keao kamman ita, sunka tše, muna zua, mu dauka yarinia nan. Daia ya tše, ni zani daukanta suna girdáma. Hakkanan yaro na wonni gari ya zakka, ya daukēta, ya kaita garinsu. Obanta ya ši labari diansa ta yi arime ; ya taši, ya hawa bissa dokinsa, ya taffi garinsu yaro nan, ya kawo diansa tšikin giddansa.

Šina da rakumi tšikin giddansa. Ya tara mutane duka, yarinia ta tše: kowane ya hawa bissa rakumi nan, ba ši fádi ba ši ne mišina.

" This girl was very beautiful; in the whole town there was no girl that surpassed her in beauty. But there were four young men, all as beautiful as she, and they said, Let us go and take the girl. One of them said, I shall go and take her for myself; so they were quarrelling with one another. In the meantime, a young man from another town came, took the girl, and carried her to his house. When the girl's father heard the news of his daughter's marriage, he got up, mounted his horse, went to the boy's town, and brought his daughter back to his house."

" He had a camel in his house. He gathered all the people together; and the girl said to them, Any of you that shall mount this camel, and not fall down, shall be my husband."

Mutane duka sun sa riga maikeao ; amma mišinta nafari ya taffo, ya dauki búsu, ya samna tšikin mutane, amma yarinia ta sanni ši ne mišinta nafari. Mutane duka sunka taši ta tše, kowane ya yi sūkuá rakumi nan saouku baši fādi ba, mišina ke nan.

Wonni ya taffo, ya hawa rukumi sunka baši būlála, ya yi sūkuá, ya fadi. Wonni ya taffo, ya yi sukua, ya fadi. Mutane duka, kowane, ya yi sukua sai ya fadi. Yarinia ta taffo, ta taffi wurin yaro šina búsú, ta tše, wa ? ga mutane, ka baši rakumi nan, ya yi sukua ? Mutane duka suka tše : mu ba mu ia ba, ši šina iawa ? Yarinia ta tše : ku hankura, ku baši, ya yi sukua kadan. Sunka tše da keao. Ya taffo, ya hawa bissa rakumi, sunka baši bulala, ya yi sukua rakumi saouku, anafudu ya taffo, ya dauki yarinia, ya ašieta bissa rakumi.

"The people all put on their best garments; but her husband, her first love, came and took a mat, and sat down among the people; the girl, however, knew that he was her husband, her first one. When the people all had got up, she said to them, Whosoever of you shall gallop this camel three times without falling down, shall be my husband."

" There came one, mounted the camel, and when they had given him a whip, he galloped and fell down; another came, galloped and fell; all the people, every one of them, galloped, but fell. So the girl came, and went to the place where the young man was sitting down on his mat, and said, Which of you people will give him the camel that he may have a run ? The people all said, What, we, we were not able, and he, shall he be able to do it ? The girl said, Have patience, give it him, that he may run a little. So they said, Very well. He came, mounted the camel, and when they had given him the whip, he run three times, and the fourth time he came, took up the girl, put her on the camel, and galloped off with her."

Oban yarinia šina da doki nakwarai šina guddu. Mutume nan šina guddu da yarinia bissa rakumi. Obanta ya taši, ya kawa bissa doki, šina sukua, ya ašie hantšin doki daidai da wuzian rakumi suna guddu. Yaro ya šigga tšikin giddansa, ya rufe kofa. Oban yarinia kaffa dokinsa ta madzu ga itatšen kofa, ya futas, ya dawoyo gidda. Ši ke nan ya kare, maganan yarinia da yara fudu.

"The girl's father had a horse, a fine one, one that could run well. The young man was running away with the girl on the camel. Her father arose, he mounted his horse, galloped, he put the horse's nose to the camel's tail as they were galloping. The boy went into his house, and shut the door. As to the girl's father, the foot of his horse was squeezed between the door-posts: he pulled it out, and returned home. This is it, it is finished, the Story of the Girl and the Four Young Men is at an end."

8. *Magana matše da mišinta.*
"*The Story of the Woman and her Husband.*"
Namiši kowotše rana šina taffia farauta ba ši kaššiewa komi ši kan taffo ga gidda. Wota rana ya taffi farauta, ya kama babe, ya nadeši daga tšikin dáši da tšiawa dayawa, ya sasi, ya darime šina taffowa gidda. Da ya taffo giddansa ya ašie. Matasa ta ganni tana tamaha nama ne, ta wanke tukunia kwarai, ta taffi, ta fura wuta, ta dora tukunia, ta taffo tana budawa, ba ta ganni ba nama, sai sansami, tana budawa ta ganni babe, ya táši. Ta tše ga mišinta : nama, da ka kawo, ya taffi. Ya tše, ha ! Matasa tana da tšiki. Ya tše mata, ki taffi, ki kamaši koénna ya šigga. Matše ta táši, ta dauki kára tana taffia ta buga fara ; fara ta táši, ta taffi, ta šída, matše ta taffi, ta buga fara, fara ta taši, ba ta ia kamawa.

"The husband went hunting every day, but when he did not kill any thing, he used to come home again. One day he went hunting and caught a locust; he rolled it up in much grass in the desert, laid it aside, tied it up, as he was coming home. When he had come in his house, he laid it aside; his wife saw it, and, thinking that it was some creature, she washed her pot well, went and lit a fire, and put the pot on; she then came, and, on opening it saw no creature, only leaves; but as she was opening it carefully, she saw the locust getting up. So she said to her husband, The creature which thou hast brought is gone away! He said, Oh! His wife was with child. He said to her, Go, catch it wherever it has gone. The woman arose, and took a head of guinea-corn, and as she was going, she struck at the locust; the locust started, went on and alighted again; the woman struck at the locust, the locust got up, and she could not catch it."

APPENDIX. 199

Fara ta taši; ta taffi tana bi, ta buga, sai fara tana taši, ba ta ia kamawa. Har maraetšie ya yi rana ta fadi, ba ta ia ganni. Ta samu kogón itatše, da girima, ta šígga, ta samna. Ga wata nan ɩa haifi danta namiši. Tana taffia ta nema abintši kadan, ta taffo, ta tši, tana bayes ga danta nono, ya ša; tana taffia tana nema abintši kadan. Kadan ta taffo, ta samna tana bayes ga danta nono har danta ya yi wayo kadan. Šina taffia wurin záki, amma zaki šina so, ši kášsiesi, ši kan yi daria; zaki ši kan berši. Zaki ya haifi diansa; kowotše rana yaro ši kan taffo wurin zaki, ši kan taffi wurin uwasa; kowotše rana zaki ši kan kaššie nama, ši kan kawo ga diansa. Yaro šina nan šina samne, šina ganni har yanzaki sunka saba dáši. Sun sanni warin mutum.

"The locust got up, again she went after it, striking at it; again the locust would get up, and she was not able to catch it; she did so until night came on, and the sun had set, and she could not see any longer. She found a hollow tree, a large one, went into it, and sat down there. In the same month she gave birth to her child, a male child. She went to look for a little food, came back, and ate it, giving the breast to her child, and he sucked. She went again in search of a little food, and came back, sat down, giving her child the breast, until her child had got a little sense. He then went to the lion's place; but when the lion wanted to kill him, he used to laugh; so the lion used to let him alone. The lion gave birth to her brood. The boy was in the habit of coming every morning to the lion's place, and then he went back again to his mother's place. The lion used to kill some creature every day, and to bring it home to his brood; the boy being there, and sitting down, saw every thing, until the young lions chose to go to the forest. They knew the scent of men."

Saodaia zaki ya kaššie nama, ya kawo ga diansa sunka tši, yaro ya taffi wurin uwasa. Ya taffo hario. Wata rana zaki ya taffi ; uwasa tana taffia tšikin daši, zaki ya ganné ta, ya kaššieta, ya kawota ga diansa. Danzaki ya ganni, ya ki tši, ya yi fúši, sunka taffi, sunka yi rami, sunka bisne uwan yaro, su(n)ka samne. Danzaki šina taffia šina golgodawa kaffansa da na uwasa, šina ganni ba daidai ba. Ši kan taffo, ši kan samna, har ya girima, ya ganni kaffasa daidai da na uwasa; ya taffo, ya samna, ya yi kibba. Dan matše šina girima. Danzaki da ya ganni kaffasa daidai da na uwasa, ya taffi, ya kamata, ya kaššieta, ya kawo ga yaro, ya tše: kai kua ka tši ; yaro ya ki tši. Su duka sunka samna babu uwa. Sunka taffi, sunka bisne uwan zaki. Samma samma dan mutum ya girima; dan zaki ya girima, su duka biu sun girima.

" At one time the lion killed some creature, brought it to his brood, and when they had eaten it (together), the boy went to the place of his mother ; he came again. A certain day the lion went; and as the boy's mother had gone into the forest, the lion saw her and killed her, and brought her to his brood. The lion's son, seeing who it was, refused to eat, and was very angry, and when they had gone, and made a hole and buried the boy's mother, they sat down. The son of the lion used to go and compare his foot (steps) with those of his mother, and when he saw that they were not alike, he would come again, and sit down until he was grown up, and saw that his footsteps were like those of his mother ; so he came, sat down, and got fat. The son of the woman was growing. And as to the son of the lion, when he saw that his footsteps were like those of his mother, he went, caught her, and killed her, and brought her to the boy, saying, Now thou must eat. The boy refused to eat. They both were sitting down without a mother; so they went and buried the mother of the lion. By and by, the son of the man was great, the son of the lion was also great, they both were great."

Samma samma yaro ya tše ga zaki, zani taffia garimu. Zaki ya tše da keao. Yaro ya tše : ina son ríga. Zaki ya tše da keao. Zaki ya taffi, ya kwanta ga hainyan fatake. Fatake sun taffo suna wutšewa, ya fada ko ya túma tšikinsu.

Mutane sunka guddu, zaki ya kawo riga dayawa, kowotše irin riga, da kore, da zanné, turkedi, da barage, da fara riga, da riga alharini; kowotše irin tufuwa ya kawo, ya bayes ga yaro. Yaro ya tše na gode. Hario ya tše, ina so maši, ina so gilma, ina so wuka, ina so kori da baka, ina so dukia. Zaki ya tše da keao ; ya taffi, ya kwanta bissa hainya. Fatake suna taffowa, ya túma, ya fáda tšikinsu. Mutane duka sunka waze, ya kawo maši, ya kawo kansakali, ya kawo wuka, ya kawo gilma, ya kawo masa duka abin da ya fadda masa. Yaro ya tše da keao. Yaro ya dauki dúkiasa, ya taffo tšikin gari, ya samna, babu wonda ya sannši, har ya yi arime.

"By and by, the boy said to the lion, I shall go to my town. The lion answered, Very well. The boy said, I want some garments. The lion said, Very good. The lion went, he laid down in the merchants' road. When the merchants came, passing that way, he fell or jumped upon them. When the people had run away, the lion brought plenty of garments, every kind of garments, both black clothes, and unmade clothing, and dyed clothes and striped, and white dresses and silk dresses: every kind of clothing he brought and gave them to the boy. The boy said, I thank thee. Again he said, I want spears, and axes. ... I want knives, I want bows and arrows, I want goods. The lion said, Very good: he went and laid down in the road. When the merchants came, he jumped up and fell upon them; and when all the people were dispersed he brought the spears, he brought the swords, he brought the knives, he brought the axes, he brought him all the things which he had told him. The boy said, Very good. The boy took his property and went to his town, and sat down: there was no one that knew him until he was

Zaki šina taffowa tšikin gari, da dere šina taffowa wurin yaro, kowonne dere hakkanan šina taffowa wurin yaro, da dere. Wota rana da dere ya taffo, ya šígga tšikin daki; šina samne da abokinsa. Matan yaro ta taffo, ta fura wuta, ta ga zaki, ta yi ufu (ko ta yi kururua), ta ši dsóro. Zaki ya hawa, ya tangana ga itatše, kaffansa biu bíssa, kaffansa biu kassa. Matše tana tšewa, akoi zaki tšikin giddamu! Yaro šina tšewa, enna ši ke? Šina tšewa, babu zaki nan. Zaki ya futta da safe, gari bai waya ba kwaraí. Ya taffo, ya tše ga yaro, kadan ka ši na yi kúka daia na mutu, kadan ka ši na yi kúku biu, ban mutu ba. Yaro ya tše da keao. Yaro sutšiasa ta gbatše. Zaki ya taffi tšikin daši, ya yi kuka saodaia, ba ši kara ba, ya mutu, Yaro ya ši, ya gerta wuka da keao tana da kaifi, ya daúka ya taffi.

" The lion came in the town by night, coming to the boy's place; every night he came to the boy's place. On a certain occasion he came by night, and went into the room, sitting down with his friend. The boy's wife came to light the fire, and saw the lion. She screamed, and was afraid. The lion climbed up, and leaned against a tree: two of his legs were upwards, and two of his legs were downwards. The woman continued saying, There is a lion in our house? The boy was asking, Where is he? and continued saying, There is no lion here. The lion went out early in the morning, the sky had not yet begun to dawn well; he came and said to the boy, If thou shalt hear me cry once, I die, if thou shalt hear me cry twice, I do not die. The boy said, Very well; but the boy's heart was broken. The lion went into the forest, he cried once, and added no more, and died. When the boy heard it, he sharpened his knife very well, it had a sharp edge, took it, and went away."

Ya tše ga matasa, zani en mutu. Ya taffi šina neman wuri enda zaki ši ke ; ya ganni zaki ya mutu ; ya dauki wuka, ya kaššie kansa, ya mutu kussa ga zaki. Su duka biú su mutu ; wonni mutum ya taffi, ya ganni yaro da zaki sun mutu wuri daia. Ya kirrawo mutanen gari, sunka daukesu, sunka kaisu, su duka biu, suka bisnesu wuri daia. Ši ke nan, ya kare, maganan mutum da matasa ; sai zaki dzakkaninsu.

"He said to his wife, I am going to die. He went looking for the place where the lion was; he saw that the lion was dead; took his knife and killed himself close to the lion ; both were dead. A certain man came and saw that both the boy and the lion had died at the same place. He called for the people of the town, and when they had taken them up, and carried them away, both of them, they buried them together. This is it, it is finished, the Story of the Man and his Wife. Alas! the lion came between them."

9. *Magana da biri.*
"*The Story of the Origin of Monkeys.*"

Biri dafari ši mutum ne.
Suna káma kīfi dayawa sun tši. Wonni lottu mutume Alla ya zakka, ya tše masu: kuna kama kīfi dayawa; rana alšima ku bersu, su tši kadan; Kowonne lottu kuna kamasu kuna tši, ranu alšima ku bersu, su kua su tši! Suka tše da keao. Matše, rana alšima ta yi, ta taffo tšikin gulbi daukan rua, ta ganni kīfi dayawa, ta kama, ta dauka rua, ta taffi gidda, ta faddi ga mása, ta tše: kuna gidda, kuna kwantše, ga kīfi sun fitto dayawa tšikin gulbi, suna tši abintši, ku taffi ku kamasu, ku kawo su, mu tši. Mása sunka tše: Mutume Alla ya taffo, ya faddi mamu, kada mu káma yao, rana daia: da mutume Alla ya taffi, ya bersu. Mata sunka tše, kadan ba ku káma kīfi ba, ba mu sonku ba.

"Monkeys in ancient times were men."
"They caught plenty of fishes, and ate them. One time a man of God came to them, and said to them, You may catch plenty of fishes, but on Sunday ye must leave them alone, that they may eat a little. Every day ye may catch them and eat them, but on Sunday ye must leave them, that they may also eat. They said, Very well. When Sunday came again, a certain woman came to the lake to fetch water: she saw many fish, caught some, took the water and went home, and told the men, saying, Ye are staying at home, and lying down, see the fish, many of them came out of the lake to eat something, go ye, catch them, and bring them that we may eat them. The men answered, A man of God came, and told us that we should not catch them to-day, this one day; and the man of God went away and left us. The woman said, If ye do not go to catch fish, we shall not love you."

Masa sunka tše, máta suna kímu, mun ki kama kífi; mu taffi, mu kama kifi. Sunka taffi, sunka kama kifi dayawa, sunka kawo gidda; mutume Alla ya dawoyo, ya tše masu: ba ku ši ba magana da na fadda maku? Mása sunka tše, mun ši, sai mátamu sunka ki ši; ya tše masu, ina tše muku, kada ku kama rana alšima. Ya tše masu: Alla ši dauka muku alberka, ku kawa wonni abu, ku šigga tšikin daši. Sunka sawoya, sunka yi wuzia, suna taffia hanu tare da kaffa, suna taka kassa, suna taffia. Ši ke nan na ši, na fadda maka, ko karia ko gaskia ban sanni ba.

"The men said, Our wives hate us, because we refuse to catch fish, let us go to catch some. When they had gone and caught plenty, and were bringing them home, the man of God returned, and said to them, Did ye not hear the word which I told you? The men answered, We heard it, but our wives would not hear it. He said to them, Verily I said to you, that ye should not catch fish on a Sunday. He therefore said to them, God will take away from you some blessing, you will be turned into something else, and go into the forest. So they were changed, and got tails, and walked on their hands and on their feet, touching the ground as they were walking. This it is, so I heard it, and told it to thee; whether it is a lie or a truth, I do not know."

10. *Magana da mutane biu.*
"*A Story about Two Men.*"

Akoi mutum daia šina da hazi dayawa, kadan ya ši almaširi, šina roko hazi, don ši samu ši tši, ši kan guddu, ši kan fitta daga bayan gidda, ši kan taffi gona, ba ya so almaširi; da ya mutu akasaši tšikin alidšana.

Akoi wonni mutum ya yi saddaka dayawa; kurdinsa šina bai ga mutane, da hazinsa šina bayes ga talakawa; da ya mutu akasaši tšikin wuta, hazinsa dayawa tšikin lahira. Mutum wonnan da ya šigga tšikin alidžana babu hazi wurinsa. Hazi daia daia šina fadawa tšikin giddansa, šina dauka, šina tši; ya tše, enna wonnan mutum ši ke? Sun tše, šina tšikin wuta. Ya tše, ku kawoši, da hazinsa duka, mu samna tare daši, mu tši hazinsa. Mutum da šina tšikin wuta sunka kawoši da hazinsa duka, akasaši tšikin alidžana, sunka samna tare dasu, wonda ya kirrawoši, ya sami alidžana, ya ši dádi.

"There was a man who had much corn: when he heard a beggar asking for corn, that he might get something to eat, he used to run away, come out and hide behind his house, or he used to go to his farm; he did not like the beggar, and when he died he was put into heaven.

"There was another man, who did many good deeds (offered sacrifices); his money he gave to the people, and his corn he gave to the poor: when he died he was put into the fire, and plenty of his corn was in Hades. The man who had gone to heaven found no corn at his place; one grain now and then fell into his house, and as he took it and ate it, he said, Where can this man be? They said, He is in the fire. He said, Bring him, and all his corn, let us sit together with him and his corn. So they brought the man who was in the fire, and all his corn, and they were all put into heaven; they sat down together with those that called him; so he found heaven, and felt sweet."

11. *Maganan matše da diata, da karnukansu.*

"*The Story of a Woman and her Daughter and their Dogs.*"

Matše da diata da kurnukansu sunka taffi tšikin gona sunka yi gidda, suka samna tšikin dáši. Karnukansu ana yi masu tuo sunka tši, anayi masu fura sunka ša. Da dere, Dodo ya taffo, ya yi kuka, suka kirrawo sunan karnukansu sunka kore Dodo. Dodo ya taffi tšikin daši, karnuka suna taffo gidda. Kowonne lottu da dere Dodo šina taffowa karnuka suna koranši. Da uwan yarinia zata taffia tšikin gari, ta faddi ga diata, ta tše: ki yi furá, ki bai karnuka, su ša, ki yi tuo, ki bai kurnuka su tši, yarinia ta tše da keao.

"A certain woman went with her daughter and their dogs to their farm, and when they had built a house there, they dwelled in the desert; and as to their dogs, they cooked food, and they did eat; they made gruel for them, and they did drink. In the night Dodo came and cried; they called the names of their dogs, and they drove Dodo away. And when Dodo had gone into the forest the dogs returned home. Every hour of the night Dodo comes, and the dogs drive him away. As the girl's mother was about going in the town, she told her daughter, and said to her, Make gruel, and give the dogs that they may drink; make food ready for them, that they may eat. The girl said, Very well."

Da uwata ta taffi tšikin gari yarnia ta kí magana uwata; da dzārarênta sunka taffo, ta yi furá, ta basu, sunka ša, ta bai karnuka sáki, sunka ki ša; ta yi tuo, ta bai ga dzararenta sunka tši, kamso ta bai karnuka, karnuka sunka ki tši. Da dere ya yi Dodo ya taffo, ya yi kuka; yarinia ta ši dsoro; ta kirrawo suna karnuka. Šato ya taffo, ya wutše, ya ki kora Dodo. Ta kirrawo Fari, ya wutše, ya ki kora Dodo; ta kirrawo Samman dunia, ya taffo, ya wutše, ya ki kora Dodo. Ta kirrawo Samma kussa, ya taffo, ya wutše, ya ki kora Dodo. Kowonne karre ya taffo, ya wutše. Dodo šina kuka ya taffo, ya šigga tšikin gidda, ya dsaya. Yarinia ta taši, ta šigga tšikin dakinta, ta dsaya. Dodo ya yi kuka, ya taffo, ya šigga tšikin daki. Yarinia ta hawa bissa gado. Dodo ya yi kuka, ya hawa bissa gado. Yarinia ta hawa bissa rafónia.

" But when her mother had gone to town, the girl disobeyed her mother's words; and when her lovers came she made gruel, and gave it to them, and they drank it: to the dogs she gave the refuse, and they would not drink it. She gave her lovers food, and they ate it; and such as was burned she gave to the dogs, but the dogs refused to eat it. When it was night, Dodo came, and made a cry; the girl was frightened, and called the names of their dogs. Shato! Shato! he came, and walked away again, and would not drive Dodo away. She called for Fāri: he came, but passed by, and would not drive Dodo away. She called Sammandunia: he came, passed by, and did not drive Dodo away. She called for Sammakussa: he came, walked about, but would not drive Dodo away. Every dog came, and went away again. Dodo was crying loud, came, went into the house, and there stopped. The girl arose, and went into her room and stood still. Dodo cried, came, and went into the room: the girl climbed on the bed."

Dodo ya yi kuka, ya šigga tšikin rafonia. Yarinia ta šigga tšikin tandu ; Dodo ya yi kuka, ya hadie yarinia da tandu duka. Uwata ta taffo da rana, ta ganni diata babu, ta tše. Dodo ya hadie yarinia, yarinia ta yi tuo, ba ta basu ga karnuka, su tši, ba ta yi fura ba, bai ga karnuka, su ša. Da uwata ta yi tuo dayawa, ta bai ga karnuka, sunka tši, sunka kóši; ta yi furá ta basu sunka ša, suka koši. Da dere ya yi Dodo ya taffo, šina kúka, karnuka suka taši suka kama Dodo, sunka kaššie Dodo. Uwan yarinia ta taffo, ta fuda tšikin Dodo ta samu tandu, ta bude tandu, ta samu diata, ta yi murna diata tana da rai, ba ta mutu ba tšikin Dodo. Uwata, tana murna, tana murna dayawa, ta sami diata !

"Dodo cried, and came on the bed. The girl climbed up on the barn. Dodo cried and went into the barn. The girl crept into an earthen pot. Dodo cried, and swallowed the girl with the pot altogether. When her mother came home the next day, she looked about, but her daughter was not there; she said, Dodo has swallowed the girl; the girl has made food, but did not give it to the dogs to eat; she has not made gruel to give it to the dogs to drink. When her mother had made plenty of food, she gave it to the dogs, and they did eat it, and were satisfied; when she had made gruel, she gave it to them, they drank it and were satisfied. In the night Dodo came crying; the dogs got up, caught Dodo, and when they had killed Dodo, the girl's mother came, opened Dodo's belly, and found the pot; she opened the pot, and found her daughter, she was glad to find her daughter still alive, she did not die in Dodo's belly. Her mother was glad, she was very glad, because she found her daughter still alive!"

12. *Magana na matše.*

"*The Story about a Woman.*"

Akoi, matše tunda Alla ya yita, ba ta yi saddaka ko daia. Saodaia wonni mutum ya taffo, kumulo ya kamaši, ya tše ga matše, ki bani kanwa kadan, kumulo ya kamani; ta baši kanwa kadan kadan, ya ša, kumulo ya taffi. Da ta mutu; ta taffi lahira, wurin wuta; wuta tana tšinta, ta dauka idonta bissa, ba ta ganni wonni abu sai kanwa da ta yi saddaka. Tana tšin kanwa har bakinta ya yi ša, ta gaši da tšin kanwa. Mutanen lahira sunka tše; ku futasda mat nan, ta taffi giddanta: sunka tše mata; ki yi sadadka ga dunia.

"There was once a woman, who from the time that God had created her, had never made any sacrifice, not even one. On one occasion a certain man came, upon whom faintness had laid hold, and he said to the woman, Give me a little kanwa (saltpetre), faintness has seized me. She gave him a very little, he drank it, and his faintness went away. When she died, she went to Hades, to the place of fire; when the fire was tormenting her, she lifted up her eyes, but saw nothing except the kanwa which she had given in sacrifice. So she was eating kanwa until her mouth was red, and she was tired of eating kanwa. The people of the Sheol were saying, Get this woman out, let her go to her house. They said to her, Make sacrifices in the world."

Da zata futta suka bugeta da karife da wuta, suka bugata bugo biu; ta kawo šaida daga dunia, ta tše masu: ku yi saddaka dayawa, wutan lahira babu keao: ta tše masu: ku ganni bayana! daga lahira akabugeni da karife da wuta, Šaida ta ke nan. Ta ši dsoro wuta lahira.

Ši ke nan, ya kare, maganan da na ši.

"When she was about to leave, they beat her with fiery iron; they gave her two blows; she brought her marks to the world, and said to the people, Make plenty sacrifices, the fire in the sheol is not good. She said to them, Look at my back, in the sheol they have beaten me with a fiery iron. This is my testimony; she was afraid of the fire of hell.

"This is it, it is finished, the story which I have heard."

13. *Tasunia da kurege, da kura, da kifi.*

"*A Tale about a Fox, a Hyena, and the Fish.*"

Akoi tasunia daia amma ban sanni ba duka, na sanni šaše.

Kurege ya taffi tšikin rua, ya sami kifi dayawa, ya futas woše, ya tši, ya kóši, ya ber saura šina tšéwa : wane šina tayani tšin kifi nan ? šina tšewa, wane šina bani tšiki da girima ?

Ya šima kadan, kura ta taffo, ya ga kura, ya tše, taffo nana kura ! kura ta taffo ; ya tše : ga nama dayawa en kin so, ki tši ; kura ta tši kifi duka, kurege šina šin haušin kura.

"There is another tale, but I do not know it all, I know half.

"There was a fox who went in the water to get some fish, he found many, pulled them out, and ate them; he did eat enough, and left the remainder, saying to himself, Who will help me to eat all these fish? Or saying, Who will give me so large a belly?

"When he had waited a little while, there came a hyena; he saw the hyena, and said to her, Hyena, come here. The hyena came, and he said to her, See all this meat, if thou dost like it, eat. So the hyena ate all the fish, and the fox felt angry with the hyena."

Sabua ta taffo, ta samna bissa itatše tana kuka: kilkal, kilkal! kura ta ganni sabua šikkinta da sānnḗ, kura ta tše : wane šina bani sanne da keao kamman sabua? Kurege ya tše ga kura : ni na yi sanne wonnan.

Kura ta tše: ba ka ba mini sanne hakka da keao? Ya faddi ga kura, ya tše ; en kina so sanne, kawo wuka da kassa fari ; kura babu hankali, ta taffi, ta kawo wuka da faran kassa, ba ta sanni ba ˃ kurege šina šin haušinta, ta tšainye masa nama ; ya dauke wuka kura ta samna šina mata šaušawa ga baya šina waka.
Ka tšainye kifina :

Ina ramawa ga šikkinta (šina tšaga da wuka, ya yi šaušawa da keao. Kura ta taffi tana šin tšïwo, kurege šina daria, ya tšaga šikkin kura.

"There came a guinea-fowl and sat down on a tree singing: Kilkal! Kilkal! The hyena saw that the guinea-fowl's body was full of dots ; the hyena said, Who is going to give me such beautiful dots like those of the guinea-fowl? The fox said to the hyena, It is I that make these dots.

" So the hyena said, Wilt thou not give me also such beautiful dots? He told the hyena and said, If thou dost want such spots, bring me a knife and some white earth. The hyena not having any sense, went and brought a knife and white earth, for she did not know that the fox was vexed with her for eating all his meat; he took the knife, and while the hyena was sitting down, cut marks into her back singing, 'Thou didst eat my fish, I am rowing on thy back.' So he was cutting with his knife, and made beautiful marks. The hyena went away full of pain, the fox laughed heartily, because he had torn the hyena's back."

THE

LIFE AND TRAVELS OF DORGU,

AS DICTATED BY HIMSELF.

One Chapter only is annexed. The rest will be published as soon as the necessary funds can be procured.

Gari enda akahaiféni Dambanas, kussa ga birnin Kantše, taffian yini daia. Daga Dambanas obana ya samna tare da uwata; sunansa Kwagé, da sunansa nabiu Adam; da sunan uwata Kande. Ta haifi kanena, Hakurau, da kanuata, sunanta Taroko. Mu woddanan uku anhaifemu ga gari daia. Obana ya samna ga gari nan siekaru dayawa; da šina kíddi da dundufansa; da šina da gonasa, karama; amma mu ba mu iawa mu yi aiki kwarai, don ba mu girima ba.

"The town in which I was born is called Dambanas, and is near to the town of Kantshe, about one day's journey. My father resided at Dambanas, together with my mother; his name was Kwage, and his second name Adam, and my mother's name was Kandee. She gave birth to my younger brother, Hakurau, and my younger sister, whose name was Taroko. We, all three of us, were born at the same place. My father lived there many years. He used to beat his set of drums; but he had also a little farm. But we children were not able to do much work, because we were little.

Da na ganni obana da uwata suna yin wohalla ga gona, na tše ga obana : ina tšī, ina ša ba na ia yin komi, ina so ka bani haiwa, en yi noma.

Ya tše mani : kai ba ka girima ba ga aiki, ka samna har ga šiekara maizakkua, kána em baka haiwa, ka yi aiki : amma ina yin kúka, don ina son yi aiki. Da muka taffi gidda, ya faddi ga makěri ya kíra mani haiwa, da makěri ya kira mani haiwa, da ya káre, da obana ya kawo mani, ina yin murna.

Da gari ya waye muka taši, muka taffi da safe ga gona; amma uwata ta samna ga gidda tana yin tuo, kadan ta kare, ta kawo muna ga gona ; kadan sun zakka ga tšin tuo, ni ba na so en zakka, en tši tuo, don na ši dádin nóma.

"So when I saw my father and my mother troubling themselves with their farm, I said to my father: I am eating and drinking, but cannot do anything: I wish thou wouldst give me a hoe, that I might do something in the garden or farm. But he said to me, Thou art too little, and canst not labour, sit down for another year, and then I shall give thee a hoe to do some work, but I cried, because I wished to do something. When we had come home, he told the blacksmith to make me a hoe, and when the blacksmith had made it for me, and it was finished, and my father brought it to me, I was glad.

"When it began to dawn we all got up, and went to the farm very early, but my mother remained at home preparing our food, and when it was ready, she brought it to us to the farm. So when they went to eat their food, I did not like to go to eat mine, because I was fond of my farm work."

Obana ši kan taffi, ši kan kawoni, ši kan tše mani: ka tši tuonka, mu mun kare namu, kana en taffi en tši tuona. Da muka ganni ga šiekara nan babu hazi dayawa ga tšikin gona nan, obana ya beri gona nan, ya yi wota kussa ga gidda; da muka noma wonnan da kussa ga gidda mun samu hazi, amma ba dayawa ba. Hario muna da wota gona ta abduga. Koyauše da ni da obana muna zua nan; amma kanuata ba ta da lafia, da uwata ta kan taffi tare damu.

Da maraetšie ya yi da muka dawoyowa daga abdugan gona, na ganni kanena daga bissa tudu (šina daga tšikin gidda), da wonni yaro karami tare daši. Uwata ta tše ga obana: wonnan Hakurau ne da Taroko! Mun yi mamaki, mun tše; kaka ta samu lafia, ta fitta woše tana yin worigi? Amma damu ka zakka da muka šigga ga tšikin gidda, na ganni yaro nan ba kanuata ba tše.

"My father used to come, and bring it to me, saying, Eat now thy food, we have finished ours; and then I used to eat my own portion. Seeing that there was not much corn in the farm that year, my father left it, and made another farm nearer home; and when we had cultivated the one nearer home, we gat some corn, but not very much. Besides that, we had another cotton-farm, and I and my father went frequently to that farm, but my sister was not well enough; my mother used to go with us sometimes.

"One evening as we were returning home from our cotton plantation, I saw my younger brother, who had been left at home, and another little boy with him. My mother said to my father, There is Hakurau and Taroko! We were much astonished, and said, How is it, is she better, that she has come out to play?

"But when we came home and entered the house, I saw that that child was not my sister."

Na yi gúddu na šigga ga tšikin daki, na kirra sunanta, na tše : Taroko ! Taroko ! ban ši ba ta amsa; na tabata ba ta yi ba mósí ; sai wuri enda ta kwanta duka ta tšikka da dalele, kána na sanni ta mutu ; na yi kuka. Da obana ya zakka, ya daukéta, ya dubéta har hawaye suka suba kassa da ga idánúnsa, da uwata kuá tana yin kuka ; amma kanena ba ši sanni ba komi, ba yaro da wayo ba ši ke. Obana ya tambayesa : ka bata fura? Ya tše : í ; ka bata rua ? Ya tše : í. Da obana ya tambaya hakka, ba ši tše ba komi ; sai obana ya tše, kadan ba ta mutu ba da yunwa da keao. Da ya kirra wonni abokinsa ya tše masa, ši ginna masa kušieya abisneta daga tšan. Da mutume nan ya ginna kušieya, ya sa kunuan itatše daga tšiki.

"I run, and went in the room, calling out my sister's name, Taroko! Taroko! but could not hear her answering; I touched her, but she did not move, and then I perceived that she had been very sick, and was then quite dead. I cried. My father came in, took her up in his arms, and looked at her, until the tears rolled down on the ground from his eyes. My mother too cried very much ; but my younger brother did not know what it was all about, he was not of an age to know what it meant. My father asked him, Hast thou given her gruel ? He said, Yes. Hast thou given her water? He said, Yes. So when my father had asked him all these questions, he said no more, but only remarked, that if she did not die of hunger, it was all right. When my father had called one of his friends, he told him to dig a grave for him to bury her in. Thus, when the man had dug the grave, he put some branches of trees in it."

Da akaruféta da zanne, ya dauketa, ya kaita, ya sata ga tšikin kušieya; ya dora itatše daga bissa ga bakin kušieya, ya rufeta duka da itatše, kana ya suba kassa daga bissa, ya rufeta da keao.

Da muka kwana, da gari ya waye, obana ya tše ga uwata: mine zamu sāyé, mu yi mata saddaka? sai ta tše masa, mu saye wáke da ayi fura akai gaba ga mainya mutane; ya tše da keao. Ya taffi, ya saye wake, ya kawo mata; da ta dauka hazi ta yi fura, ta daffa wake; muka dauka, muka kawo gaba ga mainya mutane ga dandali. Da suka tši wake, suka ša fura, suka kare, mallamai suka yi alfatia, muka taffi, muka samna.

Baya ga mutuan kanuata na ši labarin yáki šina zakkua ga garimu; muka táši da dēré, muka gúddu taffian kwana biu ko uku; aṡie karia tše ba gaskia ba.

"And when they had covered my sister with white cloth, he took her up, carried her away, and laid her in the grave. He also put some branches on the top of the grave, and covered the whole with wood, before he put earth on it, and covered the whole very nicely.

"When we had slept, and the sky began to dawn, my father said to my mother, What shall we buy to make a sacrifice for her? She replied, we cannot buy any thing but a few beans, and make some fura, to be taken before the great people. So he said, Very good. He went and bought some beans, and brought them to her; she took some millet and made gruel, and cooked the beans, and we took it and carried it before the great people in the courtyard. When they had eaten the beans and drunk the gruel, the priests offered up prayers, and then we went away and sat down at home.

"After the death of my sister, I heard the news of war coming to our country; we got up in the night, and fled about two or three days' journey; but it was altogether a false alarm, and not true."

Da gari ya waye mutane suna ganni diansu, sun gaši da taffia, ni da kaina ina yin kuka sabbada gāšiá; kadan sun ši šariri šina kuka suna tše ga uwasa : ki baši nono ya ša, don ya yi kawoi! Da muka samna daga tšikin dáši, ina tamaha woddansu mutane sun dawoyo daga tšikin gari. Da suka zakka, suka ganni garimu babu mutane, da sun zakka ga faddá, suka dawoi, suka zakka garemu.

Amma akoi wonni mutum, maisata, ya samna daga tšikin garí, ya sata abu dayawa ; ya samna har muka dawoyo. Amma da muka dawoyo, muka samu garimu aṅkoneši da wuta, don mutume maisata, ši ne, ya sa wuta ga gari ; sai giddan obāna, da giddan wota zofua, su ne, wuta ba ta tabasu ba. Amma dakin obana šiakai, da awaki, da tumaki, da káši sun šigga tšiki suna worigi.

"In the morning, as it was becoming light, the people saw that their children were all very tired of travelling; I myself cried, because of fatigue. When they heard their babes crying, they would call out to their mothers, Give them the breast, let them drink to be quiet. Having been in that desert place for some time, I think some of the people returned to our town, and, on arriving there, saw that there was nobody there to fight with us; they came back to us, and told us.

"But there was one man, a thief, who had remained in our town, and had stolen many things; he stopped there until we came back. And when we returned, we found that our town had been destroyed by fire, because the same man, that is, the thief, had set it on fire. But the house of my father, and that of a certain old person, had not been touched by the fire. The room, however, in which my father used to live was occupied by donkeys, sheep, goats, and fowls, who were amusing themselves there."

Da akoi wonni itatše, sunansa Tšedia (kunuanta da girima, ta kan haifi dia kanana, amma ba matane dayawa ba su ke tši) künuanta sun ši wuta, sun kekaše. Da na ganni kariata (kariyata) na koreta, ban sannta ba, don ta girima; sai obana ya tše mani: kada ka koreta, ba ka sanni ba, da mun guddu ka berta daga bayanka? Na tše, í, na sanni Na tše masa: da mun berta karama ta ke, amma yansu ta girimá, ya tše, í.

Da muka samu garimu babu abu da ya tabaši, sai wuta Da muka šigga, muka samna, mata suna neman tūkudne, ba su samu ba, har suka zakka ga giddan mutume nan, suka samu tukuanensu daga nan; kowolše matše ta dauka tukuniata, ta taffi ga giddanta. Mafarin šin labari yaki ke nan.

"And there was a tree close to my father's house, which is called Tshedia (the branches of it are very large, and it bears a little kind of fruit, but there are not many persons who eat it), whose branches were all destroyed by fire, and dried up. On seeing my own dog there, I drove him away from me, because I did not know him again, for he had grown much; but my father said to me, Do not drive him away, dost thou not remember that he was left behind when we fled? I said, Yes, I remember it now, and remarked, he was very little when we left him, but now he has grown very much; he said, Yes, he has.

"We found that nothing had been injured in our town except that which was done by the fire. But when we entered the houses left, and took up our abode, and the women were looking for their cooking utensils, they could not find any, until they came to the house of a certain man, and there they found their pots. Then each woman took her own pots, and went to her house. This was the first news of war we heard."

Da muka samna ko šiekara daia, hario muka ši labarin yaki daga woše wonni gari daga garemu; muka guddu muka taffi ga daši, amma ba nesa ba daga garimu, muka kwana daga tšikin daši. Da safia ta yi muka ganni mutane Fulani, bissa ga doki nesa daga garemu; kammada muka gannesu, muka yi, šigóro, ko muka hawa bissa ga itatše sai mutume daia da hankali akesaši, ya hawa bissa ga itatše, ya ganni wūráre duka ; kadan mutane suna zakkua daga garemu šina fadda muna, mu yi šíri sabbada fadda, har mutane nan suka kuma mutane, suka sa ga garinsu wuta, mu kua muna ganninsu abu da suká yi. Da suka tši gari nan suka taffi, sai hayaki muna ganni tšikin gari. Da yaro nan ya hawa bissa šina yin šígóro, ya ganni mutane biu daga nesa suna taffowa daga garemu suna yin guddu, don sun gannéši bissa ga itatše, ya fadda muna.

"When we had remained there perhaps one year, we heard again a rumour of war against us, from some other country ; we therefore ran away again, and went in the forest, but not very far from our own town, and we slept in the forest one night. In the morning we saw some persons, Phulas, on horseback, at some distance from our town. As soon as we observed them, we watched them closely, that is, we climbed upon trees ; but one man more especially, a man of sense, he was made to get upon a tree to look about in all directions, and when he saw any one coming towards us, he used to tell us to get ready to fight. Then our people caught those persons. It was found that they had set fire to their town, and we ourselves have seen what they have done. When they had destroyed the place, they left it, and there was nothing but smoke arising from that place. And when the boy who had climbed upon the tree to keep a look out, saw two persons at some distance, coming towards us, and running, because they had observed him on the tree, he told us."

*Obana da woddansu mutane biu, suka taši, suka tariésu;
da suka gammu dasu daga tšikin rŭkŭki, suka tše masu:
nắmu ko ba namu ba? Mutane nan biu suka amsa suka
tše : nắku.*

*Suka dawoyo, suka zakka garemu; muna yin murna da
mun gannẹsu, don mun sannsu. Muka tambayesu, muka
tše : kaka kun sanni muna daga wuri nan? Suka tše muna,
don mun ganni daianku šina yin šigoro bissa ga itatše.
Muka tambayesu labari tšikin gari, suka tše muna : woddansu
ańkaššiesu, da woddansu suna da rauni, da woddansu ańkắma-
su bayi. Da muna ganni woddansu mutane kussa daga garému
suna zakkua daŭkan dukiasu suna taffia ga garinsu (sunan
gari nan da akayi fadda daši Šagari) da suka fadda muna
labari, muka dawoyo, muka samna ga garimu.*

"Then my father and two other persons arose to meet them;
and on meeting them in the brush-wood they said to them,
Do you belong to us, or do you not belong to us? These
two men answered and said, We belong to you.

"So they turned back and came to us; we were glad to
see them, because we knew them. We asked them, and said,
How did you know that we were at this place? They said to
us, Because we saw one of you keeping watch upon a tree.
We asked them for all the news of the town, and they said to
us, Some persons have been killed, and some have received
wounds, and others have been made slaves. Hence, when we
saw some persons near them coming to take up their goods,
to go to their own town (the name of the town with which
they had been fighting was Sagari), and when they told
us the news, we went back and settled down in our own
town."

Baya ga fadda nan muka ši labari sarikim Bornu, Šieku Wumar šina zakkua, ya yi fadda da Kantše. Da ya taffo ba agannesi ba ; da rana ta yi akaganni kurasa, ya zakka, ya yi fadda da sarikin Kantše, ya basu kašši, ko ya bugesu, ya sa wuta ya garinsu, ya dawoi ga garinsa, ya kwasa dukiasu. Suna buga bindiga muna šinṣu daga Dambanas, har suka zakka, suka yi fadda da wonni gari, sunansa Tasau. Mutanen gari nan suka yi fadda kamman wuta, amma ba atšisu ba.

Da Sariki ya taffi ga garinsa, amma woddansu ba su taffi ba ga lottu nan akoi yuṅwa. Amma akoi wonni mutum daga gari nan, da obana ya dauka diasa, ya zakka ga obana ya tše : ba ni beri diata daga giddanka, kada ta mutu da yuṅwa. Ya dauketa, ya fušieta daga giddan obana, da ni da kanena muna kuka, don andauketa uwamu daga giddan obamu : yá kaita ga wonni gari sunansa Bangassa.

" After this disturbance, we heard the news that the king of Bornu, Sheik Omar, was coming to fight against Kantshe ; and he came without being seen; he came and fought against the king of Kantshe, and gave them battle and defeated them; he set fire to their town, and then returned to his own country, carrying away their property. They were firing guns, we heard them at Dambanas, until they came and fought with another town, the name of which was Tasau, the people of that town fought like fire, and were not overcome. And the king went to his country, but some of his people did not go with him. At that time there was a famine ; and the man whose daughter my father had taken to be his wife, came to my father and said, I cannot leave my daughter in thy house, lest she should die of hunger, so he laid hold of her, and carried her away by force, out of the house of my father, and took her to another town, called Bangassa."

Enda ya bašieta ga wonni mutum ta samma matasa, amma ba ta sonsa ba; ta kan guddu, ta kan zakka ga giddan obana. Hario ya zakka, ya maišieta ga Bangassa, amma ba ta so en samna daga gari nan. Da mišinta ya taffi gona šina šira ta kawo masa abintši, ta guddu, ta zakka ga giddamu: hario mutume nan, ko obanta, ya zakka ya maišieta. Da ya maišieta ya dawoi ga garinsa; da mišinta ya taffi ga gona ita ta samna daga gidda tana yi masa fura ta išieši ga gona; amma akoi kingi Baribari tunda aka yin faddan Kantše ba su taffi ba su duka. Da ta dauka furá da haiwata, ta noma, suka gammu da ita daga tšikin itatšé, suka kamata, suka taffi da ita. Obana ya ši labari ya zakka ya fadda muna, ya tše: uwaku ankámata, sai muka dauka hankuri muka samna.

"And there he gave her to another man to be his wife; but she did not like him, and therefore ran away from him, and came to the house of my father. Again he would come and take her back to Bangassa, but she did not like to remain in that town. So when her husband went to his farm and was waiting for her to bring him his dinner, she made her escape, and came to our house. Again the same man, that is, her father, came and took her back; and when he had brought her back he returned to his own place. When her husband went to the farm she remained at home, preparing his gruel to meet him in the farm. Now there were still some Bornu people about, from the time they had been fighting with Kantshe, for they had not all left; hence, as she had taken her gruel and her hoe to go to the farm, they met her in the woods, caught her, and went away with her."

*Da ya dauki kanena, ya bašiesa ga wonni mutum daga Ta-
sau ; ya samna daga garesa kamma dansa ; ya tše masa : Kada
ka maida mani dana sai na gammu da kai daga tšikin lâhirá.
Na yí kuka, don ya bada kanena tšan ; na samna, saí ina
tšewa ga sŭtšiáta : kadan na girima, ba na beri kanena yá
samna daga nan. Ina tamaha kanena šiekarunsa šidda ko
bokoi tunda akabašiesa. Kadan na taffi yansu, ba na
sannší ba, amma ni sannší ga šaúšāwa ; amma ši ba ía
sannina ga šaúšāwa, sai na fadda masa.*

*Baya da muka samna muka ši labari wonni sariki,
sunansa Taniman, šina zakkua ya wutše ga garimu. Da
muka ši hakka mutane suka yi šíri.*

"When my father heard the news, he came and told us, and said, Your mother has been caught! We could do nothing but bear it patiently, and sit down. Then my father took my younger brother, and gave him to a man at Tasau, that he might stay with him like his own son; and my father said to the man, Thou shalt not restore my son to me, until I meet thee in the Sheol. But I cried, because he had there given away my little brother. I sat down quietly, and only said within my own heart, when I am grown up, I shall not suffer my younger brother to remain there! I think my younger brother's years were about six or seven, at the time he was given over to that man. And if I should go thither now, I should not know him; if it were not for the marks in his face, I should not know him at all : but he, he would not know me, unless I should tell him first.

"After we had been there for some time, we heard that another king, whose name was Taniman, was coming, and on his march against us, and when we heard it, the people all made ready."

Da dere ya yi muka ši ya taffo šina wutšewa kamman fára. Ba˙ muka ši šina wutšewa Mutanen garimu suka šiefa gagaradadau matausin kofa, ko itatše da ake sawa gitšie ga bakin kofam birni. Ya tše muna, mu berši ya šigga ya ša rua, amma mun kí; ya yi fuši, ya wutše. Da woddansu zofi sun gaši, suka samna daga bayan birni, muka samesu da safe nan. Wakasa da akabaši ke nan:

> *Dere, dere, yan Kwarugom, dere, dere,*
> *Kadan ba ku sann dere ba, kura ta tšiku*
> *Babu matšictšie akussa:*
> *Táneman maibindiga,*
> *Na yado bašinni!*

"We heard him coming in the night, marching along like a swarm of locusts. When we heard that he was on his march, the people of our town made barricades before the gate, that is, they cut down large trees, and laid them crossway, at the mouth of the gate of the town. He said to us, that we should allow him to enter the town to drink water, but we refused, so he got vexed, and went away. Some old persons (belonging to him) who were overcome by fatigue remained outside the town during the night, and there we found them in the morning. The song which they made there about him is as follows:

(Keep watch) by night, by night, ye sons of Kwarugo, by
    night, by night;
If ye do not know (how to keep watch), by night the hyena
    will eat you.
There is no deliverance at hand:
Taneman is a man of guns, and
The natives of Yado are bulls (keep watch by night)!"

Da muka samna, ina tamaha daga tŝikin ŝiékára nan, muka ŝi mutanem Bornu sun ŝigga tŝikin Kantŝe; ina tamaha sarikin Kantŝe ya basu garimu su tŝi, amma ya fadda masu su yi hańkali kammada zasu tŝimu; amma sun yi wayo. Da gari ya wāyé suka zakka daia, daia, suna ŝigga daga tŝikin gari har suka tŝika garimu. Obana ya tŝe mani, en taffi en gboya daga tŝikin tŝiawa; na guddu, na gboya daga tŝikin tŝikin tŝiawa kussa ga rua, na ŝina kadan daganan. Ya zakka ŝina nemana daga tŝikin tŝiawa, ya kirrana; ina ŝinsa, amma ban amsa ba; hario ya kirrani saobiu kána na amsa. Ya tŝe mani, babu komi, sai lafia. Na tŝe, kadan lafia mu taffi gidda.

Da muka zakka gidda na samna, amma sutŝiata ba ta samna ba.

"After remaining there some time, I think it was during the same year, we heard that the Bornu people had entered Kantshe, and I think the king of Kantshe gave them our town to destroy it, but told them to beware how they were going to ruin us, and therefore they employed some stratagem. For in the morning, when it began to dawn, they came one by one into our town, until our town was full of them. My father told me to go and hide myself among the high grass, so I went and concealed myself among the grass, near to the water-side, and there I rested for a short time. My father came to look after me among the grass, and called me; I heard him, but I did not answer: he called again the second time, and then I answered him. He said to me, There is nothing the matter, all is well. I replied, If all is well, let us go home.

"When we had come home, I sat down, but my heart could not sit down."

Na tše ga matan obana (sunanta Baka, amma ba uwata ba ta ke. Obana ya fadda mani wonnan matše ya amreta tunda ši ke sarmayi, da ita kua tunda ta ke budurua, amma ban sanni ba, mi ya fušieta daga tšikin giddansa ; ko ya koréta, ko yaki ya rabásu ban sanni ba; amma ina tamaha ta šigga bauta, don tana yin maganam Baribari ; ita ya kawota, ya ašieta ga giddansa kamman uwata,) ki dauki kworiaki, da ni en dauka kibiata, da en dauka malafan obana, mu taffi ga wonni gari. Amma ta ši maganata, ba ta renani ba. Lottu nan ina tamaha šiekarata ša daia. Ta dauka kworiata, ta wutše gaba gareni, ni kua ina binta daga baya, har muka ketare rua, amma obana ba ya gidda, ya taffi ga wurin mutane šina šín labari.

" I said to my father's wife (her name was Baka, but she was not my mother: my father told me, that he had married her when he was still a young man, and when she was likewise a young maid; but I do not know what drove her away from his house; whether he had sent her away, or whether war had separated them, I do not know. I rather think that she had been made a slave, because she spoke the Bornu language; the same he brought and put her in the place of my mother), Take thy calabash, and let me also take my bow, and my father's hat (umbrella,) and let us go to some other town ; she listened to my word, and did not despise me. At that time, I think my years were eleven. She took her calabash, and walked on before me, and I followed behind her, until we had to cross a water. But my father was not at home, he had gone to the place where the people were assembled to hear the news."

Da ya zakka ga gidda, da ba ši gannemu ba, ya yi guddu, ya taffi, ya išiemu, ya maišiemu ga gidda, amma sutšiata tana raurawa. Da muka šíma kadan muka ganni wonni mutum bissa doki, ya zakka, ya šida tšikin giddamu, amma ši Bahauše ne, da wonni mutum hario ya zakka Babaribari šina son hazi sabbada dokinsa, amma mu ba mu da hazi, šina yin maganam Bornu, da matan obana tana amsa masa. Kadan ya yi maganam Bornu ni kan tambayata : mi ya fadda mata; ta tše mani šina son hazi, na tše masa : ba mu da hazi ; amma ya tše šina kirra sāmári su šigga, su ganni dakimu ; da na ši hakka ina šin dsóro. Šíma kakan muka ši sariki šina taffowa ; da maraetšie, rana ta kussa fadua kassa, muka ši wonni mutum ya zakka šina tšewa : kowonne bakko ya darime surdinsa, ya hawa bissa ga dokinsa.

"When he came home, and could not find us, he run, went, and overtook us, and made us return home; but my heart was getting up and down. When we had rested a little while, we saw a man on horseback, he came and dismounted before our house, but he was a Hausa man; and another man came soon after him, the same was a Bornu, and wanted corn for his horse. We had no corn. He was speaking in the Bornu language, and my father's wife answered him. When he was speaking Bornu, I continued asking her, What is he saying to thee? and she replied, He wants corn for his horse, I tell him that we have not got any; but he says that he will call the young men to come in, to look about in our house, and when I heard that, I was very much afraid. After a little while, I heard that the king was approaching. In the evening, when the sun was nearly down, we learned that a certain man had come into the town, and said, Let every stranger saddle his horse and mount it."

Muka ši busan sariki : *kóso, da algaita, da kālaṅgo, da kubé, da gaṅga suna yi masa kiddi; šina da tūta baba. Da suku buga bindiga kowonne bakko šina kama obangiddansa. Amma obana šina yi mani magana en zakka enda ši ke ga wota kofa, amma kaina ya giigita, ban sanni ba abin da zani yi, har mutumem Bornu, da ši ke daga tšikin giddan obana ya kámani, da obana wonni mutum Bahauše ya kamaši, amma matan obana ban sanni ba wáne ya kamata, Tšikin gari duka yara suna kuka, da uwa ta rabu da yayanta, da míši ya rabu da matasa, hakka mu duka mu ke āwāzé. Da muka wutšewa daga tšikin gari ya šani daga tšikin káya, da ni da ši, mu duka, muna daga tšikin kaya, amma ya kama dokinsa da hanu šina šana tare da doki har muka fitta daga tšikin gari.*

"We heard the music of the king; the playing of the koso,' the algaita, the kalango, the kube, the ganga; all these instruments they were playing before him, and he had large standards. Hence, as soon as they began firing guns, every stranger in the town laid hold on the master of the house in which he was. But my father had spoken to me, and told me before to come to the place where he was, to another gate of the town, but my head was giddy, I did not know what I was doing, until the Bornu man, who was in the house of my father, caught me; but as to my father, a Hausa man seized him; and as to my father's wife, I do not know who caught her. In the town all the children were crying. The mother was separated from her children, the husband was torn from his wife, so all of us were dispersed.

" As we were marching out of the town he dragged me over thorns, and both I and he, all of us, walked on thorns, for he led his horse by the hand, and thus dragged me along together with his horse, until we had come out of the town."

Amma kaya ta sosokḗni, kafata duka sai šinni. Ya hawa bissa doki, ya daukeni, ya ašieni ga bayan doki, amma ban sanni ba kaya ta sokeni, ko ba ta sokeni ba, don sutšiata tana tuna da abu da ši ke gaba garēni. Na ganni wonni yaro, abokina šina bissa bayan dokin obangišinsa, ina yin santše daši. Na tše masa : ka ganni yansu mu šigga tšikim bauta? ya tše mani : ba mu ia mu yi komi, saidai aikin Alla, har muka issa ga sansáni, muka šída. Da na woiwoya na-ganni matan obana tana bin wonni mutum da wuka ga hanunsa, har ya taffi da ita gaba ga sarikinsa. Amma na ši kaikai ga kafata, na ganni kafata duka sai šinni. Suka kawo muna gutšia, suka suba gaba garemu, amma ba mu tši ba, don ba mu da yuṅwa, da sutšia mu ba ta šin dádi.

Da suka dauka abu duka daga tšikin gari sun sa wuta ; kwoin kaza suna paššewa kamman bindiga da sun ši wuta : har gari ya waye wuta tana tšin gari.

"But the thorns had pricked me very much. My feet were all one mass of blood; he mounted his horse and took me and put me behind him on the horse. But I did not know whether the thorns had pricked me, or whether they had not pricked me, because my heart was only thinking on what was before me. I saw a boy, a friend of mine, who was sitting on the horse of his master; I conversed with him and said to him, Seest thou now we are entering upon slavery? he replied, We can do nothing except resign ourselves to the will of God. On reaching the camp we dismounted, and as I was turning round I saw my father's wife following a man who had a knife in his hand, until he came with her before the king. So when I felt my feet itching very much, I looked at my feet, and they were full of blood. They brought us some nuts, and threw them before us, but we did not eat them, because we were not hungry, and because our hearts did not feel sweet.

" When they had taken everything out of our town, they

Suka daukemu suka kaimu gaba ga sarikinsu, su godda masa bayi nda suka kama. Da ya gannemu mu duka, suka kaimu, muka samna. Mafarin bauta tawa ke nan. Kadan mun sanni zasu kamamu mu yi fadda, amma sun fayemu da wayo. Kibiamu tana da daffi; daffimu kua šina da zafi, kadan ka lása da halši šina kaššieka: hakkanan kua kadan mun yi fadda dasu, násu su mutu dayawa, da namu kua su kuššie, amma ba su yi ba fadda, kammada akedaukan gari abude, amma sun kamamu kamman yayan kaši ga asíri; amma ban ši ba ko daia ya mutu na garimu, ko wonni ya halba kibia ban ši ba.

Da muka taši daga bissa tudu enda suka šída suka taffo damu woddanda suka kama tarc dani.

"The eggs of fowls made a noise like a gun when they felt the fire; and the fire continued to destroy the town all night, and until daybreak. Then they took us and carried us before their king, and showed him the slaves which they had caught; and when he had seen us all, they took us away and we sat down. Such was the commencement of slavery for me. If we had known they were going to catch us we should have fought, but they were more cunning than we. Our arrows were poisoned, and the poison we used was very strong; if you were to touch it with your tongue it would kill you: consequently, if we should have fought with them, many of them would have died, and they would also have killed many of our people; but they did not fight, as people who take a town openly, but caught us like chickens secretly. But I have not heard whether any died of our town, or whether any shot an arrow I have not heard.

"When we had started from the hill on which they had been encamped, they came with those whom they had caught with me."

(*Ina tamaha mutane da suka kama ba su fi ba dari biu, ko dari uku; amma ina tamaha sun aike woddansu daga tšikin dere nan) muka zakka, muka wutše wonni gari kussa ga garimu, suka daukesu, ina tamaha sun yi dari fudu; muka taffi tare dasu; suka kóne garinsu. Muka taffi ga wonni baban gari muka kwana nan. Da safe suka daukemu, muka zakka ga garin kākāta, Kunduwoše sunansa. Na ganni kakata tana dsaye ga dzakkanin giddanta, da ta gannéni, šikkinta duka šina rauraẁa; ta tambayeni, ta tše, enna Adam? Na tše, ban sanni ba: sai na tše mata: sai wota rana: na wutše ina yin kuka. Na ganni taguaye biu anyašiesu bissa hainya suna yin kuka, amma ba su ia su yi magana. Muka zakka ga Zinder.*

" (I think the people whom they had caught were not more than about two or three hundred, yet I think they had sent some away during the night). We went along, and passed another town near to our own; they took the people there, and I think we were then about four hundred; so we went together, and they set the town on fire. We arrived at a very large town, and there we slept. In the morning they drove us on again, and we arrived at my grandmother's town, which is called Kunduwoshe. I saw my grandmother standing before her house, and when she saw me her whole body trembled and shook. She asked me and said, Where is Adam? I said, I do not know. All I could say to her was, May we meet again! and passed on crying. I saw two twins thrown on the road, they were crying, but they were not able to speak. And then we arrived at Zinder."

W. M. Watts, Crown Court, Temple Bar.

www.ingramcontent.com/pod-product-compliance
Lightning Source LLC
Chambersburg PA
CBHW021350230426
43666CB00006B/470